TRENDS IN MANAGERIAL AND FINANCIAL ACCOUNTING

To my parents

NIJENRODE STUDIES IN BUSINESS

Volume 1

Business is a broad field where science and business reality can and should meet to analyse and discuss old theories and to develop new ones, applicable for modern managers. One of the main objectives of the **Nijenrode studies in business** is to give a push to new developments in the multidisciplinary business area, to serve the profession as well as a wider audience.

Trends in managerial and financial accounting

Income determination and financial reporting

Cees van Dam

editor

Martinus Nijhoff Social Sciences Division
Leiden|Boston 1978

ISBN 90. 207. 0693. 4

Printed in the Netherlands.

PREFACE

In August 1976 the research seminar 'Decision-making in business' was organized at Nijenrode, The Netherlands School of Business. More than fifty scientists and practitioners from nine countries presented research papers in one of the six discussion groups. Some of them also presented some of their ideas in front of a large mixed audience at a one-day symposium. Many of the papers presented at Nijenrode were of such a high quality that the decision to publish a selection of them was an easy one. At the same time the new series *Nijenrode studies in business* was initiated. All who were involved, the policy committee of the *Nijenrode studies*, the advisory and editorial board of the series, the publisher, and the organizing committee of the seminar and symposium, acclaimed the idea of publishing three volumes in the new series. A collection of eleven papers could be grouped under the title *Trends in managerial and financial accounting*. Another collection will be published as volume 2 of this series under the title *Trends in financial decision-making*, while volume 3 will consist of papers exploring the theme *Trends in business ethics*.

The books are intended for those who are interested in new developments in the decision-making area. They are especially suitable for graduate or advanced undergraduate courses: volume 1 in managerial or financial accounting courses; volume 2 in courses on managerial finance, capital budgeting or decision-making; and volume 3 in courses on business ethics or related fields.

Many people have contributed to the success of the seminar and the symposium and made it possible for these three books to be published. In the first place, the authors of the papers who were all willing, not only to write a paper, but also to present it at Nijenrode, to discuss it with critical colleagues, and last but not least to revise it according to the capricious ideas of the editor. My thanks to all of them. But the whole enterprise would not have gotten off the ground without the great support of the members of the organizing committee of the seminar and symposium. As the president of that committee I have never made a vain appeal to any of the members. Because I am not able, nor do I wish, to discriminate between them, I will give their names in alphabetical order: Peter

Hesp, Piet Koeleman, Luud Stallaert and Tony de Wit. Of course, much had to be arranged, but the committee had dependable help in the person of Sybren Tijmstra, who was always there to bring the organizing committee down to earth. Many secretaries have made extra effort, but one of them in particular has to be mentioned because of her continuous enthusiasm before, during and after the symposium and seminar: Josée Terheggen. She did a wonderful job. Of course without the moral and financial support of the Board and different committees of Nijenrode all preparations would have led to nothing. I look back and still appreciate the year of enormous effort which went into the preparations for the congress.

It is hoped that the first three volumes of the series *Nijenrode studies in business* will be received with as much enthusiasm outside Nijenrode as was always present within the group of people who have made it all possible.

Cees van Dam

CONTENTS

Contributors to the volume

ROBERT N. ANTHONY, Ross Graham Walker Professor of Management Control at the Harvard Business School, Boston, Mass., U.S.A.

GIJS G. M. BAK, Professor of Accountancy at Tilburg University, Tilburg, The Netherlands; partner of Van Dien & Co., Accountants.

ANDRÉ J. BINDENGA, Member of the Board of Directors of the Nederlandse Dagbladunie, Rotterdam, The Netherlands.

JOHN J. CLARK, Professor of Finance at Drexel University, Philadelphia, Penn., U.S.A.

CEES VAN DAM, Professor of Business Administration at Nijenrode, The Netherlands School of Business, Breukelen, The Netherlands.

EDGAR O. EDWARDS, Ford Foundation.

HANS G. EIJGENHUIJSEN, Associate Professor of Finance at the Free University, Department of Economics, Amsterdam, The Netherlands.

MYRON J. GORDON, Professor of Finance at the Faculty of Management Studies, University of Toronto, Toronto, Canada

RICHARD H. HAASE, Professor of Statistics at Drexel University, Philadelphia, Penn., U.S.A.

PALLE HANSEN, Professor of Business Administration at the Copenhagen School of Business Administration, Copenhagen, Denmark.

JAN KLAASSEN, Professor of Accounting at the Free University, Department of Economics, Amsterdam, The Netherlands.

GERALD H. LAWSON, Professor of Business Finance at the Manchester Business School, Manchester, U.K.

TOM A. LEE, Professor of Accountancy and Finance at the University of Edinburgh, Edinburgh, U.K.

INTRODUCTION

Income determination and financial reporting are problems that have attracted the notice both of academic researchers as well as of practitioners in the accounting world. New standards, new methods, and new theories have been developed. The consequences of high rates of inflation have prompted those in the field to come to more or less uniform accounting standards. In this volume have been brought together many worth-while ideas, intended to make a positive con⁺ribution to the development of these standards.

The information process within firms and among external users of annual reports cannot always be classified as optimal. In this volume many ideas are put forward to improve these processes.

André Bindenga compares the inflation accounting method and the replacement value accounting method. After giving advantages and disadvantages of both methods, he analyses the objectives of financial statements. At the end of his paper, Bindenga develops a proposal for a method of determining the annual results of a company. He attempts to incorporate the positive elements of both methods under consideration.

Gijs G. M. Bak is interested in the information process. He considers the application of current value a means to generate relevant information for management. In order to analyse the possibilities of current value accounting, the author introduces a hypothetical computerized information system. Reporting based on current values reflects the actual price-relations the company has to deal with on its purchase and selling markets. At the same time holding gains are reported separately. Bak's paper holds the conclusion that the application of current values might result in an economic concept of income, different from the usual concept.

More about this can be read in *Edgar O. Edwards'* paper. That paper demonstrates that expectations about changes in values (new holding gains) are essential to the making of rational expansion decisions and to the determination of economic income. The accounting concept of income based on the measurement of current events (including current holding gains) contains, for Edwards, the essential data. He concludes that the current income concept is not an approximation of economic income, but rather is a primary concept essential to the derivation of its economic counterpart. Finally, this paper demonstrates that an expansion-neutral tax system, one that does not affect the choice of expansion path, must assess taxes on current holding gains as they arise and at the same rate as on other components of income.

The two contributors from the United Kingdom both give attention to an alternative system of financial reporting based on cash flows. It is *Tom A. Lee's* contention that accrual accounting, largely because of its dependence on subjective judgments for allocation purposes, has created a stockpile of problems which has diverted accountants' attention away from the more fundamental problem of finding the most suitable financial information to meet the needs of a variety of users of financial reports. According to Lee, far too much emphasis has been and still is given to the need to report individual values in financial reports. He states that cash is the key resource of most reporting enterprises. His belief is that cash flow reporting must be examined with a view to supplementing or replacing the existing accrual system.

The other U.K. author is *Gerald H. Lawson*. He was invited to write a paper on the rationale of cash-flow accounting to fill a gap in this book. He is the only contributor who has not presented a paper at the Nijenrode seminar. Lawson states that cash flow accounting is concerned with most, if not all, of the traditional purposes of accounting, and with many of the problems, notably inflation, prospective financial performance, etc., to which accounting is now seeking to adapt. The cash flow method of reporting past or prospective financial performance on a going-concern basis avoids any confusion between the functions of the income statement and balance sheet and certainly does not imply that all variants of the balance sheet concept should be cast overboard. Lawson concludes that the Hicksian concept of periodic income cannot be applied by companies in determining shareholder total periodic income. He takes the cash flow earnings equation as a yardstick for evaluating other accounting models and the Sandilands current cost accounting model.

Because of the limited significance of the balance sheet and profit and loss account for internal purposes, many firms, especially those which are basing their decisions on the use of a DCF method, require additional information.

Cees van Dam developed a new statement, the capital-income statement, that can be used as a supplement to the traditional annual statements. From that statement the expected consequences of decisions made in the reporting period and before can be read, just as the consequences of changed views, changed estimates and changed data. In his contribution to this volume, van Dam presents a variant of the statement meant to be used in firms where the net present value criterion is used and where management wishes to be informed periodically about 'the economic position' of the investment centers of the firm. He contributes to a bridging of the gap between accounting and finance.

Palle Hansen carries out an analysis to demonstrate that one cannot impose a meaningful definition onto the two basic accounting concepts of profit and of net capital value. The notion that the traditional annual statement presents a fair (conservative) picture of a company's financial position simply does not apply, according to Hansen. He abandons the traditional statements. Depreciation on fixed assets is omitted and replaced by an item of reservation for refinancing the fixed assets at the time of replacement. The concept of profit in the income statement will for that reason be similar to the concept of realized income. Hansen's suggestion is to replace the traditional balance sheet by a statement of capital administration, cleared of evaluation of the firm's possessions.

Robert N. Anthony's contribution to this book deals with accounting for the cost of interest. He proposes that interest on capital, both debt capital and equity capital, be recorded as a cost in accounting. As a matter of theory, this proposal is consistent with the treatment of interest in economics and with the fundamental cost and entity concepts that govern accounting. Anthony suggests that a 'prime equity interest' rate be established that measures the cost of equity in low-risk companies.

Corporate financial statements serve a variety of purposes. *Myron J. Gordon*'s paper is concerned with only one of them, providing information that is useful to investors for deciding whether to buy, sell or hold the common shares of a corporation. Gordon compares the usefulness of net present value, historical cost, replacement cost, and general price level adjusted cost as bases for income determination and asset valuation in providing information for investment decisions. He states that capital markets would be more efficient without financial statements insofar as there is any likelihood that the analysis of the data contained therein aids in the discovery or prevention of over- or under-priced shares.

Hans G. Eijgenhuijsen and *Jan Klaassen* analyse the relevance of stock market efficiency for the choice among financial reporting alternatives. They make a distinction between 'unbiased' and 'correct' stock prices. New information leads to changes of stock prices, but stock market efficiency has no implications for the correctness of stock prices, neither before nor after the release of new information. Therefore the efficient market concept has no meaning for the question of whether or not new information should be applied.

U.K. and American authorities specify that forecasts should be accompanied by a statement of assumptions to assist the investor in appraising the reasonableness of the forecast and the main uncertainties attached to it. However, the rules do not (a) define an assumption; (b) state the relationship between the format of the projections and the assumptions; (c) establish criteria to determine which assumptions are material and should be disclosed. The last paper of this book, by *Richard H. Haase* and *John J. Clark*, examines the role of assumptions in financial forecasting with particular reference to the assumptions implicit in the use of quantitative forecasting models.

I. A SYNTHESIS OF INFLATION ACCOUNTING AND REPLACEMENT VALUE ACCOUNTING

André J. Bindenga

This article was written in the early part of 1975. At that time, the best known system of inflation accounting was 'general purchasing power accounting'. Since then, however, much has changed, especially in the United Kingdom and the United States. Circumstances have prevented this article being published before about mid-1977, two years later than the original text was produced. As my views on a synthesis have not changed, my article needs no material alteration. Nevertheless, I must say that especially the comparison of inflation accounting and replacement value accounting in section 2 is not up to date. Inflation accounting is no longer limited to general purchasing power accounting.

In the *United Kingdom*, the Report of the Inflation Accounting Committee, Inflation Accounting, was published in September 1975 ('Sandilands Report'). It recommended a system of 'current cost accounting'. This system is not the same as replacement value accounting, but is quite different from general purchasing power accounting. Owing to criticism of the Sandilands report and the earlier proposal by the Institute of Chartered Accountants in England and Wales, a committee headed by Douglas Morpeth again studied the problem of inflation. In December 1976 it produced Exposure Draft 18, a proposal for a new statement of standard accounting practice in the United Kingdom, its contents being essentially current cost accounting with slight modifications.

In the *United States*, the Financial Accounting Standards Board has deferred its proposal for general purchasing power accounting. This deferral may have been influenced by Accounting Series Release 190 of the Securities and Exchange Commission. In this release, a start is made with current cost accounting. According to the Commission, large companies must publish the current replacement value of their assets and the cost of their sales measured at current cost. This information will be supplementary to the historic cost information. In the meantime, the Financial Accounting Standards Board has accelerated its 'conceptual framework'. Part of this framework is the study of the problem of how to measure assets, liabilities, costs and revenues. Besides this, another problem to be studied is that of the measuring unit.

Tendencies towards current cost accounting instead of general purchasing power accounting can also be seen in *Australia, New Zealand* and *Canada*.

The author of this article craves the reader's indulgence if, in the following pages, general purchasing power accounting is overemphasised as the solution to inflation in accounting.

In recent years many articles and books have been written on the influence of changing price levels on financial statements. Proposals have been made for the information to be supplied by enterprises, in most cases leading to a system of 'inflation accounting'. In the theoretical literature the system of 'replacement value accounting' has been proposed. A common notion in inflation accounting and replacement value accounting is that annual financial statements based on historic cost are not usually satisfactory, whatever the reason. The purpose of this article is, *inter alia*, to examine the reasons why there is no synthesis of these two systems. Thus, in the first section, the distinction between external and internal reporting will be considered. The second section briefly compares the two accounting methods, whilst the third section summarises the advantages and disadvantages of inflation accounting and of replacement value accounting. The fourth section enquires into the objectives of annual financial statements, after which it might be possible to select an appropriate method of preparing such statements. This section also points out the essentials of the systems in relation to the conclusions arrived at. If the objectives of financial statements can be fulfilled by taking into account the common conclusions of the different theories, the possibility of disagreement could be reduced or even minimized. If it is possible to abandon some remaining elements of disagreement, providing they are not essential to the objectives of financial statements, many difficulties could be reconciled. In the fifth and last section I give my views on the underlying principles of financial statements. A proposal will be made for a method of determining corporate annual results. The implications of this system will also be dealt with.

1. Reporting to external users and for management

The underlying notion of replacement value accounting is based on the assumption that the accounting system deals with information for management and also for the published financial statements.

Replacement value accounting is not a technique for preparing financial statements but more a means of keeping a record of capital employed and business transactions. As such, the accounting system is looked upon as an integrated system, providing management information and information for external reporting. Obviously, there is only a slight distinction between financial accounting and managerial accounting. For information on income and capital employed for internal and external users, replacement value is applied.

It must be said that many accountants throughout the world believe it is very idealistic to suppose that the accounting system could serve both purposes. They argue that managerial accounting extends beyond financial accounting to use data selectively, the foremost objective being to serve the needs of management.[1] Managerial accounting serves the needs of management and can be free from many of the restrictions imposed upon accounting information to the external users. Furthermore, managerial accounting is not bound by government rules and regulations. Managerial accounting is not forced to operate within boundaries established by the principles and procedures which govern financial accounting.

Probably one of the most important reasons for the confusion about replacement value accounting is the misunderstanding of the purposes of the system. Whereas the application of replacement values in business administration is aimed primarily at internal management, accountants feel that this system is intended for external purposes. In fact, using replacement values for published accounts is only an extension of its original function.

On the other hand, the attempts at non-historic cost information known as inflation accounting are aimed primarily at external reporting, whereas other information is probably already being used for internal purposes.[2]

In many countries there are rather stringent legal requirements for the preparation of financial statements for external purposes. Often, these regulations do not allow the use of current values or replacement values. But, it would be naive to suggest that companies compelled to follow these rules in external reporting should not make use of current values and current costs in information for managerial purposes.

The purpose of this article is to try and find a bridge between replacement value accounting and inflation accounting. Further specification of this attempt seems necessary. Inflation accounting mostly deals with external reporting, whilst totally different data are relevant for internal purposes. Replacement value accounting deals primarily with internal reporting and these different data may well deal with current values as well. It is also a question of whether managerial accounting and financial accounting can be blended in the same way

1. Carl L. Moore and Robert K. Jaedike, *Managerial accounting* (South Western Publishing Co. Cincinnati, 1972) p. 11.
2. Graeme MacDonald, *Profit measurement: alternatives to historical cost* (Accountancy Age Books, 1974).

as is in fact done with replacement value theory. It would seem better to limit the scope of the attempt dealing only with external reporting.

This article is not actually concerned with managerial accounting and this will of course introduce marked restrictions, and the problems will be reduced. The nature of this article, however, does not allow the advantages of current cost data for management decisions to be investigated.

2. Comparison of inflation accounting and replacement value accounting

Since 1920 a certain trend can be recognized in accounting literature indicating that it is incorrect to treat the profit of a business as the difference between selling price and historic cost. The reason is, apparently, that inflation has become one of the realities of economic life. Since the Second World War inflation has spread throughout nearly all civilized countries. Two main objectives of economic policy are price stability and full employment at the same time.[3]

However, to achieve full employment or, perhaps put better, to avoid large-scale unemployment, increasing prices are a necessary additional symptom. Some economists do not even believe in the possibility of full employment and a stable price level existing. Simultaneously, as the main care of economic policy is to ensure employment, inflation will last as long as this care predominates. The efforts of various groups in society to obtain higher incomes has accelerated inflation even more.

However interesting it may be, this is not the place to make a detailed analysis of the causes of inflation. Inflation is a current aspect of our lives and has influenced many writers discussing accounting. Besides this, many practitioners and professional bodies have overlooked the impact of inflation upon the determination of equity and income.

It would be rather impractical to compare the many systems with the replacement value system. Only the best-known system of inflation accounting will be discussed, viz. the system of general purchasing power accounting. No distinction will be made in terminology as between price-level accounting and inflation accounting as these are regarded as equivalents. The features of this system will be contrasted with those of the replacement value system after which the advantages and disadvantages will be summarised.[4]

3. R. Ludewig, 'The treatment of changes in the purchasing power of a country's currency in financial statements' (Paper UEC Congress, 1973) p. 9.
4. As stated in the preface, this article was written *before* publication of the Sandilands report and the proposals by accountants' organizations in Australia and New Zealand. The tendency towards

a. General purchasing power accounting

The essential characteristics of the methods to be dealt with as systems of general purchasing power accounting are:
1. The items on the balance sheet, stated at historic values, are converted into adjusted historical values mostly called general purchasing power equivalents.
2. The items in the profit and loss account, also stated at historic values, are also converted into adjusted values.
3. The conversion factor to be used in all methods of general purchasing power accounting is a general index, whatever the source of this index might be.
4. Most of the methods of general purchasing power accounting distinguish the items on the balance sheet as non-monetary and monetary items.
   The non-monetary items are usually only assets, i.e. the fixed assets and inventories. The monetary items are, in nearly all cases, current assets less inventories and long- and short-term liabilities. All monetary assets and liabilities are not normally converted with an index, but if there is a balance (assets higher), a loss on monetary items will have arisen. Such a loss is accounted for in the profit and loss account. Some methods calculate this loss in a different way because more than one general index could be applied in the profit and loss account. In the case of a profit on monetary items, i.e. net monetary working capital, this is the opposite of a loss in certain systems.
5. The equity value in the balance sheet is also converted into general purchasing power equivalents. Some methods suggest charging this equity with any loss on monetary items instead of charging the profit and loss account.

Systems of general purchasing power accounting have been advocated by professional accountancy organizations in the United Kingdom and in the United States in recent years. An 'Accounting Research Study' by the American Institute of Certified Public Accountants was published in 1963,[5] followed in 1969 by a 'Statement' by the Accounting Principles Board.[6] In 1974 the successor to the Accounting Principles Board, the Financial Accounting Standards Board,

'general purchasing power accounting' has greatly decreased since these publications. The aforementioned proposals are directed at 'current cost accounting', a quite different approach from that of the 'general purchasing accounting'.
5. Accounting Research Study No. 6: 'Reporting the financial effects of price level changes' (AICPA, New York, 1963).
6. Statement no. 3: 'Financial Statements restated for general price level changes' (AICPA, New York, 1969).

issued a 'Discussion Memorandum' on this subject.[7] In 1973, the Accounting Standards Steering Committee of the English Institute published the well-known 'Exposure Draft 8',[8] superseded in 1974 by a provisional 'Statement of Standard Accounting Practice'.[9] Moreover, one of the subjects at the European accounting bodies' congress in 1973 was 'the effects of changes in the purchasing power of money'. This interest in the problem is not new, but publications are more numerous, probably as a result of accelerating inflation.

The above-mentioned publications have a number of features in common. In the first place, the use of a general index for the conversion process is strongly recommended. The argument in favour of this is that the purpose of the methods is to measure the effects on financial statements of changes only in the general purchasing power of money. It is not intended to show current values. Secondly, in spite of the fact that the systems aim at maintaining the purchasing power of the equity value of a business, the individual balance sheet items are converted into general purchasing power equivalents. Thirdly, the common characteristic of the recommended systems is the refusal to integrate general purchasing power accounting in the traditional historical financial statements.

The systems are aimed at creating supplementary financial statements as additional information over and above the normal annual financial statements at historic cost. Last but not least, much criticism has been levelled at the various systems proposed; criticism by economists in particular was fundamental. These criticisms will be reverted to later.

b. Replacement value accounting

A brief summary is given of the principles of replacement value accounting:

1. The non-monetary assets are valued on the balance sheet at replacement value, taking into account the specific replacement values of the various assets.
2. For calculation of the net profit in the profit and loss account, costs are also based on current cost.

7. Reporting the effects of general price level changes in financial statements (AICPA, New York, 1974). This discussion memorandum resulted in an exposure draft in December 1974. In 1976 the FASB decided to defer consideration of a statement on this subject, probably because of recent developments (see preface to this article).
8. 'Exposure draft 8: Accounting for inflation' (Accounting Standards Steering Committee, 1973).
9. Because of the publication of the Sandilands report, this statement will probably be overruled by another proposal. In the meantime, a proposal has been published by the Accounting Standards Committee, resulting in Exposure Draft 18 on current cost accounting (see preface to this article).

3. Current cost is determined either by specific price indices or by replacement cost of the various assets.
4. Replacement value accounting has, in principle, provided the solution for dealing with holding gains. All holding gains on normal inventory and fixed assets are not considered as profits. Only holding gains on supernormal inventories, the so-called speculative profits, are part of business profit unless they are not realized at balance sheet date.
5. Replacement value accounting is intended as an integrated system. Therefore, the use of the method is not limited to a conversion process at the end of the period. The accounting system is organized to account for replacement values during the period.
6. Results on monetary items are not taken into consideration.

The system of replacement value accounting has been advocated especially by Dutch writers on accounting. In English and American literature a practical application was introduced by A. Goudeket.[10]

3. Evaluation of the two accounting methods

After examining the two accounting methods the stage is reached to sum up the advantages and disadvantages. No complete evaluation will be given yet; it is preferable to defer this until after examination of the objectives of financial statements in the next part of this chapter.

In the first place a comment must be made on a feature which the systems have in common. This is the fact that in these accounting systems there is a link between valuation in the balance sheet and cost in the profit and loss account. If fixed assets, for example, are valued above historic value, the basis of depreciation will be this revised value.

To my mind the background to this common characteristic is the notion that profit is the difference between two values, i.e. equity value at the end and beginning of a financial period. This is not a very revolutionary idea but rather the most obvious idea about profits. The link between value and profits is the basis of conventional accounting as well as the background for profit analysis in economic theory.

As for conventional accounting, the normal method in the past has been to calculate profit by comparing the amount of money a merchant had before he

10. A. Goudeket, 'An application of replacement value theory' (in: *The Journal of Accountancy*, July 1960).

bought and sold articles and the amount of money he had after doing so. Moreover, since the growth of modern industry, this method has been well known as 'the balance sheet approach' to profit determination. At the beginning of a financial period, a balance sheet is drawn up providing a survey of assets and liabilities, the balance resulting in a net value or equity. The same is done at the end of a financial period, arriving at a new balance and a new equity. The difference is the profit or loss. The assets and liabilities are valued at both moments as fairly and truly as possible. A very important principle in this valuation is an objective approach.

In principle, the economic approach to the determination of profit has the same method of calculating results. But economists do not believe in the concept of objectivity as conventional accounting does. Income is defined by economists[11] as 'the maximum value a person can consume during a week and still expect to be as well off at the end of the week as he was at the beginning'. In this definition, the term 'expect' calls for comment. Here we have a major element of subjectivity: income is based on expectations. The calculation of income according to economists consists of finding some sort of standard stream of values whose present capitalized value equals the present value of the stream of receipts which is actually in prospect. It is a standard stream in that it maintains some sort of constancy, as against the actual expected stream of receipts, which may fluctuate in any manner whatsoever.[12] The notion of value in this concept equals the present value of future proceeds. An asset or complex of assets has a value only if, out of this asset or complex of assets, an income can be gained. Income is the difference between two values: the value at the end and at the beginning of a period. Both values are the discounted future proceeds of the net asset value. Besides this subjectivity, the economic approach deals with proceeds in the future, or in other words: with uncertainties.

As indicated above, both conventional accounting and economic theory consider income or profit as a difference between two net asset values. The differences are very considerable however. Since profit in conventional accounting is said to be based on objective figures and valuation ex-post, economic theory determines profit with subjective figures and valuation ex-ante.

After recognizing the feature the two systems of accounting have in common and comparing its background, the advantages and disadvantages of the systems will be discussed. Primary consideration will be given to the objections to the various systems.

11. J. R. Hicks, *Value and capital: an inquiry into some fundamental principles of economic theory* (Oxford Press, Oxford, 1946) p. 172.
12. Hicks, op. cit. p. 184.

a. General purchasing power accounting

There are three elements which could be called the 'charm' of general purchasing power accounting. First of all, inflation can only be measured by the trend in the general price level. If the aim of financial statements is to demonstrate the effects of inflation, there is no denying that the general purchasing power of money has to be taken into account in some way. The second attraction of general purchasing power accounting is the simplicity of bookkeeping in the course of the financial year. No change has to be made in conventional accounting procedures. Purchases, investment, costs and sales can continue to be recorded in historical amounts as the transformation process only has to take place at the end of the period. The figures recorded in the books are not changed: conversion of the figures is only a supplementary calculation. The third advantage of general purchasing power accounting is said to be the objectivity of the conversion factor. If a general index were used by any company converting its traditional financial statements into figures corrected for inflation, much confusion could be avoided regarding the subjectivity connected with the deviation from historical amounts.

Usually, there is nothing attractive in destroying the 'charm' of anything. But I think this must be done in summing up a considerable number of objections to general purchasing power accounting.

In the first place, a major objection must be clearly stated: If the objects of the general purchasing power systems ought to be to demonstrate the effects of inflation on financial statements, the converted accounts do not, in my opinion, provide a solution. The conversion of historical amounts into up-dated amounts is artificial and automatic. The converted amounts by no means show a company management's success in the battle with inflation. The effects of inflation on financial statements should be demonstrated as if the capital invested in a business is maintained in relation to the development of purchasing power.

Converting the invested capital by means of a general index demonstrates nothing. As other people have also said: 'It is not possible to derive from the supplementary statements the success or otherwise of the managers of a business in safeguarding the shareholders' funds against the effects of inflation'.[13] In my opinion, the only way to demonstrate the more or less successful fight against inflation as regards the equity value of a business is the following: At the beginning and end of a financial period the net asset value of a business is calculated, based on real values of assets. The difference between the two net

13. Bryan Lund, 'The manager and inflation accounting' (in: *Accountancy*, October 1974, p. 36).

values is compared with the extent of inflation as given by a general index. Accordingly, the difference between the two net asset values should not include profits for the year. The reader will notice that the calculation of the net asset value introduces subjectivity and is still based on the balance sheet approach for profit determination.

Apart from this principal objection, a series of other disadvantages of general purchasing power accounting are mentioned. As a consequence of the conversion process the non-monetary assets appear on the balance sheet at a fictitious amount. Fixed assets are computed for conversion with the general index, while technological influences and specific price fluctuations are not taken into account. Inventories, too, are converted, disregarding the trend in market prices for the industry in which the business operates. The user of the supplementary statements may indeed wonder what kind of information is supplied; especially with assets acquired many years previously, the figures in the supplementary balance sheet could not at all give the value of these assets. There is an awareness of the fact that some methods try to avoid this problem. The proposed 'Statement of Standard Accounting Practice'[14] says, for instance:

In the conversion process, after increasing non-monetary items by the amount of inflation, it is necessary to apply the test of lower of cost (expressed in pounds of current purchasing power) and net realisable value to relevant current assets, e.g. inventories, and further to adjust the figures if necessary. Similarly, after restating fixed assets in terms of pounds of current purchasing power, the question of the value to the business needs to be reviewed in that context and provision made if necessary.

It is interesting, however, that much criticism of the proposed system in this proposed statement ignores this paragraph, as was argued for example by Prof. Bak at the Jerusalem Congress of Accountants in October 1974.[15] May it be suggested that by applying general purchasing power accounting, this test of lower of converted cost or market could easily be forgotten. If not, a mass of subjectivity is introduced into the system.

Another argument against general purchasing power accounting is that the suggested objectivity is false. Since the financial statements in historical amounts are drawn up with considerable subjectivity, the converted amounts cannot be objective. As was agreed by many authors, e.g. Prof. Chambers, the historic cost convention places very few limits on the exercise of judgement.[16] For the valuation of receivables, inventories, plant and equipment, subjective judgement

---

14. ED 8, proposed statement, number 21.
15. G. G. M. Bak, 'Financial reporting under inflationary conditions: trends and prospects' (Paper Jerusalem Congress, October 1974).
16. R. J. Chambers, 'General purchasing power accounting: ED 8 is not the answer' (in: *The Accountant*, July 5, 1973).

is absolutely necessary.[17] It is rather strange that systems of general purchasing power accounting are claiming to be objective while the basis is subjective. Linked to this contradiction is the use of the appropriate index. It sounds attractive to emphasize the use of one general index, but the question might arise: What is a general index? As far as is known, no country in the world publishes a general index. Indeed, retail-price indices and consumer-price indices are available statistical information, but these are not, in fact, general indices. Even assuming each country had a general index, the problem still exists for companies with a world-wide organization of subsidiaries. Does a weighted average have to be applied in the supplementary statement and what weighting factors are to be used? The advantage of one objective conversion factor is, in the writer's view, too idealistic.

A further comment must be made as to profit determination in the use of general purchasing power accounting. The fact remains that the annual financial statements to be approved by shareholders are the accounts in historical amounts. The converted statements are only supplementary and do not necessarily play a role in determining dividends. Even if shareholders were to allow for the fact that the converted profit is a better basis for dividend determination than the historical profit, it may nevertheless be dangerous to rely on such a basis. The purpose of presenting a converted profit is to demonstrate to shareholders that the historical profit is not a real profit but includes so-called holding gains. If shareholders were to think that the converted profit is a real profit, which can be distributed in full, they might be wrong. A company has to allow for replacement of its assets. As stated above, it is not at all certain that the assets converted with a general index could be replaced for these artificially computed amounts. Therefore, recognizing converted profit as distributable profit is extremely dangerous and could bring the business into difficulties. In this context, Kirkman speaks of maintaining the purchasing power of the firm.[18]

The index which is used should be related to the purchasing power of the business organization, as opposed to more general purchasing power. The invested capital is regarded as a collection of physical assets, the real value of which must have been kept constant for capital to have been maintained. Another question is: do shareholders in fact take the supplementary statements into account as a basis for their judgements? It is doubtful whether the proper way of inflation accounting is that of supplementary statements.

Another element, not really an objection to general purchasing power accounting, is the treatment of monetary assets. As is the case in general

---

17. Edward Stamp, 'Income and value determination and changing price-levels' (in: *The Accountant's Magazine*, June 1971, p. 277).
18. Kirkman, op. cit. p. 45.

purchasing power accounting, the loss on the balance of monetary assets and liabilities is charged to the profit and loss account. The financial leverage is introduced silently into the determination of profit. High gearing has a favourable effect on profits. This is a remarkable feature, which will be reverted to later in this chapter.

Another fact that should be mentioned is the deviation from the realization principle in general purchasing power accounting. In my opinion this principle is twofold. On the one hand, it has to be taken into account in profit determination as far as concerns the requirement that there must be a market transaction for the realization of profit, while no profit can be shown until the cash-cash cycle has been completed for an asset. On the other hand, the realization principle has to do with valuation; all assets are valued at historic cost until after realization. To put this briefly: the realization principle implies the rule not to take profit or higher equity unless realized. It is clear that converted financial statements do not coincide with the realization principle.

In ending this assessment, there are two final objections to general purchasing power accounting. It is often said that fiscal obligations are not properly met if the assets shown on a balance sheet are presented at amounts higher that historic cost. This relates to the famous problem of deferred income tax. In conclusion, it may be said that the conversion process seems easy but that a lot of arithmetic might be necessary in a period traditionally very busy for the officers of a company who deal with accounting.

b. Replacement value accounting

It has been said that replacement value accounting is based on an economic theory of value, seeks the correct profit, gives the correct valuation and is even practically applicable.

An effort will be made below to give the disadvantages and the criticisms, but firstly the reader's attention should be drawn to the fact that replacement value accounting is linked with economic theory more than the system already discussed. The link between value and profit is the strongest in replacement value accounting. The difference compared with economic theory, however, still exists in two respects; that is to say the aim of objective income and valuation ex-post.

The first point of criticism relates to the asserted economic basis of replace-ment value accounting.[19] Close reference may be made to an article by Professor

---

19. See e.g.: George M. Scott and Abram Mey, 'Theodore Limperg and his theory of values and costs' (*Abacus*, September 1966).

Burgert setting forth the invalidity of the theory of replacement value and income measurement.[20] As stated above, there is a close link between value and profits in replacement value accounting. The theory of value, therefore, is the foundation of the theory of income measurement. If this theory of value is invalid then the theory of income measurement loses its basis and is also invalid. Burgert has demonstrated that the theory of value is founded on an apriorism. This apriorism is the assumption that the value of a good is governed by its replacement value or its realizable value, but always the lower of the two.[21] Apart from the fact that replacement value theory does not provide any evidence for this proposition, there is something else. A value theory that does not fully allow for the possibility that there may be irreplaceable goods or that there may be goods which are more or less difficult to replace, and that these more or less irreplaceable goods can sometimes be used in different ways, cannot be very helpful in making managerial decisions. Together with the fact that in economic theory the value of a good consists of the expected future balance of proceeds and costs, the replacement value theory, considering this only as value if it is lower than replacement value and realizable value, it seems better to abandon the notion of an economic basis for replacement value accounting.

In spite of this criticism, replacement value accounting might possibly be a practical way of calculating income.

The principle of income measurement in replacement value accounting is the calculation of profits distributable on the condition that the source of income is maintained. Therefore holding gains are never considered as income unless they relate to gains on more than normal inventories. In the writer's opinion, holding gains could sometimes be distributed, depending on the way the business is financed. It is rather strange that an increase in the value of assets financed wholly or partly by long- or short-term nominal debt could never be a profit if replacement of these assets were possibly by new financial resources rather than equity. Burgert has another argument for this. He thinks the disadvantage of the theory is that it does not consider what is going to happen in the selling market once the replacement value of one or more production factors has increased. The source of income would be maintained intact only if it could be taken for granted that the future total absolute margin of profit were to remain unchanged. If the absolute margin of profit increases, the increase in value can be considered wholly or partly as income. In order to reach the same income as before, it is not essential to have the same production capacity. If the absolute margin of profit decreases,

20. R. Burgert, 'Reservations about replacement value accounting in the Netherlands': (*Abacus*, December 1972).
21. Burgert, op. cit. p. 117.

withholding the increase in the value of assets will not suffice to maintain the source of income intact.

Some other arguments against replacement value accounting may be summarized in a few words.

The deviation from the realization principle also exists in replacement value accounting. But it relates only to presentation of the equity. The problems of deferred income tax and subjectiveness in assessing replacement value also play a part. Results on monetary items are not taken into account; financial leverage seemed not to be relevant in the original replacement value accounting system.

As to other arguments against this system, reference is made to the foregoing evaluation of general purchasing power accounting. These arguments are: (a) the statements are mostly supplementary; and (b) a lot of arithmetic is required in busy periods.

Two elements of replacement value accounting must be mentioned because they relate only to this system. The first is that replacement value is not the same as current cost. The replacement value of an asset is the cost of replacing it. It is quite possible, however, for an asset to be replaced not by a non-identical asset but by one having the same function in the business. This causes an increase in the degree of subjectivity. The management of a business tries fairly constantly to suit the equipment to changing dynamic business conditions. Asset replacement depends largely on the planning of future activities: hence it is often impossible to determine objectively the replacement value of existing assets. This problem known as the problem of non-identical replacement, is practically unsolvable.

The second element is that of the accounting records. Replacement value accounting is intended to be dealt with as an integral system, and not only for the presentation of supplementary statements. The problems arising in bookkeeping are numerous.

In concluding this section it can be said that both types of systems have their shortcomings. One is inclined to say that the criticism relates essentially to the increase in the degree of subjectiveness in accounting. Maybe the refusal to abandon the link between balance sheet valuation and the determination of profit is the cause of this. The balance sheet approach, with its traditional and moreover economic basis, does not allow this linkage to be abandoned. Before deciding whether this link is absolutely necessary, the objectives of financial statements must first be examined.

4. The objectives of financial statements

There are at least three financial statements: the balance sheet, the profit and loss account and a statement of the accounting principles applied therein. A balance sheet is a summary of assets and liabilities at a certain date and is expressed in money in a certain way. The profit and loss account specifies the changes in the summary of assets and liabilities compared with a former summary. This specification is also expressed in money in a certain way. The above definitions of the balance sheet and profit and loss account consider the balance sheet as the most important statement, determining, in fact, the profits.

The profit and loss accounts gives only a specification. If this approach is still correct, it is one of the elements to study in this section.

The historical development of the basis of accounting could be summarized as follows. The old system of 'venture accounting' used by merchants was intended to determine the surplus remaining at the conclusion of their ventures. The rise of modern capitalism resulted in the creation of a growing number of separate legal entities within whose framework a series of ventures continuing over an indefinite period of time were conducted. This led to increasingly more emphasis on the importance of the balance sheet and to a conservative system of asset valuation which was designed to protect the creditors of family-owned enterprises. In the twentieth century the development of technology has created an enormous demand for capital beyond the resources of virtually any large family company. The consequence has been the divorce of ownership from management and the creation of securities markets. The result of this was that the balance sheet has remained an important document, but the dominant statement today is the profit and loss account.[22] In this account the management renders an account of its administration for the proceding financial period. The financial statements, of which the profit and loss account is the most important, provide information on the way the management has fulfilled its responsibility.

Financial statements as documents to demonstrate the way in which the responsibilities were fulfilled are not the only approach to the information function of financial statements. Another approach, leading to the concept that financial statements are information for decision-making purposes, needs a further clarification of the objectives of organizations such as modern enterprises.

A business enterprise is an organization. In economic theory the concept of the firm has been developed wherein the goal of the firm is considered to be maximization of profits. Economic theory utilizes more or less traditionally the

22. Stamp. op. cit. p. 280.

so-called holistic concept of the firm. Holistic concepts of the firm are distinguished by at least four major characteristics. They emphasize action by a collective rather than by actors in the collective. They assume predetermined rational behavior patterns. They point a clear-cut goal for the firms. They assume as external environment that creates the need for action.[23] The concepts of the firm discussed as holistic concepts stress the impersonal movements of an organism operating toward a specific goal on an environment that is objectively defined.

Many disciplines other than economic theory, however, have also studied the concepts of the firm. After the Second World War the so-called behavioral theory of the firm as an alternative to the economic theory of the firm gained ground.[24] The behavioral framework encompasses a much wider area within which concepts of the firm may be established. The common features of behavioral theories are: (a) it is not the firm that acts, but the actors within the firm; (b) behavior of actors is conditioned by personality as well as environment factors; (c) cognition, perception, beliefs and knowledge of the actors must be taken into account; and (d) the goals of the actors are often complex.

This behavioral approach to the firm is of importance for an analysis of the objectives of financial statements, since one can derive the significance of information for decision-making purposes.

The firm as an organization must be looked upon as a pattern of personal relationships of human beings, cooperating consciously or unconsciously with the goal of promoting their interests directly or indirectly. These persons cooperating in this system of relationships are called participants. The participants work together because they feel that the inducements they receive have greater utility for them than the contributions they have to offer. The cooperation is viable when the sum of inducements is not lower than the sum of contributions. These inducements are not necessarily money, for the total pattern that is the firm also includes a complicated set of status systems established formally, and by age, position, etc. According to the behavioralists, the willingness of each member of the firm to serve, and thus the adhesive that holds the firm together or makes it viable, is dependent upon the net inducements offered to each member, which must be positive.[25]

It should be understood that the participants in the firm are internal as well as external. All participants offer a contribution and are offered an inducement.

23. Joseph McGuire, *Theories of business behavior* (Prentice Hall, Englewood Cliffs, 1964).
24. Richard M. Cyert and James G. March, *A behavioral theory of the firm* (Prentice Hall, Englewood Cliffs, 1965).
25. Herbert A. Simon, 'A comparison of organization theories' (in: *Models of Man*, Wiley and Sons, New York, 1957).

The following summary gives an idea of this:

Participants	Contribution to the organization	Inducement from the organization
External		
Shareholders	Money	Dividends
Bankers	Money	Interest
Suppliers	Raw material	Money
Customers	Money	Products
Government	Legal system	Taxes
Internal		
Management	Labor	Money, status
Employees	Labor	Money, satisfaction

The viability of an organization means, in fact, that all participants must continue to be willing to cooperate in the pattern of relationships. They are willing if the utility of the inducements is higher than their contributions. Since it is very difficult to measure the intangible inducements, one could limit the sum of contributions and inducements to tangible things, measurable items. These tangibles are the flow of income and the flow of expenses, both in a broad sense. In this article this will be called the 'concept of continuity'; in traditional accounting it may be called the 'going-concern concept'. To define it more precisely: *a business has a continuity when the flow of income is not lower than the flow of expenses, these flows to be considered in the minds of the participants.* One is aware that this is a rather vague concept. Many readers will say: 'How do I know if, in the minds of my shareholders, the dividends have greater utility than the money which they have given to me' or 'How do I know if my banker will lend me money if I pay him interest of $x\%$ or $y\%$'. Of course this concept of continuity is vague, but it has to be demonstrated that analyzing business behavior must take into account all the participants.

All participants, external and internal, frequently make decisions. One of these decisions is to stay in the organization. As Simon wrote, the participants do not make all the decisions rationally. He rejects the notion of omniscient rationality and substitutes for this an idea of limited or bounded rationality. Man in the organization recognizes that the world he perceives is a drastically simplified model of the real world. He is content to leave out of account those aspects of reality that are substantially irrelevant at a given time. He makes his choices using a simple picture of the situation that takes into account just a few of the factors that he regards as most relevant and crucial. All the participants attempt, however, to be as rational as possible within the limits set for them by their personalities and by the environment. The business organization becomes an imperfect decision-making model, forced continually to choose from alternatives without knowing exactly what the results of each choice will be.

Under such conditions it becomes evident that men in business cannot know the best alternative in all cases where choices must be made.[26]

Let us now revert to the subject of the objectives of financial statements. Financial statements give information and may be regarded as an instrument for management to demonstrate the way it has used its responsibilities. In my opinion, the information in financial statements serves far more the information needs of participants in providing alternatives for their decisions. The financial statements are part of the information for their decision making. One ought to realize this important function of financial statements to a greater extent. In this context an extremely important decision process is the allocation of resources. Shareholders, investors, bankers and potential investors want the optimum investment of their resources. Financial statements of enterprises are information for them and help them in their decisions to invest or to reinvest. The investors want to know periodically if their decision to invest in a certain company was a good decision.

This idea of financial statements being useful in making economic decisions is a concept already recognized by accountants in the United States of America. In 1966 the American Accounting Association published a statement[27] which emphasized the fact that economic information should meet the needs of the users. To draw a conclusion about the contents of accounting, a study is necessary of the users' decision processes. The American Institute of Certified Public Accountants has also said that accounting should be defined as:[28] 'a service activity to provide quantitive information, primarily of a financial nature, about economic entities that is intended to be useful in making economic decisions'.

Financial accounting has to do with financial statements which give *inter alia* information about economic activities that is useful in making economic decisions.

The financial statements provide information on results. The analysis of results in the financial statements of today is not satisfactory, Earnings per share, for example, are not comparable in the various accounting principles applied.

26. Herbert A. Simon, *Administrative behavior* (Wiley and Sons, New York, 1947) p. 55.
27. A statement of basic accounting theory' (American Accounting Association, 1968).
28. Statement No. 4 of the Accounting Principles Board: 'Basic concepts and accounting principles underlying financial statements of business enterprises'. (AICPA, New York, 1970).

The financial statements constitute an instrument for external participants to put them in a position to judge the conduct of the business organization. As a matter of fact, one should realize that the information in financial statements should largely meet the users needs.

When financial statements are drawn up, one should envisage the kind of decisions the user wants to make. In other words: to judge whether the objectives of financial statements are fulfilled one ought to know the user's decision model. This may seem a quite different approach from financial accounting. The information in financial statements should be dictated by the information needs for users' decision making, not the willingness of management to give information on its abilities.

Thus, financial statements are information. It is realized that today they are intended more as stewardship accounts of management than information accounts for decision-making purposes. The management gives an account of its conduct, the financial consequences thereof being incorporated in financial statements. The results of its conduct are said to be found in the financial statements. To judge if management has succeeded in attaining its goals, a periodic presentation of results is necessary. Before determining the principles underlying financial statements, the goals of management must be determined, because the financial statements present the degree to which these goals have been realized.

Derived from the above considerations on the behavioral approach to the firm, the main goal of management is to maintain the cooperation of the participants. In other words: the viability of the coalition of participants. This is called: maintaining continuity in a broad sense.

If then, the principles of financial statements are formulated, it can be said that:

1. Financial statements are in principle documents for demonstrating the way in which responsibilities are fulfilled, but are also used as information for decision-making purposes.
2. The continuity of the organization is the main goal of management.
3. Financial statements give information on the realization of this main goal.

It must be said that accounting principles in many cases more or less assume the continuity concept. The going-concern concept is a sort of or basic postulate. Frankly speaking, this cannot be a postulate; it should be the aim to demonstrate this in financial statements.

An attempt will now be made to evaluate the systems of general purchasing power accounting and replacement value accounting, taking into account the above considerations.

As a common feature of the systems, the balance sheet approach to profit determination has been recognized. The results of a financial period are determined by comparing two balance sheets. The profit and loss account gives only a specification of the changes in equity value. In fact, profits are defined as an increase in net asset value. There is an awareness of the fact that not all systems completely adopt this approach. Defining profits as an increase in net asset value may be described as an 'all-inclusive income-statement'. Replacement value accounting in particular does not produce such a statement, but rather a 'current-operating-income statement'. This latter characteristic is somewhat irrelevant in distinguishing the common feature since it is desired to oppose the balance sheet approach as such. If it is intended to give financial statements the function either of demonstrating the way the responsibilities have been fulfilled or giving information for decision-making purposes, the net asset value would not seem to be so important.

In the financial statements the user wants to read: (a) information on the degree of realization of the organization's goals (the element of demonstrating the way responsibilities have been fulfilled) and (b) information for preparing his decision-making.

In my opinion, the profit and loss account is the most essential document for both elements. The results of the management's activities to ensure the viability of the organization (in other words, the care for the continuity of the enterprise) are shown in the profit and loss account. Investors are interested in earnings per share and the degree of growth of future earnings for preparing their decisions. Employees base their claims for more income on the results of the organization.

The first conclusion is that the profit and loss account is the prevailing document in the financial statements. The balance sheet approach to profit determination must be abandoned. The net asset value and changes therein are not entirely unimportant, but the strong accent on equity should be altered largely to emphasize the profit and loss account. As will be demonstrated in the next section, it is not a cast iron law that profits or losses are the difference between the two net asset values.

Nevertheless, there are some good things in the systems of accounting described. Maintenance of organization's purchasing power, which one tries in some way to reach by replacement value accounting, is such a thing.

In order to ensure the continuity of the business, it might be necessary to leave the assets intact. In the endeavour to maintain a flow of income greater than the flow of expenses, the assets of the business need to be replaced. However, it is not an automatic rule that maintenance of the assets guarantees continuity. The goal of maintaining the assets is only part of the aim for continuity. But, taking into account current prices of assets is in fact a step in the struggle for continuity.

As to maintaining the general purchasing power of the equity, this could also be part of the aim for continuity. Investors may look to earnings at first; if the business weakens through not maintaining its equity, the guarantees of survival diminish.

Thus, maintaining the purchasing power of the business and the general purchasing power of the equity have been recognized as useful elements in the described systems. However, some other important elements must be added to the systems in order to fulfill the objectives of financial statements.

These supplementary elements have at least four aspects. The first element is clearly the most important; this is the pivot on which everything turns, since the intention is to demonstrate in the financial statements the way in which the management has tried to safeguard the continuity of the enterprise. As already stated, maintaining the purchasing power of the business and maintaining the general purchasing power of the equity is not sufficient. In order to hold the organization together (or in other words, to ensure its viability) it is necessary to guarantee a certain flow of income in the future. Two important factors can cause this maintenance of the purchasing power of the assets to be insufficient for the purpose. In the first place, assets having a certain function in a business might be replaced by quite different assets. These other assets migh even have a quite different technical function but the same economic function. A simple example: A newspaper publisher with his own composing facilities makes use of lead-type composing machines. He has about fifteen such machines in operation. Current prices of such machines are known and it would be possible to maintain the purchasing power of the enterprise. Everybody in this industry, however, knows that lead-type machines require a lot of labor. If the battery of fifteen machines were to be replaced, then they would surely be replaced by one photographic composing machine and the employment of computers.

At this moment the price of this machine is known and is much higher than the current prices of fifteen old machines. Moreover, a lot of research has been done to improve the new method and the price of the new machine is estimated to be even higher at the actual replacement date. A guarantee of continuity would mean depreciating the old machines on the basis of an estimated price of a machine not to be purchased at present. In this case, the replacement machine still has the same technical function, but it may be that a totally different line of products is to be made instead of the former products. The second factor causing maintenance of the purchasing power of assets to be insufficient relates to the dynamics of society. To have a certain guarantee of the survival of an enterprise (i.e. to hold together the coalition of participants), growth, expansion, diversification, etc. may sometimes be necessary. It would, therefore, be idealistic to assume that the maintenance concept safeguards continuity.

The second element that should be incorporated in the systems is to dispense with the ambiguity of supplementary statements. Such statements confuse the user. It is essential for a company's financial statements to consist of only one set of statements. Since, in the writer's opinion, the profit and loss account is the main document, he wants to advocate a single account.

The third element relates to the assumptions of the systems that there can only be one result. Replacement value accounting, especially, has this approach. Not every user of financial statements is satisfied with the same profit. There are users who think that profit based on historical cost serves their information needs. Other users believe that profits with cost at current basis are the best for their needs. If it is possible to show more that one result in the profit and loss account, this should be done.

The fourth element concerns the financial structure of a business. As already pointed out, general purchasing power accounting takes the financial leverage into account in a certain way. As far as a balance exists between monetary assets and liabilities, a loss is included in the supplementary profit and loss account. Neither current cost accounting nor replacement value accounting deal systematically with the leverage effect, although this is a necessary addition for profit determination.

Before an attempt is made to suggest a synthesis, this section can conclude additions also introduce a greater degree of subjectivity.

One should realize, however, that this subjectivity also exists in historical cost accounting. It is necessary to admit subjectivity in financial accounting; it would be strange to disregard reality in this context. Once subjectivity is accepted, a sharp distinction between profit determination and profit retention is arbitrary as well. This aspect will be dealt with in the next section.

If this were not the case, profit distribution (or retention in the business) might be a correction of the profit determination according to the subjective views of the management.

Realizing the consequences of the basic postulate, we can formulate five starting points for proposing a synthesis, summarized under the following headings: (1) *replacement prices;* (2) *subjective view;* (3) *financial leverage;* (4) *profit and loss statement;* and (5) *valuation.*

Re 1. Replacement prices
In order to maintain the continuity of the enterprise, it is necessary for it to have a continual flow of income to satisfy the needs of the participants. Out of this income the fixed and current assets, e.g. the means of production, will at some time have to be replaced in order to fulfill the same function in the enterprise, or rather the same function in gathering of income. The income of the enterprise

must be sufficient to maintain its activities to the extent expected by the participants. Income not needed for substitution (or: replacement) of means of production is distributable. In principle, in calculating profits it is therefore necessary to take into account replacement prices of at any rate the price of means and goods that are substitutes for the means and goods used in production. Replacement prices should be understood to be economic replacement prices.

Re 2. Subjective view
The maintenance of the enterprise as an organization is not guaranteed if profits are determined at replacement prices, even if replacement is defined as economic replacement. In endeavouring to maintain the coalition of participants, expansion is sometimes necessary. For financing of such expansion profits may have to be retained. The percentage of profits to be retained as related to total profits depends on the subjective view of management regarding the determination of economic replacement value, and on still greater subjectivity in weighing the necessary growth and therefore the necessary retention of profits.

5. A proposal for a synthesis

In this section my ideas will be given regarding the information to be provided in financial statements. In these ideas an attempt is made to incorporate the positive elements of the systems of general purchasing power accounting and replacement value accounting. Moreover, the attempt to arrive at a synthesis includes the four elements mentioned as shortcomings of the systems.

Based on the assumptions for the goals of an enterprise, the basis postulate can be formulated with the following idea:
The basis requirement of principles for financial statements is that information is supplied concerning the results of a period, indicating at least the results which are to be distributed so far as they are not necessary for maintaining the continuity of the enterprise as an organization.

This basis postulate has two important consequences which must first be realized. Sufficient evidence has been given in the preceding sections in support of the argument that attempts to maintain continuity are largely influenced by subjectiveness and uncertainty. Objectivity in profit determination should signify that two persons calculating independently of each other would arrive at the same result for a period. This seems an unattainable ideal. In normally conventional historical cost accounting, there are a number of subjective interpretations and estimations as well as in current cost accounting and replacement value accounting. It is true that the postulate of maintaining continuity has even greater subjectivity. However, it is believed that if it is demonstrated where subjectivity plays a role, there is no objection to this. A further consequence of this postulate and subjectivity is the significance of the distinction between profit determination and profit distribution. If profits could be determined objectively in an objective sense, there might be a rather sharp distinction with the distribution of profits.

A strict distinction in the information on results as regards profit determination and profit retention is not therefore necessary.

Re 3. Financial leverage

The financial structure of an enterprise is of great importance in determining results. If means of production are financed to some extent with long- or short-term debt, and assuming this method of financing is also possible in the future, profits need not be calculated *completely* on the basis of replacement prices. Or in other words: part of the difference between replacement prices and historical prices may be considered as distributable profits. This does not mean that profits should not be based on replacement prices but that holding gains need not always be retained in the enterprise. The results would have to be determined in such a way that economic substitution of means of production is possible. This does not mean complete depreciation based on the replacement value of fixed assets nor that all other costs are entirely on a current basis. As for financing the replacement, the results should be based on replacement values but only to such extent as the ultimate replacement will be financed from the equity. The financial leverage that is desirable and necessary must be taken into account and not the financial structure which exists at the time profits are determined.

Re 4. Profit and loss statement

As stated earlier in this article, the profit and loss account is the main document in the financial statement. The annual financial statements give information on the activities during the financial period as regards the maintenance of continuity. Therefore, the balance sheet is of minor importance. In the first instance, the profit and loss account was defined as a specification of the changes in net asset value. After this examination of the objectives of financial statements, the profit and loss account can no longer be considered to have this function. The function is, in the writer's opinion, to give information on the extent to which continuity has been maintained. The 'cast-iron law' that results consist of a difference in value is thus not as cast-iron as it sounds. It would be better to abandon the link between valuation in the balance sheet and costs in the profit and loss account.

Re 5. Valuation

A balance sheet was defined as an assessment in money of the values of assets and liabilities. This assessment contains a number of subjective elements. Moreover, it would be necessary to estimate the value of the assets which will in reality replace the existing assets. It seems rather strange to put these values in the balance sheet. Nevertheless, in presenting and calculating the information in the profit and loss account, it is necessary to take current and even future values into account. The determination, or rather the estimation, of economic replacement value is necessary. However, these values are considered as having a function only in profit determination and not in valuing the assets in the balance sheet. Consequently, presentation of assets and liabilities is most neutral if based on historic cost.

The profit and loss account will not then specify net asset value, as already stated in point 4, but the equity value in the balance sheet will still have to be adjusted for changes in the purchasing power of money. For proper understanding: not the adjustment of individual assets and liabilities for increased prices, but only adjustment of the equity value for changes in the organizations purchasing power and in general purchasing power. These adjustments appear in the profit and loss account, since they form part of maintaining continuity.

Obviously in adopting this view a number of scientific analyses of economic theories will be abandoned as well as the common thoughts in traditional accounting. Since this examination of the objectives of financial statements largely takes into account the behavioral aspects of continuity, the conclusion is indeed that the level of abstraction of economic theory should be rejected.

After classification of the basis postulate, realization of the consequences and presentation of the five starting points, the stage has now been reached for making a proposal for a synthesis. Firstly, the proposed contents of the profit and loss account; thereafter comments thereon:

Contents of profit and loss account

Sales, at historical prices	S
Cost at historical amounts, excluding depreciation and interest	C
Balance of operations (cash flow)	E
Less:	
Depreciation based on historic values	D_h
Balance	B
Less:	
Interest paid less interest received	I
Result 1	R_1

Less:
1. Additional depreciation of fixed assets based on replacement values, in so far as necessary for financing the replacement from the equity D_r
2. Difference between replacement prices and historic prices for other costs, in so far as necessary for financing the replacement from the equity C_r
3. Taxes on income T

M_1

Result 2 R_2
Less:
Maintenance of general purchasing power of the equity, if higher than $D_r + C_r$ M_2

Result 3 R_3

Distribution of result 3
Dividends to shareholders r_a
Profit sharing for personnel r_b
Management bonuses r_c
Retained for expansion to maintain continuity r_d
Balance, if any r_e

R_3

Contents of balance sheet

Fixed assets at historic prices	A_h	Equity at beginning	E
		Plus:	
Inventories at historic prices at lower of cost or market	S_h	$D_r + C_r$ Plus: (eventually)	M_1 M_2
Monetary assets	A_m		E
		Plus . (after approval)	r_d
			E
		Monetary liabilities	L_m
	T		T

The first comment on the above exhibits relates to taking financial leverage into account as in determining the amounts of D_r and C_r. The writer's view is that in determining these amounts management must bear in mind what financial structure is desirable and possible. As a means of asset financing, the equity and all interest-bearing indebtedness must be considered, but not suppliers' credit. If the equity debt leverage ration were, for instance, 60:40, the leverage could be illustrated as follows:

Fixed assets	a	Equity	c (60)
Current assets less		Interest-bearing debts	d (40)
non-interest bearing			
liabilities	b		
	a + b		a + b (100)

In determining amounts D_r and C_r, only 60% (if this leverage is desirable and possible) of additional depreciation and the difference between current cost and historic cost is charged to profit and loss account. This means in fact that gains from financing assets with indebtedness are included in profits. In other words: all holding gains not needed for maintaining the purchasing power of the enterprise are considered as profit. Maintaining the purchasing power of the enterprise is part of the endeavour to maintain continuity.

Another observation is that the proposal breaks the link between asset valuation and profit determination. The assets and liabilities are valued at historic cost, which seems to be the most acceptable method in most countries. The equity value in the balance sheet, however, is maintained in terms of general purchasing power. This is considered desirable especially in the United Kingdom and the United States. The way the equity adjustment is reached is less arbitrary than in inflation accounting systems. Moreover, a compromise has been found as between those advocating taking specific price levels into account and those advocating taking general price levels into account. Amounts D_r and C_r relate to specific prices, whilst the additional amount M_2 relates to the general price level. For a deficit completeness, it may be added that amount M_2 can never be a deficit. If $D_r + C_r$ is greater than M_2 no adjustment is needed. The amount M_2 if existing – always a surplus – is the balance of equity converted at the beginning of the period less equity not converted at the beginning of the period, less amounts $D_r + C_r$. If these latter amounts are higher, the amount M_2 being a deficit, no addition to profits can ever be made since amounts $D_r + C_r$ are needed to maintain continuity.

A further comment on the proposal is that the profit and loss account shows more than one result. Every user of the financial statements can take that result which is convenient for his purposes. Furthermore, a result based on historical cost is given. In international comparisons of companies this still seems to be a relevant figure. In judging the return on total invested capital this result can be compared with the sum of the equity and long- or short-term interest-bearing debt. The cash flow can also be compared. I am aware of the criticism that no indication is given of assets values.

This may be a major factor in assessing the return on investment. The return on investment of a company with 'old' assets may be higher than that of a company with 'new' assets. If the proposed system is supplied in the right way, the latter company has more depreciation on historic cost than the former company. Moreover, the company with the 'old' assets takes only part of the additional depreciation into account. It must be confessed that this is true. The solution seems to be that the notes to the statements should indicate the real value of the assets. This is also necessary to comply with certain statutory requirements regarding the annual financial statements of companies.

Two final observations: firstly, one can say that the problem of deferred income tax is not a major factor as far as it relates to asset evaluation. Normally, the taxable profit is R_1; taxes are included in the profit and loss account based on this result.

Finally, the proposed profit and loss account incorporates the element of subjectiveness in items D_r, C_r and r_d. Since amount M_2 is also included, a reasonable objectivity factor is also included. If one feels inclined to admit the element of subjectivity in business accounting there is no longer any problem.

II. A STUDY IN CURRENT VALUE ACCOUNTING

Gijs G. M. Bak

1. Introduction: the ideal management information system

Suppose, we have to develop a management information system (MIS) for a company, trading and/or manufacturing some kind of goods; and also suppose that there are no budgetary constraints as to computer costs and expenses of systems design and implementation. The creation of such ideal circumstances – even if they are only imaginary – gives us a useful background for discussion on some essential aspects of management and financial accounting. We can disregard conventional ideas about the kind of information that could be generated by an accounting system and we may feel entirely free to choose the information the system should produce.

Of course, after our excursion to such an ideal MIS, we must return to our dull daily practice, where budgetary and other contraints are normal. Nevertheless our excursion could be a very useful one if it helps us to try to make the best of what we have. In other words: from an analysis of an ideal MIS we could try to find approximations, or simplified applications for our day-to-day practice.

My paper will follow the lines set out above under the constraint that only one aspect of the MIS will be studied; the use of prices and values as a means to generate information for economic decisions. Other aspects (such as planning and control) will be dealt with only as far as necessary for the main theme of this paper. In my description of the ideal MIS the use of current value will take a central position. Reasons for this approach will not be given now, but I will try to demonstrate its usefulness with help of the (ideal) system itself. After that it will have to be considered which of the advantages of the current value approach can be kept in the approximations or simplified applications we have to design under the normal constraints of practice.

'Current value' is used in this paper as a concept of entry value referring to the actual position of the company on the market. The amount of money needed at the amount (n) to acquire an asset – or an economic equivalent of it – is considered to be the current value of that asset at that moment (CV_n).[1] This concept is basically the same as the concept of current costs, used by Edgar O. Edwards in his paper. I prefer 'value' to 'costs' because we are really dealing with (entry) values as also stated by Edwards: costs are measured at current values, giving current costs.

Also there seems to be no real difference between my concept of current value and the concept of replacement value as used by André Bindenga in his paper. I prefer 'current' to 'replacement' because replacement does not play an essential part in the concept of entry value used. This concept has nothing to do with an actual replacement of assets that will (or will not) take place; I hope to demonstrate this by my definition of current value (see above).

Before we start our investigation into the MIS that we want to develop, we should consider the users of the information to be generated by the system. First of all we have to provide all the different levels of management with the information they need for decision making and for measuring the effects of their decisions. This means that we are entering the area of 'management accounting'. Secondly we have to produce the information required for the periodical financial statements of the company, which is the field of 'financial accounting'. Although both areas of accounting are different in many aspects they have enough in common to justify an integrated approach from the outset when we study an advanced MIS, making use of all facilities of modern computers.

Our analysis of the system should also indicate to what extent the information requirements of outside parties – being the basis of financial accounting – tally with the requirements of management, and to what extent extra information is needed for use in the financial statements made available to third parties.

2. Current value, part of the system's basic data

Our (so called) ideal MIS is supposedly built around a data base, where we find, *inter alia*, a large number of records with data concerning the fixed assets and the materials the company is dealing with: raw materials, work in progress, finished products and/or trade stock. For purposes of planning, control and reporting the physical flow of those goods through the company is followed closely by our information system. All transactions and the most important internal movements are registered under a key indicating the specific class of items concerned. For each item (fixed assets and other goods) a basic record is

---

1. See: the list of symbols at the end of this chapter.

maintained giving the basic data such as: reference key, description, relevant features ... and ... the current value (per unity).

In order to keep those basic data up to date they may be changed under certain conditions (except for the reference key!). Changes of the current value result automatically in a calcuation of an amount called 'revaluation'. Revaluation is defined as: quantity of the item available (in stock) times the change in its current value per unity

$$[R = Q_{st} \times (CV_{n-1})]$$

In the company a special department (which can be called the CV-Department) acts as a guardian for the current value data available within the system. The main task of this department is to keep the current value data reliable and up to date. To some extent the system itself provides for automatic adjustments on the basis of relevant data available from new transactions. The CV-Department formulates proposals for the systems design as to such automatic adjustments in close cooperation with the systems development department. On the other hand the CV-Department has to gather relevant external information in order to keep current value data up to date. Resulting changes have to be registered through a manual input device.

Cost figures can be generated in our system in two ways:
(a) the current value at a certain moment of a single item (CV_n), of a certain quantity of an item ($Q \times CV_n$), or of a set of items ($\sum Q \times CV_n$);
(b) the current value of a stream of items, measured at different moments, ($\sum Q \times CV_{1,...,n}$).

Two examples might explain this:
(a) If someone in the company wants to know the cost-price of a certain product that has to be assembled from different parts, the system will give this information on the basis of $\sum Q \times CV_n$.
(b) If someone wants to know the cost of sales of one item during a certain period ($p, ..., q$) the system will give this information on the basis of $\sum Q \times CV_{p,...,q}$. This means that CV has been measured at the moments the quantities have been sold.

Of course the stream figures have to be built up somewhere in the system either on the basis of individual transactions or by adding the relevant data for each item between fixed intervals.

3. Purchases, sales and stock

Now we turn to the part of the information system that normally will be covered by the bookkeeping department: the registration of purchases, sales and stock.

When a purchase-transaction enters the system the following data are necessary:
– the quantities added to the stock of specific items Q_p
– the amount of costs per item according to contract and/or invoice C_p.
The system automatically generates a calculation of D_p, the 'difference of a purchase transaction':

$$Q_p \times (CV_n - C_p) = D_p$$

D_p is automatically compared with a constant factor T, being the acceptable margin between CV_n and the costs of a purchase transaction.

If: $D_p \leqslant T$ The transaction will be accepted by the system as far as price controls is concerned.

If: $D_p > T$ The system may provide one of the following facilities:
– An automatic reassessment of CV_n as described in section 2 (above), and accordingly acceptance of the transaction.
– Ditto + an immediate announcement to the CV-Department of the reassessment made.
– Stop the recording of the transaction, combined with a message to the CV-Department, that has to analyse the nature of D_p and take action according to its findings.

The total amount of purchases during a certain period $(p, \ldots, q)$ might be analysed by the system as follows:

$$\Sigma Q \times C_p = \Sigma Q \times CV_{p,\ldots,q} + \Sigma D_p,$$

where ΣD_p may have been authorized in detail according to the facilities described above.

The choice of the factor T determines to a large extent the effectiveness of control over (the registration of) purchase transactions.

When a sales transaction enters the system the following data are necessary:
– the quantities sold of each specification Q_s
– the sales price according to contract and/or invoice P_s.
The system automatically generates the calculation of sales $(Q_s \times P_s)$, cost of sales $(Q_s \times CV_n)$ and gross profit of the transaction: $GP = Q_s(P_s - CV_n)$.

Under the conditions of the system each sales figure is combined with its own gross profit figure (GP).

An important factor in the system as described above is the timing of current value measurement for each transaction. As CV is determined only in relation to (n) the choice of (n) may have an important impact on the financial information about a transaction. Moreover we should bear in mind that both purchases and sales of a commodity are interrelated to each other, in a way we must think of 'earnings cycles'. In order to get into a position to formulate rules for this timing problem we have to decide as to the preferable approach:
− *A purely economic approach,* whereby the impact of the physical flow of the goods is left aside. According to this approach an earnings cycle is determined by the period the company bears the risk of changes in the current value of the goods concerned. A purchase transaction will be registered at the moment of agreement with the supplier about all conditions including the (purchase) price. A sales transaction will be registered at the moment of agreement with the customer about all conditions including the (selling) price. According to this approach we account for the 'economic stock' which changes only at the moments of completed purchase and sale contracts and not at the moments of physical input or output of stock. The results of both purchase and sales transactions are measured accordingly against CV_n, (n) being the moment of concluding the contract. The registration of the physical flow of goods between contract and delivery has no impact on the calculation of gross profit nor does it result in the calculation of a difference between purchase price (C_p) and CV on the moment of delivery.
− *The other approach is based on the accounting convention* or on the rules normally kept in the field of financial accounting: according to this approach an earning cycle is determined by the period the goods concerned are at the disposal of the company. A purchase transaction will be registered at the moment of delivery, which mostly coincides with the moment the invoice is received. A sales transaction will be registered at the moment the bill is sent out and/or the goods are delivered.

The results of transactions are measured against CV_n, (n) being the moment of physical change of stock. Changes of CV between contract and delivery − although irrelevant for the results of an earnings cycle from an economic point of view − have an impact on the measurement of results under this approach.

From this exposition on the two different approaches to the problem of timing of measurement of CV_n it will be clear that we found a first indication of a possible difference between the requirements of management accounting from those of financial accounting. To what extent a real difference should be made in this respect depends largely on the type of business. When only a short time elapses between contract and delivery both approaches normally will lead to (almost) the same results. As a matter of fact, however, it is not the time between contract and delivery that counts, but the changes in CV that could occur during this period.

Accounting for fixed assets and the calculation of depreciation will follow the same lines as set out above. A change in the replacement cost of an asset is registered in the record of that asset. At the same time a recalculation is made of the book-value on the basis of the new replacement costs, without changing the existing depreciation method. Revaluation (R) in the case of fixed assets is then the difference between the book-value before and after the change in replacement costs. By applying the above method both book-value and depreciation are kept at current value level. Adjustments of depreciation in previous periods (backlog depreciation) will not be made.

Instructions for the CV-Department

A very important section of the whole system is the instructions for the CV-Department. The methods applied by this department in order to assess current value have direct impact on the information on Gross Profit (GP) and Revaluation (Holding gains). As it is the task of the CV-Department to maintain up-to-date data on current value in the records of the system, there is no need for them to reflect all changes in current market prices of articles and fixed assets, in their current values. The CV-Department should try to make a distinction between incidental price changes caused by special circumstances or market conditions and structural changes of the prices. This is not an easy job, of course, but there is some help from outside.

The CV-Department receives indications from an analysis of internal figures (especially D_p!) and from external information, such as market quotations, index figures and the like. The CV-Department will discuss the determination of CV with those who are ultimately responsible for the operating results, and who are supposed to have a thorough knowledge of the relevant markets. Analogy can be found in the processes of determination of useful lifetime of fixed assets and the preparation of departments budgets.

As to materials this discussion will be directed especially to the situation on the relevant markets. As to fixed assets this discussion will mainly be about the influence of technical developments on the CV of existing machines etc. By no means will every change in replacement costs of a machine lead to a change in the CV of that machine; this depends also on the development of new types with a different efficiency.

4. Benefits from the use of current value

Having dealt with our 'ideal information system', the possible benefits that can be expected will now be considered, once such a system has been designed and implemented.

The most important benefit stems from the use of current values as such. The CV-Department is permanently involved in gathering relevant data about current values of the materials and fixed assets the company is dealing with. Every user of information knows that it is based on current values, and that it reflects as a consequence the actual relations between purchase and selling markets for the relevant items. Changes in these relations are shown immediately reflecting all aspects of the company's operations. This is particularly true for the (detailed) information relating to gross profit on sales. In a period of rising prices the profit margin is adapted without delay to actual level, regardless of the temporary (!) gains that may or may not be earned on existing stock, bought at lower prices.

On the other hand the system provides for a permanent registration of holding gains. As described in section 2 (above), for every change in CV of an article the corresponding amount $R = Q_{st} \times (CV_n - CV_{n-1})$ is calculated and accounted for. If necessary R can be broken down by item for every reporting period.

The pattern of information that is typical for our system can be summarized as follows (see figure 1):

Basic data

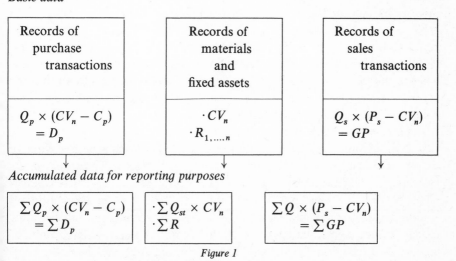

Records of purchase transactions	Records of materials and fixed assets	Records of sales transactions
$Q_p \times (CV_n - C_p)$ $= D_p$	$\cdot CV_n$ $\cdot R_{1,\ldots n}$	$Q_s \times (P_s - CV_n)$ $= GP$

Accumulated data for reporting purposes

$\sum Q_p \times (CV_n - C_p)$ $= \sum D_p$	$\cdot \sum Q_{st} \times CV_n$ $\cdot \sum R$	$\sum Q \times (P_s - CV_n)$ $= \sum GP$

Figure 1

The four basic elements of periodical reporting are $\sum D_p$; $\sum Q_{st} \times CV_{(n)}$; $\sum R$ and $\sum GP$. For each of these basic elements the necessary specification has to be indicated by the users of the reports, and this will depend largely on the type of business we are in. Nevertheless we can go into a little more detail as to the meaning of the information generated by the four basic elements of reporting mentioned above:

– $\sum D_p$ normally is a figure without any economic meaning as such. It only indicates to what extent the CV-Department did succeed in keeping CV_n really up to date. Accordingly the amount for a period will be kept within narrow limits. It is also possible, however, that this figure comprises some incidental profits or losses resulting from purchase transactions at prices below or above CV_n at that moment. As a result of the control system developed for the purchase transactions there has been a day-to-day reporting of such elements during the period, so they can be reported separately if material. So, using CV_n as a norm figure, given by a special department, management gets informed to what extent CV_n has been the reflection of the (purchase) market during the period. On the other hand there is a system of exception-reporting for relatively high or low purchase prices (compared to CV_n). For a good judgment those exceptions should be explained further, as the purchase price is of course only one of the conditions for a purchase transaction.

– $\sum Q_{st} \times CV_n$, being the current value of stock at hand or of fixed assets in use. This figure is clearly defined as long as it is clear to everybody in the organization what the meaning is of CV_n. The value of stock does not depend on the movement of stocks in connection with the changes in the relevant historic costs as is the case with such methods as FIFO or LIFO. The value of stock depends on current value as assessed and kept up to date in a well-defined process. Wherever the total value of stock at hand is used for the calculation of ratios, such ratios are always based on the amount invested, calculated at current value. Changes in such ratios indicating a tendency towards a more (un)favourable position of the company come to the attention of management without the delay caused by the historic cost valuation.

E.g.: – Working capital needed for the financing of stocks;
    – Gross profit/sales in relation to working capital.

– $\sum R$, the amount of revaluation during the period for each article or group of articles or fixed assets. The meaning of this information for management is quite obvious. $\sum R$ indicates the change of equity as a result of changing current values of the commodities held by the company. This change in equity is reported separately from the change in equity as a result of Gross Profit, calculated against current values. Separate reporting of such different items is important for management, whatever we call them. So, whether we want to call the amount $\sum R$

'Profit' or not it remains useful for management to receive a separate reporting of this particular change in equity.

As far as the information is used as a yardstick for the performance (of a certain department) of the company, this performance will be measured in different ways when it is clear to management what part of change in equity results from merely changing current values and what part results from Gross Profit against current value. As far as the information is used as a basis for extrapolation of future results, management in most cases has less reason to expect a continuing contribution from changing current value then it has to expect a continuing Gross Profit. In other words factors influencing the one are quite different from factors influencing the other.

– $\sum GP$, the amount of gross profit. Gross profit for a period being calculated on the basis of current value has a definite meaning for management. It reflects the actual position of the company on the (purchase and selling) markets. It does so for reporting on every article or group of articles, but also for reporting on sales and gross profit in particular parts of the total market (a country, a group of clients).

Using the information elements given in this section (4), periodical reporting on the results of operations could be done in the following format:

Gross profit for the period	$\sum GP$
Profit (loss) on purchases	$\sum D_p$
	$+$
Current value profit	CVP
Holding gains/losses	$\sum R$

This way of reporting[2] is consistent with a valuation of stock at current value:

$$\sum Q_{st} \times CV_n$$

It should be realized, however, that only $\sum GP$ is calculated on the basis of realization and of matching costs to realized sales. This way of reporting will certainly be useful to management, but it is not in conformity with accounting principles based on historic costs. In order to comply with those principles an adaptation is necessary which could be calculated on the basis of a different stock valuation at the beginning and the end of the reporting period. For that reason

2. Both CVP and $\sum R$ are parts of current income as defined by Mr. Edwards in his paper (current operating profit and new holding gains); The element of 'net financial income' is not relevant for the exposition in my paper and consequently left out.

reporting should be extended with the amount of stock valued at FIFO, LIFO, or whatever method the company wants to apply. We call the difference between $\sum Q_{st} \times CV_n$ and stock against the conventional valuation $D_{st/n}$; $D_{st/n}$ can be characterized also as the unrealized holding gain (loss) on stock at the end of the reporting period. In the case of fixed assets $D_{st/n}$ is calculated at the difference between book-value at moment (n) on the basis of replacement costs and historic costs.

The schedule of reporting can be modified accordingly:

Gross profit for the period	$\sum GP$
Unrealized holding gain (loss)	
previous period	$(+) \quad D_{st/n-1}$
Profit (loss) on purchases	$(+)\sum D_p$
Holding gains/losses	$(+)\sum R$
Unrealized holding gain (loss)	
at the end of period	$(-) \quad D_{st/n}$
Realized holding gain (loss)	
for the period	$\dfrac{\sum R}{HCP} +$ (realized)
Historic cost profit	
Unrealized holding gain $(= D_{st/n})$	$\sum R$ (unrealized)

From this exposition it will be clear that the application of an accounting system based on current value does not impede periodical reporting on historic cost basis, whereas the problem of stock valuation remains the same as before, and for fixed assets the calculation of historic cost depreciation has to be carried out.

On the other hand it does not seem very useful to provide such information for management purposes. As soon as holding gains are calculated as a separate item, there is little advantage in applying the matching principle to such gains. In fact such holding gains show little relation to the amount of sales during the period, so there is no logic in applying the matching principle in this case. It seems better to either eliminate holding gains from profit entirely or add them to profit as soon as they are calculated. In both cases it is the breakdown of profit and holding gains together that counts rather than the profit figure alone!

We must return now to the problem of timing of measurement of transactions against current value as discussed in section 3. The analysis of the information produced by the system, as given in this section is correct only under the conditions of the so-called economic approach. According to this approach measurement against current value is applied at the moment the transactions are realized in an economic sense, i.e. when the company has taken over the risk of changes in current value (by entering into a purchase agreement) or when the company has transferred the risk of changes in current value to a customer (by concluding a sales order). Only then can $\sum R$ be characterized as 'holding gains (or losses)' without restriction, and only then $\sum D_p$ and $\sum GP$ reflect the results of transactions in the light of the actual market position of the company. Under the approach based on the accounting convention the moments of measurement may deviate from the economic relevant points of time as described above. As a consequence part of the changes in current value is accounted for in the wrong category. This can be demonstrated using a simplified example of a group of transactions for one article:

Moments of measurement	$CV_{(n)}$	C_p	P_s
Entering into the purchase agreement	10	10	
Delivery by the supplier (invoice)	12		
Concluding the sales order	14		18
Delivery to the customer (billing)	15		

In this example it is not difficult to analyse the relevant figures from an economic point of view:
– Purchase price (C_p) is exactly at current value at the moment of contract, giving $D_p = 0$.
– Gross profit (GP) is 4 $(18 - 14)$, being the difference between sales price (P_s) and CV at the moment the sales order was concluded.
– Holding gain (R) is 4, being the change in current value during the period the company bore the risk of such change.

However, applying the system under the conditions of the accounting convention will give quite other information:
– Purchase price (C_p) is below current value, at the moment of delivery $(12 - 10 = 2)$, giving $D_p = 2$!
– Gross profit (GP) is 3 $(18 - 15)$ being the difference between sales price (P_s) and CV at the moment the order was delivered and/or billed.
– Holding gain (R) is 3 being the change in current value during the period the commodity was at the disposal of the company.

There are several solutions to this problem:
(a) ignore it and stick to the accounting approach; in many cases this is a practical solution, because of the relatively small time-lag between contract and delivery;
(b) combine the two approaches into one system; this also means that at the moment of realization measurement of CV must be done as at the moment of

contract. This solution therefore is a very complicated one, applicable only for an enterprise that enters into a relatively small amount of large contracts. For this type of business – e.g. in the building industry – the whole accounting system will be based on the individual contracts. The information system will be directed anyhow towards an analysis of the risks of changing prices;

(c) strict separation of the accounting system into two sections: one based on the economic approach and the other based on the accounting convention. As a matter of fact this should be done in companies dealing with goods with a world market quotation, such as cacao, timber etc., where it is common practice to conclude long-term contracts resulting in the fixing of the purchase and/or selling prices for a long period. The results calculated on a contract basis may differ widely from the results calculated against CV per the moment of delivery.

In the situation given under (c) we discover a possible antithesis between the requirements of our management information system and the requirements of financial accounting based on the conventions of public reporting. I will not go further into this question except to say that the accounting convention seems to be a rather inadequate basis for the reporting of companies of which profits are to a large extent determined by contract concluded several months before re-alization.

5. Simplification of the system

As stated in section 1, we have to consider the situations where we have less facilities available than in our highly advanced and expensive computer application. We have to look into methods of simplifying the system; as simplification is hardly needed in the case of fixed assets, we will concentrate ourselves in this paragraph on other items. I suggest that simplification could be found in three ways:

– we can abandon the CV-Department (see next paragraph (a))
– we can simplify the system keeping the main features of it (see subsequent paragraph (b))
– we can try to find methods of approximation, in order to attain (almost) the same results without the detailed information the system produces (see subsequent paragraph (c)).

(a) The easiest way to simplification is to abandon the CV-Department. I call this the easiest way because this department was introduced mainly for the purpose of my paper. As a matter of fact, it is not the department that counts but the procedures described for the assessment of current value. It is important that CV

is not introduced as a *deus ex machina* at the end of the year as an element of stock valuation or as a problem of presentation of fixed assets in the financial statements. The CV-based information plays an important role during the year in all reports to management at different levels of the organization. The task of the CV-Department can be carried out by the purchase department under supervision of the accounting department, or – in an industrial company – by a department that also is responsible for the calculation of standard costs. Essentially the instructions mentioned in section 3 remain the same!

(b) The main feature of the system is the permanent registration against current value of the flow of goods. The sophisticated way of keeping CV up to date for every article and at every moment could easily be replaced by a more simple method. If we could agree that it is fair enough to work with current values that are adapted to the real situation only at certain intervals, it is possible to limit the accounting procedure of revaluation to that of a periodical revision of the current values in the records of our system. A monthly or quarterly batch processing would do in that case! If we think that the trouble lies especially in the assessment of current value we could simplify otherwise: we can then work under the hypothesis that current value is always equal to the purchase price of the last purchase transaction ($CV_n = C_p$). In that case we can combine the revision of CV_n and the calculation of R with the process of accounting for purchase transactions in the stock records. According to my experience in practice it is possible without many difficulties to run a system, simplified as indicated above, by using a mini- or an office-computer. Generally speaking the capacity of the records is big enough to allow for the 4 to 6 numeric positions needed for the CV data; the programming load is hardly influenced by these requirements. A further simplification of the system can be obtained by gathering the information about revaluation (R) only on an overall basis, without the breakdown per item as described in section 4.

It depends on the type of business and the information requirements of management how far simplifications as indicated above will be justified in each case. However, the main feature of the system can be maintained only if a detailed registration of stock and stock-movements is part of the system. Such registration will not primarily be installed for the periodical assessment of Gross profit ($\sum GP$) and Revaluations ($\sum R$) but for purposes of planning and control. In many cases it will be useful to aim at an integrated system serving both requirements.

(c) If a detailed registration of stock and stock-movements is not considered to be necessary, or when it is not practicable to use at the same time such registration for planning and control purposes and for the assessment of periodical financial results we are forced to apply methods of approximation. The following schedule indicates the headlines of these methods as compared to the methods described earlier in this paper. In the system given, the information required is built up from a registration per item, giving the following elements:

$$Q_{st/b} \times CV_b + \sum Q_p \times C_p + \sum D_p + \sum R - \sum Q_s \times CV_n = Q_{st/e} CV_e \quad (1)$$

and

$$\sum Q_s \times P_s \qquad\qquad - \sum Q_s \times CV_n = GP \qquad (2)$$

In words:
+ Stock at the beginning of the period at current value at that date
+ Purchases according to invoice and/or contract
+ Differences on purchase transactions ($= Q_p \times (CV_n - C_p)$)
+ Revaluations
− Cost of sales against current value at the moment of sales
= Stock at the end of the period at current value at that date
and:
+ Sales
− Cost of sales
= Gross profit for the period against current values.
    Approximations will always be based on a restatement of formula (1):

$$[Q_{st/b} \times CV_b - Q_{st/e} \times CV_e] + \sum Q_p \times C_p = \sum Q_s \times CV_n - [\sum D_p + \sum R] \quad (3)$$

In words:
If only the stock against *CV* is available at the beginning and at the end of the period, together with the amount of purchases for the period, the amount of cost of sales at *CV* will be found inclusive of the amount of revaluation (including $\sum D_p$) during the period. Whereas a direct assessment of one of these elements is not possible under the restrictions given above, we will try to calculate $[\sum D_p + \sum R]$ by means of a special treatment of $[Q_{st/b} \times CV_b - Q_{st/e} \times CV_e]$.

    It is easy to see how corrections in the valuation of $Q_{st/b}$ and/or $Q_{st/e}$ to the amount of $[\sum D_p + \sum R]$ will lead to the required amount of cost of sales against current value: $\sum Q_s \times CV_n$!

    In this respect the following statements could help in finding methods of approximation:
(i) if − for each article or on an average for a group of articles − $Q_{st/b} = Q_{st/e}$ and also $= Q_{st}$ at the relevant moments of revaluation, the amount of revaluation $[\sum D_p + \sum R]$ is equal to $Q_{st/b} \times (CV - CV_b)$.

(ii) if – for each article or on an average for a group of articles – $Q_{st/b} \neq Q_{st/e}$ we can apply statement (i) to $Q_{st(b)}$ and limit our approximation problem to the quantity of $Q_{st/e} - Q_{st/b}$. In fact we have to do only with $CV_e - C_p$ for this quantity on a FIFO basis.

(iii) the correction of $[Q_{st/b} \times CV_b - Q_{st/e} \times CV_e]$ following from LIFO stock valuation is equal to $[\sum D_p + \sum R]$ only under extremely rare conditions.

From these statements it follows that the application of fixed stock valuation (see (i) and (ii)) gives the best results, as an approximation of $\sum GP$ against CV. Nevertheless it will be necessary to investigate into the actual movements of stocks and of the relevant current values before the results of fixed stock valuation can be seen as a reasonable approximation of what should have been the result of the application of CV as such!

6. Summary and conclusion

Financial reporting to outside parties as well as to management should provide for information that is relevant from an economic point of view. An information system based on current values is set up to reflect the actual position of a company between its purchase and selling market. As it is the main economic function of a company to generate an income from the simultaneous price differences on both markets, the information produced by such an information system is considered to be relevant from an economic point of view.

The counterpart of current value based information on transactions is information on holding gains on assets held by the company. As it is a secondary (but inevitable) economic function of most companies to run the risk of changing values of their assets, information that reflects the quantitative effects of this function is relevant from an economic point of view.

A company trading and/or manufacturing some kind of goods may try to take advantage of the access to its markets in order to realize holding gains as a byproduct to its main activities. To this end the company will accelerate or postpone purchase or sales transactions. Reporting on holding gains may be a means of quantifying the effect of such policy. From an economic point of view it seems to be important to generate information on the results of such specific activities of the company.

Accordingly, the MIS described in this paper can be considered to produce information that is relevant from an economic point of view. Simplifications and approximations – as considered in section 5 – are necessary in many cases because of 'budgetary constraints', but a simplified system may produce information of the same economic tenor on a less sophisticated basis.

Determination of current value should not be seen as a pure accounting problem. It is necessary (and useful) to stimulate a well-defined process where the assessment of current value is an integrated function in the organization of the company.

Current value accounting therefore is based on an economic approach to accounting and to financial reporting. This is not the same as saying that current value accounting as such provides us with the key to the economic concept of income as it is found in economic literature. I refer to the paper of Mr. Edwards dealing with this economic concept of income and also with a concept of current income which is based on the same conceptual framework as developed in this paper. His most important considerations on the relationship between current and economic income demonstrate the economic character of both concepts. For the same reason I consider recent proposals, as launched in the UK by the Sandilands Committee and formulated in ED 18 of the Accounting Standards Committee, to be milestones in the development of accounting. The calculation of current operating profit and of holding gains marks the transition from bookkeeping to the production of economically relevant data.

Looking at the results of Mr. Edwards' study we might even expect that general acceptance of current value accounting will result, one day, in the filling of the gap between the accounting and the economic concepts of income.

List of symbols

CV_n	= Current Value	The amount of money needed at the moment (n) to acquire an asset or an economic equivalent of it.
Q	= Quantity	Quantity of an item.
Q_{st}	= Quantity in stock	Quantity of an item available (in stock).
R	= Revaluation	$R = Q_{st} \times (CV_n - CV_{n-1})$.
Q_p	= Quantity purchased	Quantity added to stock at a purchase transaction.
C_p	= Cost of a purchase transaction	Cost of an item purchased.
D_p	= Difference of a purchase transaction	$D_p = Q_p \times (CV_n - C_p)$.
T	= Tolerance	Acceptable margin between CV_n and C_p.
Q_s	= Quantity sold	Quantity of a sales transaction.
P_s	= Price of a sales transaction	Sales price.
GP	= Gross Profit	$GP = Q_s \times (P_s - CV_n)$.
CVP	= Current Value Profit	Profit calculated on the basis of CV, exclusive of holding gains.
HCP	= Historic Cost Profit	Profit calculated on the basis of historic costs.
D_{st}	= Difference of stock valuation	Amount of difference between historic cost valuation of stock and $Q_{st} \times CV_n$.

III. THE PRIMACY OF ACCOUNTING INCOME IN DECISIONS ON EXPANSION: AN EXERCISE IN ARITHMETIC

Edgar O. Edwards

1. Introduction

'Accounting records the past and the present; economics considers bygones to be bygones and treats with the present and the future.' Many professionals in both fields have been content with this division of responsibility. Accountants, in particular, in determining the present values of future events have drawn in large part on the economists' arsenal of analytical tools. More recently, in their efforts to fashion income concepts that take into account future prospects as opposed to past accomplishments, some accountants have conceded that the economic concept of income is the ideal.[1] In this view, the accounting concept of income will differ from the economic concept only because practical difficulties of measurement prevent accountants from directly measuring the ideal itself.

The attempts to treat accounting income as an approximation to economic income do both interested professions a disservice. In particular, the approximation approach fails to do justice to the independent character of accounting income and to the role that expectations about accounting income and its components must play in determining economic income. Finally, by treating one as an approximation of the other, the task of reconciling the two concepts is not even confronted.

This paper seeks to establish 'current income,' an accounting concept, as a basic analytical tool and to expose the deficiencies of the approximation approach (1) by deriving a stream of economic incomes from a stream of expected, independently defined current incomes, (2) by showing that the two concepts of income are indeed different, and (3) by demonstrating the relationship between the two. These tasks are undertaken in the context of

The author is undebted to Philip W. Bell for perceptive comments on an earlier draft. (The views expressed are not necessarily shared by the Ford Foundation.)
1. The Inflation Accounting Committee, for example, has taken the following position (1975, p. 30): 'In practice ... other concepts (of profit) must be considered which approximate to (economic income) and which are capable of practical application.' We shall argue that the Committee may be selling its own concept short. See also Lawson, 1975.

expansion decisions – the analytics of choice among alternative future expansion paths. Finally, it is shown that an expansion-neutral tax system, one that does not affect the choice of expansion path, must assess taxes on new holding gains as they arise and at the same rate as on other components of current income.

The conceptual relationships, which are the subject of this article, can be most clearly exposed by leaving aside problems of measurement, without, however, suggesting that these problems are not of very real importance in matters of practical accounting application. It is therefore assumed throughout the article that past and present market values of assets and liabilities exist and are known, and that future market values will become determinate as time overtakes them.

The task will be further simplified by assuming no changes over time in the general price level. Such changes could be grafted on to the model, but doing so would only complicate the presentation without affecting the fundamental relationships we seek to disclose.

We also assume that firms act to maximize profits; that future events, including changes in specific asset and liability values, are uncertain but expectations about them can be entertained by individuals and corporations and can be represented as single-valued in nature; that time horizons are finite; and that expansion is internally financed.

Finally, differences between exit and entry prices and the possible effects of taxes on the choice of expansion path will not be discussed until the basic model has been presented.

We accept as the economic concept of income most appropriate to this discussion that concept attributable to Fisher (1906), Lindahl (1939), and Hicks (1946), according to which income is 'the maximum amount which an individual can spend this week and still expect to be able to spend the same amount in real terms in future weeks' (Hicks, 1946, p. 173). Note two points, however. The definition assumes that the assets in which income lodges are fungibles and an individual need not in fact spend his income or limit his spending to this income.

The accounting concept of income employed in this article is termed 'current income'. With minor modifications, it is the concept called 'business profit' in Edwards and Bell (1961, Chapter IV). It represents the increase in the net current value, as measured by market prices, of resources committed to the firm, before dividends and excluding new stockholder investments. Current Income has three components.

1. *Current Operating Profit* – the excess of the current value of output sold over the current cost (in some instances, net realizable value) of the related inputs.
2. *Net Financial Income* – the excess of interest and other financial income over interest and other financial expense.

3. *Current Holding Gains* – changes arising during the period in the current cost (in some cases, net realizable value) of the firm's assets and liabilities.

Current Income differs from traditional historic-cost based accounting income in two major respects. First, all realized capital gains, the excess of realized values over historic costs, are *excluded* from Current Income whether these are realized through direct sale of an asset or as cost savings, the excess of the current cost of inputs at time of use over their historic cost. In traditional accounting, cost savings are intermingled with operating profit. Second, all increases (decreases) in the current value of assets (liabilities) held for any time during the period are included whether realized during the period or not. These gains arising from current revaluations are 'Current Holding Gains'. Current Income is therefore a current value concept that includes all increases in value arising during this period (and no other) whether through operating or holding activities. It implies position statements that are stated in current values.[2]

Current Operating Profit and Net Financial Income are normally 'realized' during the period in question. If 'Realized Holding Gains', namely gains accruing in past and the current period which are realized in this period whether through sale or use, are substituted for Current Holding Gains, we obtain 'Realized Income' (Edwards and Bell, 1961, Chapter IV). Realized Income is equal in total to traditional accounting income but realized cost savings are classified with Realized Holding Gains and not included in Current Operating Profit. If, however, the realization of holding gains is considered to be simply a change in the form of values which have already been recorded in the Current Incomes of this and prior periods, as we do here, Current Income represents a complete summary of all of the accounting income events occurring during this period.[3]

2. Valuing an expansion path

If assets and liabilities are fungibles, a firm can at any point in time exchange one set for another without affecting the net market value of the set. Hence, market

2. Current Income is entirely consistent with Bak's formulation in another paper in this volume. Specifically, it is the sum of his 'Current value profit' and 'Holding gains/losses'. For a comparison of various profit concepts, see Parker and Harcourt (1969, Chapter 1) and Enthoven (1973, Chapter 13).
3. The Current Income of most firms will include some of all three components and the relationships among them in the decision-making process merit analysis (in another context). The components themselves may also provide a basis for the classification of firms for some analytical purposes, according to whether the majority of a firm's income takes the form of one component or another, – for example, 'operating', 'financial' and 'investment' firms. Such uses depend, of course, on the accurate and comparable reporting of the three components.

values provide no basis for preferring one array of assets and liabilities over another. It is differences in the streams of expected future earnings associated with the various arrays of assets and liabilities contemplated by the firm that lead the firm to prefer one array over others.

It is also safe to say that the firm's expectations about alternative future income streams are not shared by everyone else, for then market values would have adjusted so that every array of assets and liabilities would yield the same rate of return, and the firm, and everyone else holding assets for profit, would be truly indifferent about its asset composition. The firm's expectations are unique, internal and subjective; they cannot be inferred from market values or the expectations of an outside observer.

The firm can, however, state its expectations about forthcoming events and use them as a basis for selecting its own expansion programme from among the alternatives it considers. A simple example of one of these alternatives will serve as the basis for further discussion.

The firm has a time horizon of three years and an initial composition of assets and liabilities having a net current value in the market of 100. The market value of goodwill, if any, should be included among the assets. If the firm commits its net current value to the expansion path under consideration, it expects that over the years within its time horizon its Current Income will be composed of the components and dispositions shown in table 1.

Table 1. Components and dispositions of current income.

	Period		
	1	2	3
Current operating profit	30	25	27
Net financial income	−5	−7	−8
Current holding gains	10	5	15
Current income	35	23	34
New commitments	23	11	22
Dividends	12	12	12

'New Commitments' represents increases in net current value retained by the firm in order to generate income in subsequent periods. The phrase is used to distinguish it from 'investment' which normally refers to the acquisition of new assets. 'New Commitments' includes, in addition, increases in the net current value of assets and liabilities previously held and now retained by the firm.

From current incomes to subjective goodwill

We now seek to demonstrate a basic theorem in both its weak and strong forms. The weak version is that subjective goodwill, the variable to be maximized in choosing among expansion paths requiring the same investment, can be derived using Current Incomes as one of the inputs. In its strong version, the theorem states that subjective goodwill *cannot* be determined without reference to the expected events composing Current Incomes, and in particular without reference to expectations about changes in values. Hence, we shall argue that expected Current Incomes (or the events composing them) are essential to the making of profit-maximizing expansion decisions.

The critical link in the argument is Commitments. It follows from the definition of Current Income that the net current value expected at the end of the planning period is necessarily the arithmetic sum of (1) the initial net current value committed to the expansion programme and (2) subsequent New Commitments – in our example, 156. Moreover, any other definition of the 'final' net current value is arbitrary and will introduce arbitrary elements into the expansion decision.

To pursue the example, assume that the expected discount rates employed by the firm are 15 per cent, 10 per cent, and 15 per cent in the three consecutive periods, yielding discount factors (see mathematical note for formula) of .87, .79, and .69 respectively. The basic relationships on which the case for Current Income rests are depicted in table 2.

Table 2. The basic data for computing subjective goodwill.

	Period				Present value
	0	1	2	3	
Current income	0	35	23	34(+156)	179.22
Commitments	100	23	11	22	143.82
Dividends	(−100)	12	12	12(+156)	35.40
Cumulative commitments	100	123	134	156	

The proof of the theorem lies in the algebraic relationship among the first three rows. If any two rows are known, the third can be determined. Moreover, two rows must be known; *the expansion path cannot be fully described by reference to one row alone.* In mathematical terms, the three rows represent three equations in three unknowns, the present values. But the definitional identity among the present values, PV (Current Income) − PV (Commitments) = PV (Dividends), makes a fourth equation. This identity permits us to eliminate *one* of the row equations, but only one.

In order to confirm the importance of this relationship, consider the methods available for computing subjective goodwill. The basic method for determining the subjective goodwill associated with this expansion path is that shown in table 2, namely to subtract its costs, i.e. the present value of commitments, from its benefits, i.e., the present value of the 'Current Income stream' composed of (1) Current Incomes and (2) the expected net current value of the firm at the end of the planning period.

A second method is to subtract the present value of the 'Optional Income stream', composed of (1) the incomes which could be earned if Cumulative Commitments at the beginning of each period were employed to earn interest at the discount rates and (2) the final net current value, from the present value of the Current Income stream. The equivalence with the first method can be demonstrated by showing that the present value of Commitments is identical to the present value of the Optional Income stream, as in table 3.

Table 3. Optional income has zero subjective goodwill.

	Period				Present value
	0	1	2	3	
Optional income	−	15.00	12.30	20.10 (+156)	143.82
Commitments	100	23.00	11.00	22.00	143.82
Subjective goodwill					nil

Clearly the subjective goodwill associated with the 'Option' must be nil. It follows that the subjective goodwill of the 'Action' plan represents the excess of the subjective value of Action over Option.

Alternatively, one can subtract Optional Income, the interest foregone on cumulative Commitments at the beginning of each period, from the Current Income of the period and discount the resulting stream of Excess Current Incomes without reference to net current value at the end of the planning period.[4] This yields subjective goodwill directly, as shown in table 4.

4. The latter method was explored in Edwards and Bell in a little noticed appendix (1961, pp. 66–69).

Table 4. The present value of excess current income equals subjective goodwill.

	Period			Present value
	1	2	3	
Current income	35	23.0	34.0	71.99
Optional income	15	12.1	20.1	36.59
Excess current income	20	10.7	13.9	35.40

A fourth method, the mainstay of the economics profession, is to substract the initial investment from the present value of the dividend stream, including as a 'final dividend' the expected net current value at the end of the planning period.

While the fourth method yields the right answer, it has mislead some analysts in both accounting and economics to the view that the operation of the firm can be adequately revealed through the cash flows into and out of it, without considering changes in the market values of its other assets and liabilities. The confusion follows from the basic indeterminancy of analyses based on only one of the three fundamental equations (rows).

The indeterminacy arises in that the dividend stream, detached from Current Income and Commitments, provides no selfcontained explanation for the 'final dividend'. While arithmetic consistency can be recaptured by generating three related cash flow equations, the value then obtained for goodwill is inconsistent with those obtained in the previous examples.

Suppose that a purely cash flow analysis is applied in our example, the nature of the expansion path remaining, however, unchanged in all respects. We adjust Current Income to a cash flow basis by eliminating all valuation items – substracting new holding gains (10,5, and 15 in respective periods, assuming none are expected to be realized within the time horizon) and adding back depreciation (say, 5 per period) as in table 5.

Table 5. From current income to cash flows.

	Period		
	1	2	3
Current income	35	23	34
Less: current holding gains	−10	−5	−15
Plus: depreciation	+ 5 − 5	+5 0	+ 5 −10
	30	23	24

We assume no other adjustments (for example, for accruals and deferrals) are required. We can now derive the cash flow relationships shown in table 6.

Table 6. The present value of cash flows alone.

	Period				Present value
	1	1	2	3	
Cash flow	–	30	23	24 (+141)	157.69
Investment	100	18	11	12	132.60
Dividends	(−100)	12	12	12 (+141)	25.09
Cumulative investment	100	118	129	141	

These three 'equations' reflect cash flow alone and they are arithmetically consistent. But in order to keep the arithmetic consistent, we have been forced to use as our 'final dividend' in computing 'goodwill' the amount of 141, which is simply the sum of the initial net current value and subsequent cash flows retained. There is no information in the equations for determining values. Unfortunately, such a procedure is economic nonsense and the present values so derived are only curiosities. The analyst must either derive the 'final dividend' as the sum of Commitments, which include changes in values (see table 2), or make an independent valuation that yields the same answer. The very idea of an independent valuation implies that the expected net current value at the end of the planning period can be determined without reference to the expected behaviour of values throughout the planning period.

There are some circumstances in which cash flows appear to be sufficient unto themselves – if the project is expected to be liquidated within the planning period or if the time horizon defining the planning period is indeed infinite. Even in these cases, however, the question must be raised (and answered) as to how expectations about the amount and timing of cash flows can be formulated without reference to expectations about value changes.[5] Obviously, they cannot. When to buy and sell and how much will be paid or received depend on expectations about changes in values, among other things.[6]

We conclude then that the value of the expansion programme under consideration can be determined by using any of the methods outlined above

5. To my knowledge, this question has not been seriously addressed in the cost-benefit and project appraisal literature although it is fundamental to the determination of expectations about both the amount and timing of at least some cash flows. See, for example, Little and Mirrless (1974, pp. 7–11) on 'The Basic Data Required.'
6. This is not, however, to argue the observe, namely that planning can take place solely in terms of values without reference to form (of which cash is one, but only one).

provided that the 'final dividend' used in those methods requiring it is the cumulative sum of Commitments, which include changes in values. We conclude also (1) that Current Holding Gains are an essential component of Current Income, whose inclusion does not involve double counting, and (2) that Subjective Goodwill cannot be determined without reference to expectations about Current Holding Gains.

Exit or entry values

The nature of changes in values is still ambiguous, however, because entry and exit values have been assumed to be the same. Philip Bell and I are among those who have argued that, for the going concern, entry values – in particular, the current cost of purchasing the services used in production and the assets and liabilities on hand – will usually be appropriate (Edwards, 1954, 1961, 1975, Edwards and Bell, 1961, and Bell, 1971). It is clear, however, that for almost every going concern, *some* of its assets should appropriately be valued at less than current cost because the decision has been made to dispose of the asset either through use or resale (Edwards and Bell, 1961, pp. 98–103). Hence, the modification of the current cost approach by the Inflation Accounting Committee (1975, pp. 57–60 and 161–2), suggesting 'value to the business' as a concept with encompasses valuation at less than current cost when that is appropriate, is a useful refinement following Solomons (1966). The proposal is that current cost should be the basis of valuation except where it exceeds both Present Value (of expected net receipts) and Net Realizable Value (exit value) in which case the higher of the other two bases should be employed.[7]

But some have argued that exit values (Net Realizable Value) should be generally preferred over entry values (Chambers, 1966 and Sterling, 1970). It would follow that expectations of values at the end of the planning period (and therefore during its course and at the outset) should be entertained in terms of the cash that could be realized from disposal of the firm. The end of a planning period does not imply, however, an expectation that a going concern will terminate, but only that at the present time events beyond the time horizon are too uncertain to entertain firm expectations about them. Indeed, plans are being

---

7. My quibble is with the use of Present Value in the only case in which it would arise, namely when an asset or a group of assets is to be disposed of through use in preference to resale. The Present Value of the firm's expectations of the net receipts to be derived from asset use is subjective in nature. An Appraisal Value determined by an independent source (which might, of course, use present value methodology) would be preferable. Baxter's 'cost savings' may be an even more promising alternative (1975, pp. 129–31).

continuously revised and the time horizon is never reached as it too extends into the future with the passage of time. A finite time horizon does not destroy the concept of the going concern on which the use of current cost as a basis for valuation rests. It follows that the value expected at the end of the planning period should be the net current value of the firms as a going concern including the market value of goodwill, if any.

3. The relationship between current and economic income

The subjective value of the expansion programme under consideration is the sum of the initial net current value committed to the programme and the subjective goodwill associated with it. Subjective goodwill is itself the first item in the series of economic incomes, representing as it does an increase in value over the initial commitment occasioned by the choice of this expansion path. It is essentially a subjective capital gain arising from the identification and choice of an expansion path that is more profitable than simply investing at market rates of interest. Subsequent items in the economic income series can be determined as interest on subjective value at the beginning of each period. They are defined in the Hicksian manner. In our example the discount rates are 15 per cent, 10 per cent, and 15 per cent in the three consecutive years, so the series set out in Table 7 can be directly determined.

Table 7. Deriving goodwill from economic income.

	Period				Present value
	0	1	2	3	
Economic income	35.40	20.30	14.40	21.90 (+156)	186.72
Commitments of subjective value	135.40	8.30	2.40	9.90	151.32
Dividends	(−100)	12	12	12 (+156)	35.40

The arithmetic still holds in that subjective goodwill can now be determined as the present value of Economic Income less the present value of Commitments of Subjective Value. The fact that in this 'fifth method' subjective goodwill must be known *before* it can be computed sustains two further conclusions, namely, (1) Economic Income cannot be determined independently of Current Income (and expectations about it) and indeed must be derived from it, and hence (2) Current

Income is not an approximation to Economic Income but is a fundamental concept in its own right.

It can also be demonstrated that the difference between the two concepts is entirely one of timing. Table 8 shows that the arithmetic sums of Current Income and Economic Income are identical.

Table 8. The relationship between current and economic income.

| | \multicolumn{4}{c}{Period} | | |
	0	1	2	3 (+156)	Sum	Present value
Current income	0	35.00	23.00	34.00 (+156)	248	179.22
Economic income	35.40	20.30	14.40	21.90 (+156)	248	186.72
Difference	−35.40	14.70	8.60	12.10	0	−7.50
Commitments of:						
Current value	100.00	23.00	11.00	22.00	156	143.82
Subjective value	135.40	8.30	2.40	9.90	156	155.32
Difference	−35.40	14.70	8.60	12.10	0	−7.50

Moreover, the excess in each period of Current Income over Economic Income is precisely matched by the excess of Commitments of Current Value over Commitments of Subjective Value. Finally, if subjective goodwill is positive, Economic Income will on the average occur earlier than Current Income – it represents an anticipation of events – and this will be reflected in its higher present value.

4. The evaluation of expectations

We have shown that Economic Income is derived from expectations about those current events which make up Current Income. In a very real sense Economic Income reflects subjective events whereas Current Income represents market events. It follows that any objective evaluation of expectations must be conducted by comparing expectations about those current events which make up Current Income with actual market events as they transpire. *Ex post* Economic Income may differ from *ex ante* Economic Income for the same period in two ways – because current events of the period differ from the expectations originally entertained about them, and because expectations about still future events have changed. It is only the first set of expectations that can be assessed against actual market events of the period and it is that set from which expected Current Income for the period was derived.

The point is that subjective goodwill is expected to be translated into objective market values (net current value). In our example, the translation is expected to occur as shown in table 9 (cf. Edwards, 1961, and Edwards and Bell, 1961).

Table 9. The expected translation of subjective goodwill into current market values.

| | Period | | | |
	0	1	2	3
Subjective value	135.40	143.70	146.10	156.00
Net current value	100.00	123.00	134.00	156.00
Subjective goodwill	35.40	20.70	12.10	0
New commitments of:				
Net current value		23.00	11.00	22.00
Subjective value		8.30	2.40	9.90
Decreases in				
subjective goodwill		14.70	8.60	12.10

In each period the excess of the increase in net current value over the increase in subjective value represents a decrease in subjective goodwill, the amount having been 'realized' in the form of objective market values.

Over the planning period as a whole subjective value is expected to rise by less than net current value. Indeed, the difference over the planning period is precisely equal to subjective goodwill at the outset. Hence at the end of the planning period, if actual events correspond to expectations, all subjective goodwill entertained at the beginning will have materialized in objective market values. Evaluation should be directed toward determining whether or not actual increases in net current values correspond in all respects to those expected and if not, why not.

The deviation of actual events from expectations gives rise to unexpected income or windfalls (cf. Hicks, 1946). It is the detailed and refined analysis of these deviations that provides the basis for modifying expectations and improving the decision-making process itself. It is these deviations that are truly 'extraordinary gains' and they can arise with respect to any component of income, not only with respect to holding gains, (cf. Inflation Accounting Committee, 1975, pp. 20–23).

5. Expansion-neutral income taxes

It would be usual, of course, to introduce taxes into the analysis while formulating expectations about the Current Income stream. Our purpose is not, however, to take account of taxes expected to be paid according to ongoing tax systems, but rather to infer from our model the nature of an income tax system that would be expansion-neutral in the sense that its imposition would not alter preferences among alternative expansion paths.[8] We shall argue that such a system should have the following characteristics:

1. Taxes should be assessed on Current Incomes as they arise.
2. Taxes may be prepaid or postpaid with interest being earned or accrued as the case may be at the discount rates.
3. Tax rates should be the same for all components of Current Income.

Perhaps the most controversial feature of this system is that holding gains would be assessed when they arise (not when realized) and at the same rate as other components of income.

We have shown that subjective goodwill is the excess of the present value of the Current Income stream over the present value of Commitments and that this is equivalent to the excess of the subjective value of 'Action' over 'Option', where optional income is earned in each period on the net current value at the beginning of the period at the discount rate expected to prevail in that period. In order to analyze taxes, a third alternative must be considered, one in which taxes would be nil because current incomes are nil. With a constant price level that alternative is holding cash; we merely assume that the same Commitments are made as before, but that they are held in the form of cash over each period. This alternative is depicted in table 10.

Table 10. Holding cash has negative subjective goodwill.

	Period				Present value
	0	1	2	3	
'Cash' income		0	0	0 (+156)	107.23
Commitments	100	23	11	22	143.82
Subjective goodwill					− 36.59

8. We do not argue that such a criterion should be the only consideration entertained in formulating tax systems. Indeed, a government may wish to use the tax system to bias expansion paths in particular directions if only because many social costs and benefits do not enter into the private calculus of those making expansion decisions.

Given the option of earning income at the discount rates, the subjective goodwill associated with holding non-interest-earning cash must be negative. The present values associated with the expansion path (Action), investment at market rates of interest (Option) and holding cash (Cash) are compared in table 11.

Table 11. Present values of 'Action', 'Option', and 'Cash' compared.

		Present values	
'Action'		179.22	
	over 'Option'	143.82	35.40
'Option'		143.82	
	over 'Cash'	107.23	36.59
'Action'		179.22	
	over 'Cash'	107.23	71.99

The present value of 'Action over Cash' is the appropriate basis for assessing taxes representing as it does the present value of earning income over simply holding cash. *It is the present value of taxable income.* Indeed, the present value of 'Action over Cash' can be obtained directly as the present value of expected Current Incomes, excluding net current value at the end of the planning period. Hence, if taxes are assessed directly on Current Income (say, at 10 percent), the present value of taxes can be obtained directly as the product of the tax rate and the present value of Action over Cash, as demonstrated in Table 12.

Table 12. The present value of taxes on current income.

	Period			Present value
	1	2	3	
Current income	35	23	34	71.99
Taxes	3.5	2.3	3.4	7.20

Hence, the subjective goodwill associated with this expansion path should be reduced for taxes by 7.20 from 35.40 to 28.20.[9]

The firm can be given the option of paying its taxes in advance or delaying payment provided only that it receives interest on prepayments and accrues interest on delayed payments at the discount rates. Hence, the firm could settle its

9. Obviously, the introduction of taxes may affect the discount rates. We are therefore assuming that the discount rates we have been using (and Optional Incomes) are already net of tax effects.

taxes for the planning period (subject to renegotiation on windfall profits) by (1) paying 7.20 at the outset, (2) making current payments on Current Income, or (3) delaying payments with interest accruing. But the basis of assessment should be Current Income, and the standard for judging whether or not payments are 'on time' should be the timing of taxes so assessed.

Suppose, for example, that the firm has two possible expansion paths both having, before taxes are considered, the same pattern of Commitments and the same Current Incomes as those used in our running example. However, in Path A, Current Income is composed of Current Operating Profit alone while in Path B it is made up of net rental income of 12 per period and the rest is New Holding Gains. Without taxes, the two paths would have the same subjective goodwill. A tax system that is expansion-neutral should leave the post-tax subjective goodwills equal.

Suppose, however, that taxes are assessed against realized income only and that all holding gains in Path B are expected to be realized only at the end of the planning period. Assume further that Commitments must be maintained as originally expected in order to generate expected Current Incomes before tax. The payment of taxes must now reduce the dividend streams associated with the two paths from 12 per period to the figures shown in table 13.

Table 13. The differential effect of taxes based on realized incomes.

	Period			Present value
	1	2	3	
Path A				
Realized incomes	35	23	34	
Taxes	3.5	2.3	3.4	7.20
Dividends	8.5	9.7	8.6	
Path B				
Realized income	12	12	12 (+56)	
Taxes	1.2	1.2	6.8	6.67
Dividends	10.0	10.8	5.2	

Path B should now be preferred to Path A because its subjective goodwill has been reduced by taxes by only 6.67 as compared to 7.20 for Path B. Hence, taxation on a realized basis introduces a clear bias in favour of expansion paths in which realization is postponed, i.e., generally in favour of holding gains over operating income, even if the tax rates are the same.

The differential effect of taxes can be remedied, however, by assessing taxes on

Current Income in Path B (equal to realized income in Path A) and charging interest on deferred payments. Path B can then adopt the dividend stream in Path A, reinvest its tax savings in Periods 1 and 2 (2.3 and 1.1 respectively) to earn the interest being charged by the tax authorities. The tax payment required in Period 3 will then become 7.57 and the present value of taxes will rise to 7.20, the same as for Path A. Expansion-neutrality is recovered.

Assessing taxes on the different components of Current Income at differential rates will have obvious effects on choices of expansion paths. Such a system will bias choices in favour of those expansion paths in which income takes the form that is taxed the least.

Most existing tax systems tax holding gains at lower rates than other forms of Current Income and assess those gains only upon realization. We conclude, therefore, that most existing tax systems favour expansion paths dominated by holding gains whose realization is postponed as long as possible. Whatever the merits these tax systems may have, they are not expansion-neutral.

6. Conclusion

In recent years, the accounting profession has been moving in a growing number of countries toward the recognition of current costs in both the income and position statements of the firm. That movement merits commendation and is properly gathering strength and support from some governments and business firms. Unfortunately, the rationale for adopting current cost accounting has often been that it is a means of approximating economic income. The weakness of that foundation may retard the widespread adoption of current cost accounting.

This article has sought to demonstrate that Current Income, an accounting as opposed to an economic definition of income, is a fundamental analytical concept necessary for the determination of Economic Income and not at all an approximation to it. It should therefore be adopted in its own right and on its own very considerable merits.

Mathematical note

The basic relationships discussed in the article follow directly from definitions. They can be summarized as follows:

Let n equal distance of planning horizon and, in Period t, let

i_t = discount rate

d_t = discount factor = $\dfrac{1}{(1 + i_1)(1 + i_2) \ldots (1 + i_t)}$

B_t = Current Income

I_t = Commitments; $I_0 = 100$

D_t = Dividends = $B_t - I_t$

Q_t = Optional Income = $i_t \sum\limits_0^{t-1} I_t$

Define present values (PV) as follows:

C_w = PV of $\sum\limits_0^n I_t$

B = PV of Current Incomes

B_w = $B + C_w$

Q = PV of Optional Incomes

Q_w = $Q + C_w$

D = PV of dividends

D_w = $D + C_w$

I = PV of Commitments

G = Subjective goodwill

Then, in the three-period case, we have

(1) $C_w = d_3 \sum\limits_0^3 I_t.$

(2) $B_w = d_1 B_1 + d_2 B_2 + d_3 B_3 + C_w.$

(3) $I = 100 + d_1(B_1 - D_1) + d_2(B_2 - D_2) + d_3(B_3 - D_3).$

Subtracting (3) from (2) shows that

(4) $G = B_w - I = D_w - I_0 = d_1 D_1 + d_2 D_2 + d_3 D_3 + C_w - 100.$

The present value of the Optional Income stream is given by

(5) $Q_w = d_1 i_1(100) + d_2 i_2(100 + I_1) + d_3 i_3(100 + I_1 + I_2) + C_w.$

Substituting $d_3(100 + I_1 + I_2 + I_3)$ for C_w, and making use of $d_t i_t = d_{t-1} - d_t$ from $i_t = \dfrac{d_{t-1}}{d_t} - 1$, this can be rewritten as

(6) $Q_w = (1 - d_1)(100) + (d_1 - d_2)(100 + I_1) +$
$\qquad\qquad\qquad + (d_2 - d_3)(100 + I_1 + I_2) + d_3(100 + I_1 + I_2 + I_3),$

which reduces to

(7) $Q_w = 100 + d_1 I_1 + d_2 I_2 + d_3 I_3,$

demonstrating that

(8) $Q_w = I$.

Hence

(9) $G = B_w - Q_w = B - Q$.

and goodwill is simply the present value of excess current incomes.

Now assume that Q_w and the discount rate are net of tax effects. Noting that C_w is simply the present value of Commitments accumulated in the form of cash to the end of the planning period, the present value of taxable income can be obtained directly from Equation (2) as

(10) $B = d_1 B_1 + d_2 B_2 + d_3 B_3$,

from which it follows that if taxes are assessed against incomes other than B_1, B_2, and B_3 (excepting incomes that are proportional to or temporally adjusted from B_1, B_2, and B_3), B will be affected arbitrarily and taxes will not be expansion-neutral.

References

Baxter, W. T., *Accounting Values and Inflation* (McGraw-Hill, 1975).

Bell, P. W., 'On Current Replacement Costs and Business Income', in R. R. Sterling, ed., *Asset Valuation* (Scholars Book Co., 1971).

Chambers, R. J., *Accounting, Evaluation and Economic Behavior* (Prentice-Hall, 1966).

Edwards, E. O., Depreciating Policy under Changing Price Levels, *The Accounting Review* (April 1954).

Edwards, E. O., 'Depreciation and the Maintenance of Real Capital,' in J. L. Meij, ed., *Depreciation and Replacement Policy* (North Holland, 1961).

Edwards, E. O., 'The State of Current Value Accounting,' *The Accounting Review* (April 1975).

Edwards, E. O. and Bell, P. W., *The Theory and Measurement of Business Income* (University of California Press, 1961).

Enthoven, A. J. H., *Accountancy and Economic Development Policy* (North-Holland, 1973).

Fisher, I., *The Nature of Capital and Income* (Macmillan, 1906).

Hicks, J. R., *Values and Capital*, 2nd ed. (Clarendon Press, 1946).

Inflation Accounting Committee, *Inflation Accounting* (Her Majesty's Stationery Office, 1975).

Lindahl, E., *Studies in the Theory of Money and Capital* (Allen & Unwin, 1939).

Little, I. M. D. and Mirrlees, J. A., *Project Appraisal and Planning for Developing Countries* (Heinemann, 1974).

Parker, R. H. and Harcourt, G. C., eds., *Readings in the Concept and Measurement of Income* (Cambridge University Press, 1969).

Solomons, D., 'Economic and Accounting Concepts of Cost and Value,' in M. Backer, ed., *Modern Accounting Theory* (Prentice-Hall, 1966).

Sterling, R. R., *Theory of the Measurement of Enterprise Income* (University Press of Kansas, 1970).

IV. THE CASH FLOW ACCOUNTING ALTERNATIVE FOR CORPORATE FINANCIAL REPORTING

Tom A. Lee

1. Introduction

Financial accounting theory began to take its present form around the turn of the century. It crystalized into what are now the various orthodox rules and ways of perceiving things by the 1930's. Recently, signs of major change have become visible. Perhaps the majority of academic theorists now reject the historical cost rule. And many theorists are attempting far more sweeping changes than this. Many writers, especially the younger theorists, are trying to reconstruct financial accounting on entirely new foundations.[1]

Thomas thus summarises the present situation in financial accounting and reporting. Winds of change are blowing throughout the accounting world, and reporting accountants are having to cope with a seemingly endless stream of recommendations, requirements and amendments. It is reasonably clear that the greatest attention is being given to two main areas – that is, the objectives of reporting systems (in particular emphasising the various needs of different user groups); and income and value measurement systems (with specific regard to the problems arising from significant rates of price inflation). In addition, the prevailing debate has made one matter abundantly evident – historic cost accounting has a limited utility for reporting purposes, and the major problem over the next few years will be to find suitable alternatives which meet report users' known needs, adequately reflect economic reality, and can be implemented in practice.

The traditional accounting underlying corporate financial reports is based on accruals – that is, the financial data generated in the accounting system are allocated to the specific reporting periods to which they are judged to relate. The main practice adopted for this purpose is the familiar matching principle whereby revenue outputs are related to allocated inputs when measuring periodic income. Readers will very probably know of no system other than that defined above, and it is understandable that accountants react strongly against

1. A. L. Thomas, 'The Allocation Problem in Financial Accounting Theory', *Studies in Accounting Research 3*, American Accounting Association, 1969, p. 105.

any attacks on its adequacy. However, the number of attacks have been few and, consequently, the accrual basis to financial reporting has remained virtually unscathed over the years.Indeed, a review of the history of accounting thought and practice would reveal that accountants have been concerned, almost exclusively, with problems within the accrual accounting context. Unfortunately, most of these problems remain unresolved, despite attempts to standardise practice.

It is therefore my contention that accrual accounting, largely because of its dependence on subjective judgments for allocation purposes, has created a stockpile of problems which has diverted accountants' attention away from the more fundamental problem of finding the most suitable financial information to meet the needs of a variety of users of financial reports. For example, they have been far too busy with the problem of how to allocate fixed asset depreciation to bother to investigate whether depreciation is vital to the needs of report users. Even now, when the crucial question of price-level accounting is being debated, the framework for discussion remains the accrual process. The implicit assumption must therefore be that accountants, on the whole, are satisfied with this judgmental allocation system as a proper structure for their financial reports. There is no evidence to suggest otherwise.

2. Challenges to date

The validity of such an assumption deserves to be challenged. It is much too fundamental a point to be left unquestioned for so long. The number of sustainable challenges, however, have been few – the most detailed and direct outside the U.K. being that of Thomas,[2] with Chambers[3] and Sterling[4] also contributing in a somewhat different manner. The U.K. experience is similarly sparse, but will be looked at in detail in the following sections.

Thomas has concluded that the allocation or accrual process is indefensible in terms of attempting to measure information which adequately describes the real world:

Excepting rare instances where productive processes do not interact, and very high levels of input aggregation, financial accounting's allocation assertions are ambiguous and incorrigible. They may be employed to code the accountant's communication of estimates

2. Thomas, *op. cit.;* and 'The Allocation Problem: Part Two', *Studies in Accounting Research 9*, American Accounting Association, 1974.
3. R. J. Chambers, *Accounting, Evaluation and Economic Behaviour*, Prentice-Hall, 1966.
4. R. R. Sterling, *Theory of the Measurement of Enterprise Income*, University Press of Kansas, 1970.

about the firm, but allocation assertions do not reflect anything that exists in the external world, and do not correspond to any aspects of the firm's economic state or activities.[5]

Thomas' main argument, therefore, is that the arbitrary nature of accounting allocations leads to false descriptions of the reality of economic phenomena in reporting entities. His main solution is the production of allocation-free financial statements – in terms either of exit values or cash flows.

Chambers and Sterling, on the other hand, arrived at their exit value reports when considering the most relevant type of financial information to meet the needs of decision makers, rather than by specifically attempting to resolve the allocation problem. It can therefore be argued that their recommendations avoid the allocation problem whilst remaining within the familiar income and financial position framework. However, their work represents a significantly different approach to financial reporting as compared with other systems depending on accrual accounting.

3. The U.K. example

In the past, several U.K. writers have hinted at the possibility of a cash flow alternative to accruals – that is, a system based on cash transactions. However, to date, only Lawson[6] and myself[7] have investigated the proposal in any depth. As with Thomas, the Lawson-Lee case rests on a fundamental dissatisfaction with accrual accounting and also on doubts about the absolute utility of the income concept. The accountancy profession has remained relatively silent on these matters, but cash flow reporting has achieved a limited support in the recent Sandilands Committee report (although it was felt that it could not easily be accommodated within the present U.K. legal requirements).[8]

There are therefore grounds for hoping that a wider acceptance of cash flow reporting may eventually be forthcoming. With this in mind, the remainder of this paper will be concerned with my own arguments for such a system as they have developed over the years. In no way can they be regarded as entirely original nor, indeed, are they complete. However, at this stage, they fall into three

5. Thomas (Part Two), op. cit., p. 156.
6. See, for example, G. H. Lawson, 'Cash-Flow Accounting', The Accountant, 28 October 1971, pp. 586–9, and 4 November 1971, pp. 620–22; 'Distributable Profits and Dividends', Management International Review, Vol. 12, No. 2/3, 1972, pp. 113–19; Memorandum Submitted to the Inflation Accounting Committee, Manchester Business School, 1974; and 'The Rationale of Cash Flow Accounting', Investment Analyst, pp. 5–12.
7. These writings will be referenced in appropriate parts of the remainder of this paper.
8. 'Inflation Accounting', Report of the Inflation Accounting Committee, Cmnd. 6225, HMSO, 1975, p. 156.

groupings – conceptual (being related particularly to the objectives of financial reporting); measurement (being concerned with the validity of accrual accounting, and the relevance of income reporting); and comprehension (being directed at the communications problems facing report users). Each will be discussed in the following sections, and interested readers will find in the appendix to this paper outline cash flow statements, together with exit value statements based on the same data.

4. The conceptual argument

A conceptual study of accounting for goodwill gave rise to my initial thoughts on cash flow reporting.[9] Typically, such an asset tends either to be ignored or summarily dismissed in financial reports. However, if it is to be accounted for properly, it requires to be continually recognised and valued. But market values do not exist for such a purpose – goodwill cannot be purchased in the market place in the same way as plant or inventory. Its value therefore must depend upon some form of present value calculation involving the discounting of future income benefits to be derived from it. In other words, economic principles of valuation would require to be introduced into the accounting measurement process.

My eventual recommendation was therefore for the reporting of historic and forecast flows for the entity as a whole in order to give decision makers relevant data for purposes of making their own estimates of its economic value (including its goodwill resources). I felt this would prevent the rather dubious exercise of decomposing the total flows in order to value individual assets. The reporting of historic and predicted data, together with explanations of material differences between the two, and disclosure of forecasting assumptions, were also felt to satisfy both the decision making and stewardship objectives of reporting.

These initial proposals were tentatively made but they did contain one firm recommendation – that the reported flows should be measured on a cash rather than an accrual basis, thereby avoiding the inherent problems of the latter. In addition, I believe that forecast cash flows provide a more appropriate basis for discounting purposes than do accrual-based flows. Arbitrary accounting allocations (such as for depreciation, inventory, deferred taxation, etc.) would appear to distort the timing element with which the discounting process is designed to cope in present value calculations.

9. T. A. Lee, 'Goodwill: An Example of Will-O-the-Wisp Accounting', *Accounting and Business Research*, Autumn 1971, pp. 318–28.

Initially, therefore, I saw the advantages of a cash flow reporting system as follows:

1. Financial report users would be provided with a data base which could be used by them for purposes of deriving valuations necessary for decisions – for example, for the investor estimating future dividend flows for his share price model.
2. Managerial accountability would be improved by the reporting of actual and forecast data, coupled with explanations of material differences.
3. The major problem of allocation in financial accounting would be largely avoided, although cash flows would require some temporal segregation.
4. The attendant problems of price-level variations could also be largely avoided by using money cash flows, to which a money time preference rate could be applied in discounting by decision makers.
5. All resources (tangible and intangible) of the reporting entity would be represented in its total net cash flow, thereby avoiding incomplete reporting.
6. The classical Hicksian model of income and capital could be applied by decision makers by obtaining opening and closing entity capital from a discounting of forecast cash flows.

In other words, I envisage a system of reporting entity cash flows which avoids the traditional problems of accounting, although introducing new ones – particularly in the area of forecasting. I also see it as a system which distinguishes two separate functions – that of measurement and reporting of relevant data (which I believe to be the domain of the reporting accountant) and that of *overall valuation* (which I believe to be the responsibility of the decision maker when he makes use of reported data). Far too much emphasis has been and still is given to the need to report *individual* values in financial reports. In my view, this has given the impression that the reporting accountant is attempting to give an overall valuation of the entity to decision makers. This is clearly not the case. Whilst I would take issue with the proposition that all forecasting should be left to report users, it is my belief that overall valuations of the entity, or shares in it, should be made by them, and that cash flow data are more relevant than accrual-based data for this purpose. I also believe that they should be provided with entity management's quantifications of future activity as a basis for their personal forecasts.

These conceptual arguments for cash flow reporting have been developed further in two relatively recent papers[10] and, coupled with those contained in my

10. T. A. Lee, 'The Relevance of Accounting Information Including Cash Flows', *The Accountant's*

goodwill paper, have been grouped into three main categories – the need for change; the key factor of cash; and maximising objectivity.

4.1. The need for change

The traditional objective of financial reporting is stewardship or managerial accountability but there now appears to be an almost universal acceptance of economic decision making as the major reason for financial reports. Thus, accountants must ensure that reported data adequately meet the latter need, either in terms of historic information with a reasonable predictive ability or in terms of forecast data with a reasonable credibility – or possibly a combination of both.

The predictive ability of historic accounting information is relatively uncertain, either in historic cost or current value terms. Surprisingly, this aspect of accounting has remained inconclusive and unproven,[11] although there is a school of thought which suggests that no form of historic information should be used for predictive purposes.[12] This approach can be summarised as follows:

The primary goal of financial reporting should be to 'feedback' data about values of resources held by the firm as distinct from the shareholders. ... For present and past measurements to be selected on the basis of their capacity to predict future valuations of the same (distorted) measurements ... involves a circularity of reasoning unlikely to be of real use to investors in the end. Investors, after all, want for prediction purposes private information they can trade upon to their exclusive advantage. But accounting messages are public data and, hence, are best used for the verification of expectations.[13]

In other words, there is a very persuasive argument for treating historic information as control information, and for decision makers to use it only within such a context.[14] Additionally, there is evidence (which would apply to historic

Magazine, January 1972, pp. 30–34; and 'A Case for Cash Flow Reporting', *Journal of Business Finance*, Summer 1972, pp. 27–36.

11. The difficulties of assessing predictive ability can be seen in such studies as W. H. Beaver, 'Market Prices, Financial Ratios and the Prediction of Failure', *Journal of Accounting Research*, Autumn 1968, pp. 179–92; M. C. O'Connor', 'On the Usefulness of Financial Ratios to Investors in Common Stock', *Accounting Review*, April 1973, pp. 339–52. Altogether there have been little more than 20 empirical studies in this area between 1966 and 1975. All have been either restrictive in their coverage or tentative in their conclusions.

12. For example, M. N. Greenball, 'The Predictive-Ability Criterion: Its Relevance in Evaluating Accounting Data', *Abacus*, June 1971, pp. 1–7.

13. K. V. Peasnell, 'The Usefulness of Accounting Information to Investors', *Occasional Paper*, International Centre for Research in Accounting, 1973, p. 20.

14. There is evidence to suggest that, in relation to annual financial reports, investors use them for purposes of verifying information made public earlier in other sources such as interim reports – see,

cost or replacement cost systems, but not to realisable value systems) that the accrual process can introduce variations likely to affect the predictive ability of the resultant data – for example, different accounting techniques and allocations applied to the same situation can result in materially different decisions;[15] and fluctuating income series can be smoothed by companies for reporting purposes, thereby masking the true situation.[16] However, due to the limited nature of this evidence, I would be reluctant at this stage to condemn entirely the predictive ability of historic-orientated reporting systems which depend on accrual accounting. But I do believe that the frailties which appear to exist in them are sufficient to warrant investigation of reporting models which appear better suited to meet the needs of decision makers.

In particular, there appears to be merit in the argument for the formal provision of predictive data in financial reports. This recommendation has been made several times in the past and, despite doubts about its credibility, has been used for some years in the U.K. – albeit in the limited context of corporate acquisitions and mergers.[17] My doubts about forecast data concern not so much their inherent subjectiveness (which is unavoidable and can be allowed for by decision makers), but more the additional subjectivity which is created if the accrual basis is adopted as the measurement process. In my opinion, cash flow forecasts are more credible than accrual-based forecasts. They avoid the variability and manipulation which can result from the use of accrual accounting. I also feel that adequate descriptions of the assumptions underlying cash forecasts would be necessary to improve their credibility; as would explanations of material differences between actual and forecast performance (for example, distinguishing between variances due to economic circumstances and variances due to forecasting errors). This would mean the provision of forecast data for predictive purposes and actual data for 'feed-back' purposes – all on a cash and, therefore, allocation-free basis.

for example, R. Ball and P. Brown, 'An Empirical Evaluation of Accounting Income Numbers', *Journal of Accounting Research*, Autumn 1968, pp. 159–77.

15. See, for example, N. Dopuch and J. Ronen, 'The Effects of Alternative Inventory Valuation Methods – An Experimental Study', *Journal of Accounting Research*, Autumn 1973, pp. 191–211, for evidence of effects on individual decisions. At an aggregate level, however, evidence suggests the market is not 'fooled' by these variations – see R. Ball, 'Changes in Accounting Techniques and Stock Prices', *Empirical Research in Accounting: Selected Studies*, 1972, pp. 1–44. Presumably individual decision variations are compensated at the aggregate level.

16. For example, R. M. Copeland, 'Income Smoothing', *Empirical Research in Accounting: Selected Studies*, 1968, pp. 101–16. These results as with other similar studies, were tentative only, and require replication.

17. As under the provisions of *The City Code on Take-overs and Mergers*, Issuing Houses Association, revised 1976, p. 19 and pp. 39–41.

4.2. The key factor of cash

Whereas the previous section has emphasised certain failures of the traditional reporting system which give rise to the need to examine the cash flow proposal as a suitable alternative, this next section outlines the main reasons why cash flow reporting is of value, *irrespective of the frailties of the accrual system*. My main argument in this connection is that cash is *the* key resource of most reporting enterprises. Irrespective of the vital importance of other resources in business (such as workers and managers), the cash flow of an entity is essential to its very existence. Not to recognise this is to ignore the harsh realities of the business world. Cash is the life blood of a business entity.

In other words, no business entity can survive over the long-term without an adequate and positive net cash flow from its trading operations. Profitability is not enough and reasonable liquidity is required too. However, the traditional financial reporting system, with its considerable emphasis on profitability, is not specifically geared to highlight the key resource of cash. Funds statements are a considerable help in this respect, but they are not universally produced in practice and, in any case, are based on the income-orientated, accrual-based accounting system which does not necessarily identify the stark reality of cash flows. Admittedly, income contributes to liquidity but it is not the only factor to do so, and funds statements are somewhat inadequate for the purpose of isolating pure cash inflows and outflows. Cash is such an essential ingredient in the survival of reporting entities that it is very surprising that reporting accountants have paid so little attention to it. Some emphasis has been given through the use of accrual-based funds statements which are often, and misleadingly, termed cash flow statements (cash flow being defined as reported income after deduction of tax and addition of the depreciation provision). But, as previously mentioned, funds statements are no more than imperfect substitutes for cash flow statements.

It is also equally surprising that the needs of report users in relation to cash data have been virtually ignored. For example, the generally accepted share investment decision model is based on predictions of dividend flows which, in turn, depend to a large extent on the existence of distributable cash in the future. Accrual-based historic information cannot be said to be ideally suited to meet these particular needs. Nor can it be said to meet the needs of creditors anxious to assess a reporting entity's ability to pay its way both in the near-present and future (for example, with regard to interest and capital repayment commitments). Likewise, the employee and his official representatives concerned with wage negotiations, job security, and entity investment performance would find cash flow data more directly relevant to these needs than income-orientated information. In other words, just as a business will collapse through lack of cash, report users would appear to be equally disadvantaged through lack of information relating to cash. This applies whatever the economic climate, although it is most evident in times when cash is in short supply.

4.3. Maximising objectivity

One of the most fundamental and influential guidelines in traditional financial accounting is that reported information should be as objective as possible. There has been a significant switch of emphasis by accountants in recent years – away from the rather rigid interpretation of this concept in terms of being able to verify independently the fairness of reported information in relation to available evidence, towards the increasingly accepted view of informational neutrality vis-à-vis report users. This change has evolved from a growing awareness on the part of accountants that reported information is in many ways a compromise. In particular, it must be relevant to its users but at the same time it must be credible in their eyes. The problem is therefore one of finding an optimal mixture of the essential features of financial reports. They cannot be completely relevant; nor can they be completely objective. However, they can be reasonably relevant and reasonably objective. With this in mind, I have come to the following conclusion in relation to the utility of cash flow data:

... if objectivity is accepted as an important criterion of accounting, production of the type of information which appears to present the most reasonable balance of relevance and objectivity should be aimed for at all times – because of its overall utility to the user. Cash flow information appears ... to satisfy these conditions best. Firstly, in its historic form, it is perhaps the most objective information possible, avoiding most of the subjectiveness which enters into the technical adjustments involved in the traditional accrual accounting; it is also the most relevant information for purposes of comparison with forecast information should this be measured on a cash basis. Secondly, forecast cash flows, although involving a great deal of uncertainty (however, no more so than budgeted profits on the accrual basis) clearly avoid the necessary subjectiveness of accrual judgments and opinions. Therefore, they appear to be far less subjective in a *total* sense than profit forecasts.[18]

I would therefore have thought that a cash flow reporting model would be considerably attractive to accountants, in the sense that it appears to increase the relevance of financial reports whilst also increasing the objectivity of historic data and minimising the subjectivity of forecast data. In addition, it tends to switch the burden of responsibility for reporting away from the reporting

18. Lee (A Case for), *op. cit.*, p. 30.

accountant (by eliminating the absolute necessity for accounting allocations and valuations) towards entity management which, after all, is ultimately responsible for the quality of financial reports. If cash flow reporting were implemented, the onus would be on management to produce credible forecasts and not to manipulate historic flows by accelerating or decelerating cash transactions.

5. The measurement arguments

The conceptual arguments for cash flow reports have one thread running continuously through them – that of the frailty of accrual accounting. So far in this paper the latter has been examined mainly in terms of the element of subjective judgment involved. But it also gives rise to the need to look more closely at, first, the way in which traditional accounting is conducted (particularly the flexibility of accounting practice) and, secondly, what is accounted for (with specific regard to income and value measurement). Both these areas appear to me to contain matters which should be closely questioned when considering the suitability of the cash flow alternative.

5.1. Flexibility in accounting

It almost goes without saying that the measurement of past income and financial position on the accrual basis, without any guidelines or standards, is likely to reduce financial accounting to ultimate chaos due to the inherent flexibility of practice and the lack of a suitable mechanism to remove irrelevant or obsolete practices. Nevertheless, the accountancy professions in many countries have operated under such a laissez-faire system for several decades. The result has been the predicted chaos, increasing criticism, and the eventual implementation of programmes of standardisation.

It is not the purpose of this paper to describe in detail the degree of flexibility which exists in present-day financial reporting. Evidence of this can be found in various surveys of financial reporting practices now produced by professional accountancy bodies in many countries. Additionally, as part of my argument for cash flow reports, I have conducted empirical studies of the problem in three areas (goodwill accounting, disclosure of business combinations, and funds reporting)[19] and, in each study, evidenced substantial differences of approach, both between companies and over time.

19. Respectively, 'Accounting for Goodwill', *Accounting and Business Research*, Summer 1973, pp.

The various programmes of standardisation which are now in operation have helped to reduce considerably the absolute level of flexibility in accounting practice. Major problems have been identified, and suitable solutions have been made mandatory for the reporting entities to which they have been judged to apply. Despite this, several problems remain which, in many ways, are as fundamental as the original problems to which the standardisation process was directed. They appear to me to be as follows:

1. Prescribed accounting standards cannot eliminate the flexibility of accounting practice entirely. For example, a standard which states that inventory should be valued at the lower of cost or net realisable value, without stating how cost should be determined, reduces flexibility only marginally. Additionally, it may not be possible to standardise certain areas of practice which depend entirely on subjective judgment – for example, with regard to the probable life of a depreciable fixed asset or the estimation of irrecoverable debtors. Finally, standards can include provisions allowing reporting entities the right to deviate from a prescribed practice if a reasoned case can be advanced for so doing; again with the effect of perpetuating possible flexibility.

2. There is a considerable danger that prescribed standards, once stated as such, remain as the advocated practice beyond the point of time at which they become irrelevant or obsolete. In other words, unless they are constantly reviewed, and amended or abandoned where necessary, financial reporting will suffer from the 'stockpiling' effect that standardisation, in part, was designed to eliminate. This puts a considerable onus on professional bodies to police prescribed standards.

3. The question of who is ultimately responsible for producing and implementing accounting standards appears to be unclear at the present time. The obvious favourites are reporting accountants and their professional bodies and, in the U.K. and elsewhere, this appears to have been the course followed. However, this leads to problems because accountants are not usually responsible by law for financial reports (this normally being the function of entity management) and, in any case, standards may involve issues going beyond the boundaries of accounting. A possible solution may be to incorporate accounting standards into legislation, but this tends to place them within a context which is extremely difficult to amend except in the long-term.

4. The proliferation of accounting standards in recent years has resulted in a similar proliferation of standard-setting bodies. Whilst it is gratifying to find so

175–96; 'Accounting for and Disclosure of Business Combinations', *Journal of Business Finance and Accounting*, Spring 1974, pp. 1–33; and *The Funds Statement*, The Institute of Chartered Accountants of Scotland, 1974.

much interest in the problems of accounting and financial reporting, I cannot help but feel uneasy at the situation which could arise over the years whereby different bodies prescribe different solutions to the same problem. This is reasonably easy to cope with so long as the reporting entity is confined within its own national boundaries. But the same is not the case for the international or multi-national entity. In these instances, they will have to decide which of several standards they have to apply; a situation remarkably similar to the condition of flexibility which standards were aimed at minimising.

5. Finally, the development of accounting standards has resulted in an ever increasing disclosure of explanations of particular practices utilised in individual financial statements. Although it is wholly desirable for reporting accountants to make adequate disclosure of their accounting messages, I find it rather perturbing to see financial reports become more and more complex in order to improve their content. As a later section of this paper will explain more fully, a considerable number of report users are unable to use and understand the present form of financial report. Standardisation, and its related disclosure, does nothing to ease these problems.

Taken together, these various points force me to the conclusion that accrual accounting creates a problem of variability in practice which, to some extent, can be reduced by standardisation, but only by creating further problems for both the consumer and producer of financial reports. For this reason, I am not very impressed by the standardisation programme. In my view, it is simply another example of accountants looking for ways of repairing the accounting framework; ignoring the fact that it may not be capable of adequate repair and, instead, should be replaced. Unfortunately, at least in my view, the thinking which has taken place on the question of flexibility in accounting has caused accountants to ignore the possibility of alternative systems of financial reporting. Cash flow reporting would, after all, avoid many of the difficulties mentioned above in relation to accrual accounting and its standardisation.

5.2. The relevance of income

As an accountant educated in the tradition of income measurement and reporting, I find it hard, and more than a little confusing, to build my case for cash flow reporting to a large extent on the irrelevance of income measures. After all, over many decades, financial accountants have concentrated their attention almost exclusively on ways of improving income measurement – that is, in relation, first, to historic cost allocations (and standardisation thereof); secondly, to resolving the monetary purchasing power fault inherent in historic cost accounting; thirdly, to investigating current value alternatives to historic cost; and, fourthly, to examining ways of incorporating purchasing power and current value changes to derive measures of so-called real income.

I have examined these particular matters at length, sufficiently to conclude that income is akin to a very flexible piece of elastic. It can be as long or as short as its manipulator wishes; indeed, it is almost infinitely variable. In other words, there is no such thing as *the* income of a reporting entity for a defined period. Instead, there are many possible income measures, each dependent on the particular rules and judgments applied by the reporting accountant. Of course, the theoretical possibility of a large number of income measures, based on the same economic data, exists. And, of course, there is reassurance in the knowledge that reporting accountants usually operate within a fairly limited set of income rules. But there is also cause for concern in the fact that, by changing these rules, accountants are capable of describing entity income in an entirely different way to that previously entertained.

This is particularly important in relation to report users, for periodic income is a major factor in their assessment of reporting entities. It can be, and presumably is, used as a means of judging the success or failure of an entity and its management and, therefore, can be used as an indicator of future performance. Moreover, in relation to consumption and investment, it is a means of determining how much an entity can afford to distribute, and how much it must retain in order to maintain, expand, or change its existing operations.

In light of these matters, it is vital to define income in a consistent and acceptable way in order that report users can make rational judgments about the matters referred to above. Unfortunately, income does not lend itself to easy definitions, nor to any definitions likely to receive general acceptance. Much depends on the way in which a number of matters are treated. Put briefly, income cannot exist unless capital exists. But capital exists only if the resources underlying it have a value to the entity. Thus, resource valuation is one variable to be resolved before periodic income can be determined – differing values resulting in different capital measures, thereby producing different capital increments or decrements for purposes of determining income.

The next income variable with which reporting accountants have to cope concerns the decision about how much of each periodic capital increment or decrement should be treated as income – that is, the familiar capital maintenance decision. Again, the range of possible answers is wide, depending on the question of what is regarded as the appropriate capital to maintain. Subjective judgments have a considerable influence on this matter. For example, in the U.K., the Sandilands Committee has recommended that holding gains which result from its current cost variant of replacement cost accounting should not be treated as income, and, instead, should be taken to reserve.[20] If implemented as an accounting standard, this particular treatment of holding gains would eliminate the need for capital maintenance judgments. However, as seems likely, if the matter is left to the discretion of the reporting entities and their accountants, the judgmental aspect of accounting will be increased beyond present levels.[21] In other words, what is capital and income to one entity may not be the same for another entity. Indeed, what is capital and income to an entity in one period may be different in another period. Income is therefore not only variable in nature between entities, it is also temporally variable within the same entity.

In summary, periodic income can be measured and perceived in many different ways. Much of the variability exists because of the number of accounting procedures and resource valuations which can be applied to its measurement. But the judgmental aspects associated with capital maintenance decisions are likely to have an increasing impact on the potential variation of income. I would have sympathy with these problems if I felt that income was absolutely essential to the various users of financial reports. In my opinion, it may be of some use but it certainly does not appear to be of paramount importance to, for example, the investor assessing future dividend flows; the employee seeking wage increases or job security; the lender examining the ability of the entity to meet its loan commitments; and the tax authority computing entity taxation liabilities. Each of these matters can be satisfied without recourse to income measurements. Cash flow reports could provide all the necessary information for these purposes, thus avoiding the elasticity of income.

6. User comprehension

My earlier studies of the cash flow alternative to income were all in the areas described in the previous sections – that is, they were concerned exclusively either with purely conceptual points or with the measurement problems inherent in the income-orientated, accrual-based reporting system. This meant that one further matter had been largely ignored – the ability of report users both to use and understand the existing form of financial report. Even if the existing reporting system was free of the conceptual and measurement faults already mentioned, I can hardly argue for its overall utility unless I am convinced that it can be reasonably used and understood by those persons to whom it is directed. With

20. 'Inflation Accounting', *op. cit.*, p. 162.
21. This is precisely what has happened in 'Current Cost Accounting', *Exposure Draft 18*, Accounting Standards Committee, 1976, pp. 5–6.

this in mind, it seemed appropriate to examine the extent to which report users make use of traditional financial reports, as well as the degree to which they appear to understand the accounting messages contained in these reports. The subjects looked at to date have been private shareholders in limited companies – typically in the U.K., they hold a substantial majority of shareholdings, without necessarily holding a majority in terms of value. In comparison with institutional investors employing a great deal of accounting and financial expertise, they appear to be at the greatest risk in relation to the complexities of financial statements prepared on an accrual basis.[22]

To date, financial reporting systems have been based on general-purpose financial statements – that is, statements designed to meet the needs of as many potential users as possible, irrespective of their abilities, background, and experience in such matters. So long as financial reports remain uncomplicated documents, no major problem of use or comprehension would appear to exist. When they become complex, technical statements, written in a specialist language, these problems are all too apparent. But, so far, no attempt has been made by reporting accountants to meet this challenge. Indeed, the reverse appears to be true, with financial reports appearing to become more complex day by day as amendments and additions are made to the existing accrual structure.

A small number of studies have revealed that accounting and financial messages are likely not to be understood by a majority of people.[23] The research with which I have been associated supports these earlier findings, the level of understanding of the private shareholders questioned being usually very low – the only exceptions being for those with an accounting background or experience. The greatest difficulty was found to exist with valuation procedures and accounting terminology used in financial reports, and with financial ratios. In particular, balance sheet terminology was very badly understood.

So far as use of financial reports was concerned, the overall finding was that the annual report was generally little used, with the chairman's report being the

22. This research has been conducted in association with Dr. D. P. Tweedie of the University of Edinburgh. The detailed findings are contained in the following list of publications, and have been summarised for purposes of this paper: T. A. Lee and D. P. Tweedie, 'Accounting Information: A Study of Private Shareholder Usage', *Accounting and Business Research*, Autumn 1975, pp. 280–91; 'Accounting Information: A Study of Private Shareholder Understanding', *Accounting and Business Research*, Winter 1975, pp. 3–17; 'The Private Shareholder: His Sources of Financial Information and His Understanding of Reporting Practices', *Accounting and Business Research*, Autumn 1976 (forthcoming), pp. 304–14; and '*The Private Shareholder and the Corporate Report*', The Institute of Chartered Accountants in England and Wales, 1976 (forthcoming).
23. See F. J. Soper and R. Dolphin, 'Readability and Corporate Annual Reports', *The Accounting Review*, April 1964, pp. 358–62; J. E. Smith and N. P. Smith, 'Readability: A Measure of the Performance of the Communication Function of Financial Reporting', *The Accounting Review*, July 1971, pp. 552–61; and M. D. Still, 'The Readability of Chairmen's Statements', *Accounting and Business Research*, Winter 1972, pp. 36–9.

most thoroughly read part. Financial press reports were the best used of other sources of financial information. But the most alarming finding was that the thorough reader of the annual report tended also to be the thorough reader of other information sources – many shareholders appearing to make little or no use of *any* source of information about companies. This was even more disturbing in light of two other results – thorough readers of financial information tended to have a substantially better understanding of accounting matters than less interested readers, and tended also to have a relevant accounting background or experience. In fact, there is clear evidence to suggest that many private shareholders must be unable to use existing financial information due to its complexity. It appears, therefore, that accountants have produced a reporting system which is capable of being read thoroughly and reasonably understood only by accountants or equivalent professionals. This is particularly significant when it is realised, at least from our findings, that the vast majority of the private shareholders concerned were making their own invest- ment decisions without any expert help or advice. Many therefore must be making their decisions blindly, and a considerable number who do make use of financial reports must be in obvious danger of misunderstanding their content.

Armed with this knowledge, and coupled with suggestions from responding shareholders, two alternative and possibly complementary recommendations were made – first, to devise means of simplifying the present accrual-based annual report (both in relation to its complexity and terminology); and, secondly, to devise alternative systems to that of accruals which are likely to meet the needs of report users (and this could include cash flow reporting). Similar research is being conducted into the needs of institutional users but, meantime, the following conclusion warrants attention:

Financial reports must not be conceived solely in terms of the so-called sophisticated user. To do so would be to ignore the needs of the majority of shareholders in most companies. It could also result in the ignoring of the particular needs of other financially unsophisticated groups which, undoubtedly, are likely to be major recipients of company financial reports – for example, company employees.

Otherwise, to adapt the familiar Orwellian statement:

'All shareholders are equal. But some shareholders are more equal than others.'

Such appears to be the unintentional reality in financial reporting. It needs to be remedied. The remedy lies in the hands of members of the accountancy profes- sion.[24]

My own firm belief in this respect, conceived from an earlier conceptual

---

24. Lee and Tweedie, ('The Private Shareholder'), *op. cit.*, pp. 234–5.

standpoint, and confirmed from empirical evidence briefly discussed above, is that cash flow reporting must be examined with a view to supplementing or replacing the existing accrual system. It could simplify financial statements (because less disclosure of accounting methodology would be required); it would avoid the complexities of accruals and remove much of the language of accruals (such as income, depreciation, reserves, assets, debtors, inventory, and accrued charges); and it would appear to be more directly compatible with the needs *and* abilities of its potential users (particularly those lacking in accounting qualification and experience).

7. The future

It would be wrong of me to suggest that the case for cash flow reporting rests or falls entirely on the basis of the above briefly-described arguments. This position can only be reached when the system has been empirically tested in relation to both the needs of sophisticated and unsophisticated report users, and its feasibility in practice. Work therefore has to be conducted in the construction of cash flow reports, using both historic and forecast data. Once this stage has been completed, and only when this is so, the resultant reports can be tested on shareholders and other users to find out whether these can be used meaningfully (both in relation to decision making and control), and whether they are able to understand cash flow data significantly better than the present accrual-based data.

I have no intention of condemning conventional accounting absolutely. It is a system which, despite its acknowledged faults, has received general acceptance in the accountancy profession and business world. It is also a system which is likely to be used for some time to come even if cash flow reporting received immediate support. There may even be a case for reporting on both bases, or the arguments for cash flow reporting may ultimately be found to be unacceptable. Indeed, cash flow reporting may not be the only conceivable alternative to accrual accounting. Therefore, whatever the future holds for financial reporting, I only ask that the case for cash flow reporting be examined fully, debated adequately, and implemented if it is found to be useful.

Appendix: specimen cash flow and exit-value financial statements

This appendix has been prepared using invented data, and on the basis of a cash flow reporting format described originally in T. A. Lee. 'A Case for Cash Flow Reporting', *Journal of Business Finance*, Summer 1972, particularly pp. 32–5. It is not a complete reproduction of such a system, and is intended only to give the reader an impression of what it might be like in practice. Much work has yet to be undertaken on the precise contents of cash flow statements, and the undernoted should be regarded as for discussion only.

Exit-value balance sheets have been appended to the cash flow report because there are convincing arguments to suggest that they complement it rather well, and prevent the loss to report users of statements of financial position. Both the cash flow report and the exit-value report have been derived from data which are described first in the traditional historic cost format. For purposes of simplicity, the latter has not been prepared in accordance with any U.K. or E.E.C. regulations.

Traditional historic cost financial statements

1. *Income Statements – calendar years 1975 and 1976*

	1975		1976	
	£	£	£	£
Sales		677,000		759,000
Less: raw materials	420,000		498,000	
direct labour	101,000		117,000	
direct overheads	37,000	558,000	41,000	656,000
		119,000		103,000
Less: indirect labour and overheads	5,000		6,000	
irrecoverable debts	2,000		12,000	
loan interest	3,000		2,000	
depreciation	55,000	65,000	61,000	81,000
		54,000		22,000
Less: loss (gain) on sale of:				
plant	—		6,000	
motor vehicles	—		(3,000)	
investments	—	—	(10,000)	(7,000)
		54,000		29,000
Less: taxation		35,000		13,000
		19,000		16,000
Less: dividends		15,000		15,000
		4,000		1,000
Add: retained income brought forward		26,000		30,000
Retained income		30,000		31,000

2. *Balance Sheets – year-ends 1975 and 1976*

	1975		1976	
	£	£	£	£
Fixed Assets				
Land and buildings (cost)		100,000		100,000
Plant and machinery (cost)	250,000		265,000	
Less: accumulated depreciation	100,000	150,000	139,000	126,000
Motor vehicles (cost)	25,000		40,000	
Less: accumulated depreciation	20,000	5,000	8,000	32,000
Research and development (cost)		—		28,000
		255,000		286,000
Current Assets				
Stock and work in progress	180,000		206,000	
Debtors	75,000		83,000	
Investments	30,000		15,000	
Bank	10,000	295,000	—	304,000
		550,000		590,000
Less: Current Liabilities				
Creditors	190,000		196,000	
Bank	—		65,000	
Taxation	35,000		13,000	
Dividends	15,000	240,000	15,000	289,000
		310,000		301,000
Less: loan		30,000		20,000
		280,000		281,000
Share capital		200,000		200,000
Reserves		50,000		50,000
Retained income		30,000		31,000
		280,000		281,000

3. *Funds Statement – calendar year 1976*

	£	£
Sources of funds		
Income before taxation		29,000
Add: transactions not involving movements in funds:		
depreciation	61,000	
net gains on sale of assets	(7,000)	54,000
		83,000
Proceeds from sale of assets:		
plant	15,000	
motor vehicles	8,000	
investments	25,000	48,000
		131,000

Less: *Application of funds*		
Purchase of assets:		
plant	50,000	
motor vehicles	40,000	
Research and development costs	28,000	
Repayment of loan	10,000	
Taxation paid	35,000	
Dividends paid	15,000	178,000
		(47,000)

Decrease in working capital

Increase in stocks and work in progress	26,000
Increase in debtors	8,000
Increase in creditors	(6,000)
Decrease in bank	(75,000)
	(47,000)

Outline cash flow statements

1. *Statement of total cash flow*

	Calendar Year			
	1976			1977
	Forecast	Actual	Variance	Forecast
	£	£	£	£
Bank balance brought forward	10,000	10,000	–	(65,000)
Operational transactions flow	120,000	64,000	56,000	130,000
Financial transactions flow	(10,000)	(10,000)	–	(10,000)
Capital transactions flow	(104,000)	(77,000)	(27,000)	(12,000)
Taxation transactions flow	(35,000)	(35,000)	–	(13,000)
Net distributable flow	(19,000)	(48,000)	29,000	30,000
Interest and dividends	(17,000)	(17,000)	–	(21,000)
Undistributed bank balance	(36,000)	(65,000)	29,000	9,000

2. *Statement of operational transactions flow*

	Calendar Year			
	1976			1977
	Forecast	Actual	Variance	Forecast
	£	£	£	£
Cash received from customers	765,000	739,000	26,000	800,000
Cash paid for:				
raw materials	(502,000)	(513,000)	11,000	(499,000)
labour	(100,000)	(116,000)	16,000	(121,000)
overheads	(43,000)	(46,000)	3,000	50,000)
Net operational flow	120,000	64,000	56,000	130,000

3. *Statement of financial transactions flow*

| | Calendar Year | | | |
| | 1976 | | | 1977 |
	Forecast	Actual	Variance	Forecast
	£	£	£	£
Repayment of loan	(10,000)	(10,000)	—	(10,000)

4. *Statement of capital transactions flow*

| | Calendar Year | | | |
| | 1976 | | | 1977 |
	Forecast	Actual	Variance	Forecast
	£	£	£	£
Cash paid for:				
plant	(66,000)	(61,000)	(5,000)	—
motor vehicles	(40,000)	(36,000)	(4,000)	—
research and development	(25,000)	(28,000)	3,000	(12,000)
	(131,000)	(125,000)	(6,000)	(12,000)
Cash received for sale of:				
plant	18,000	15,000	3,000	—
motor vehicles	9,000	8,000	1,000	—
investments	—	25,000	(25,000)	—
Net capital flow	(104,000)	(77,000)	(27,000)	(12,000)

5. *Statement of taxation transactions flow*

| | Calendar Year | | | |
| | 1976 | | | 1977 |
	Forecast	Actual	Variance	Forecast
	£	£	£	£
Tax paid	(35,000)	(35,000)	—	(13,000)

6. *Statement of interest and dividend payments*

| | Calendar Year | | | |
| | 1976 | | | 1977 |
	Forecast	Actual	Variance	Forecast
	£	£	£	£
Loan interest paid	(2,000)	(2,000)	—	(1,000)
Dividends paid	(15,000)	(15,000)	—	(20,000)
Total distribution flow	(17,000)	(17,000)	—	(21,000)

Note: The above statements contain a 'stewardship' accounting of the cash flows for the immediate past period, compared and contrasted with the forecasts made for the same period and originally reported in the previous financial report. I would also recommend a disclosure of explanations by management of the variances resulting from the comparison of actual and previously forecast data. The possibility of an audit of these explanations would have to be considered.

Forecast data relating to the next period are provided for purposes of decision making. I believe it to be important to ensure that these are supported by adequate managerial statements of the assumptions on which they are based. Again, the question of audit would require to be considered. (Ideally, forecasts for more than one future period should be contemplated. However, given the inherent subjectiveness of these data, it may not be feasible or credible to go beyond a one year forecast in the first instance.)

Finally, I would recommend that a ten year summary of historic cash flow should be reported in a separate statement similar to that described above as Statement of Total Cash Flow. This would provide report users with a relatively simple trend of cash flow data.

Outline exit value balance sheets

Year-ends 1975 and 1976

	1975		1976	
	£	£	£	£
Fixed Assets				
Land and buildings		360,000		396,000
Plant and machinery		80,000		67,000
Motor vehicles		9,000		31,000
Research and development		—		175,000
		449,000		669,000
Current Assets				
Stock and work in progress	115,000		136,000	
Debtors	75,000		83,000	
Investments	40,000		18,000	
Bank	10,000	240,000	—	237,000
		689,000		906,000
Less: Current Liabilities				
Creditors	190,000		196,000	
Bank	—		65,000	
Taxation	35,000		13,000	
Dividends	15,000	240,000	15,000	289,000
		449,000		617,000
Less: loan		30,000		20,000
Realisable Capital		419,000		597,000
Less: opening realisable capital				419,000
Increase in Capacity to Adapt				178,000

V. THE RATIONALE OF CASH FLOW ACCOUNTING

Gerald H. Lawson

1. Introduction

As a method of measuring financial performance, cash flow accounting is concerned with most, if not all, of the traditional purposes of accounting and with many of the problems, notably inflation, prospective financial performance (Lawson, 1969), etc., to which accounting is now seeking to adapt.

Whereas virtually all variations of the historic, current and replacement cost bases of accounting studiously adhere to the principle of disclosing financial information through the profit and loss account and balance sheet media, developments in cash flow accounting in the last decade have emphasised (Lawson, 1969; Lee 1972) the income aspect of financial performance alone.

There are convincing reasons, well rooted in economic theory, why the axiomatic connection between the balance sheet and profit and loss account, which has often been too readily assumed in the past, should be severed. Thus, it might be argued, the proprietorship of a company quoted in the stock market can dispense with the balance sheet because it can observe the market value of its wealth on a daily basis. Moreover, a proprietorship desirous of the enjoyment of its full periodic income in the celebrated Hicksian[1] sense must anyway, as this paper explains, trade some proportion of its shares in the market. Market value criteria cannot therefore be ignored. But none of this implies that the balance sheet should be abandoned.

If the value of proprietorship wealth (value of a business in use) representing capitalised future dividends, which, in turn, derive from current and future earning power, is quoted in the market place, it is arguable that the balance sheet should reveal the market or exchange value of the net assets of the business (break-up or disposable value). A comparison of a company's value in use with its value in exchange yields important information from a resource allocation standpoint, not to mention the interests of its owners.

1. '... we ought to define a man's income as the maximum value which he can consume during a week, and still expect to be as well off at the end of the week as he was at the beginning' (Hicks, 1946).

The cash flow method of reporting past or prospective financial performance on a going-concern basis avoids any confusion between the functions of the income statement and balance sheet and certainly does not imply that all variants of the balance sheet concept should be cast overboard. Though this paper ignores the balance sheet and concentrates on comparisons between historic cost, current cost and cash flow bases of reporting annual income, a statement of financial affairs which is completely consistent with cash flow accounting can readily be devised.

Apropos some of the other principal purposes which accounting data are normally expected to serve, a number of important claims for cash flow accounting may be made. These include:

1. Whilst cash flow accounting is no more than receipts and payments accounting it is, contrary to what many accountants and others seem to have supposed, backed by sound economic principles (Lawson and Stark, 1975). Indeed, it is entirely consistent with both classical capital theory and modern capital market theory.[2]
2. Cash flow accounting is completely consistent with the principles of tax neutrality. Put more strongly; cash flow accounting is the only way of giving operational effect to the principles of tax neutrality (Lawson and Stark, 1975; Sumner 1975).
3. On a more pragmatic level, cash flow accounting is the only basis of corporate taxation which effectively has inbuilt safeguards that can prevent the kind of financial crisis suffered by British industry in 1974. This crisis resulted from an interesting combination of technical factors which, even now, have not been properly understood (Lawson and Stark, 1975; Lawson, 1974b).
4. Cash flow accounting is the only system of accounting that correctly captures relative price changes. It therefore succeeds in measuring periodic financial performance in terms of periodic purchasing power. That is to say, it compares like with like and also satisfies the necessary conditions for handling changes in the general level of prices (Lawson, 1974a).

The impression should by now have been given that cash flow accounting is a somewhat involved subject and that its protagonists are willing to have it judged against stringent criteria. This said, we may now turn to some of the details of the subject.

2. It is probably because accountants and others have failed to appreciate the relevance of the equilibrium assumptions of capital market theory that such irrelevant methods of accounting for financial performance in conditions of inflation have recently been proposed.

2. Cash flow accounting and shareholders

Cash flow accounting (CFA) is an accounting model which measures the return to shareholders in precisely the manner in which that return is enjoyed. The CFA model therefore explicitly allows for the existence of the individuals who are entitled to the proprietorship income which the historic cost-based conventional accruals accounting model (CAAM) allegedly measures. One of the most perplexing features of the CAAM is that it does not have shareholders in it and does not therefore specifically allow for the financial relationship between them and their company. Nor does the CAAM allow for the existence of capital markets.

Unless the financial relationship between a company and its shareholders is made explicit in, or as an adjunct to, the corporate income accounting process, there must at least be a strong presumption that, whatever the accounting model employed actually does measure, it is unlikely to reveal the (observable) manner in which consumable or reinvestable income is actually transferred to or received by shareholders. A realistic accounting model must also take cognisance of capital markets and share prices.

The foregoing propositions and some of their implications are elaborated in the following pages.

3. Return to shareholders

In defining the return which individuals or institutions obtain from *any* investment bought in the market place, it is useful to distinguish between the single period return (or periodic income) and the multiperiod return. The distinction between investment returns and the *disposal* (i.e. consumption and/or reinvestment) of those returns is also a matter of some consequence in the interpretation of periodic returns.

3.1. Single period return

The single period *rate of return*, r_e, obtained by an equity shareholder is the value of r_e which satisfies the equation

$$P_0 = \frac{D_1 + P_1}{1 + r_e} \tag{1}$$

whence

$$P_0 r_e = D_1 + (P_1 - P_0) \tag{1a}$$

(P_0 and P_1 are the entry and exit prices of the share at end-years 0 and 1 respectively; and, D_1 is a dividend received at the end of year 1.)

Both the L.H.S. and R.H.S. of (1a) define the single period return (as opposed to rate of return) to the investor.[3] The R.H.S. is however of *greater importance* in that it defines the *components* of the single period return and, in turn, raises a major category of considerations about the corporate income measurement process.

The single period return obtained by a shareholder is represented by a dividend paid directly to him[4] by his company *plus* the change in the market price of his share.[5] Assume that $P_1 > P_0$ and that the shareholder desires to consume (or reinvest elsewhere) the *whole* of his periodic income. If so, he must realise the proportion of his end-year 1 shareholding given by $P_1 - P_0$. He thereby maintains his initial (money) capital intact and therefore disposes of a periodic income measured in the classical Hicksian economic sense.

It must be emphasised that in order to realise (i.e. consume and/or reinvest) his *full* (Hicksian) income, the shareholder *must* transact in the market place. It is in this way, and only in this way, that the second component of the full periodic (Hicksian) income can be obtained. To state that the single period return to a shareholder is the sum of a component delivered directly by the company to shareholders, i.e. dividend, and a capital gain (or capital loss) which can only be obtained by making use of the capital market, is not to assert that capital gains (or capital losses) must necessarily be realised by shareholders annually. *What it does however imply is that, contrary to what has often been advocated, the Hicksian concept of periodic income cannot be applied by companies in determining shareholders' total periodic income.* All that companies can ever determine is the 'directly delivered' component of periodic income, the expected future values of which are at the root of the complex market capitalisation process which results in observable share prices.

As the writer has pointed out elsewhere (Lawson, 1975), the Sandilands Inflation Accounting Committee was wholly in error in stating that it is because a company's capitalisation rate and its expected future dividend stream both defy

---

3. L.H.S. and R.H.S. denote left and right-hand sides respectively.
4. A policy of zero dividends in no way negates the analysis which follows.
5. Should the shareholder provide further capital, B_1, for his company, equation (1a) needs to be adjusted to:

$$P_0 r_e = D_1 - B_1 + (P_1 - P_0). \tag{1b}$$

quantification that the Hicksian concept of income cannot be applied *by companies* (*Inflation Accounting*, 1975). The share prices which can be observed in the market place are the consequence of an automatic market capitalisation process and are precisely the values which are needed by investors (as opposed to companies) to give effect to the Hicksian concept of periodic income. The Hicksian concept of periodic income cannot generally be fully implemented by companies because the periodic income given by $D_1 + (P_1 - P_0)$ can only be paid out by companies when $P_1 = P_0$. In all other cases, i.e. in general, the company can only pay out D_1. The Sandilands Committee's suggestion that a company cannot pay out $D_1 + (P_1 - P_0)$ because P_1 and P_0 cannot be quantified is not only observably false; it is, conceptually speaking, also an error of double-counting (Lawson, 1975).

3.2. Multiperiod return

The familiar geometric mean *rate of return* obtained by a shareholder who holds for n years is given by the value of r_e which satisfies (2).

$$P_0 = \frac{D_1}{1 + r_e} + \frac{D_2}{(1 + r_e)^2} + \ldots + \frac{D_n + P_n}{(1 + r_e)^n} \tag{2}$$

The sequence of single period rates of return: $r_1, r_2, \ldots, r_3$, from which the geometric mean rate, r_e, is derived, is defined by equation (2a), namely,

$$P_0 = \frac{D_1}{1 + r_1} + \frac{D_2}{(1 + r_1)(1 + r_2)} + \ldots + \frac{D_n + P_n}{(1 + r_1)(1 + r_2)\ldots(1 + r_n)} \tag{2a}$$

whence,

$$P_1 = \frac{D_2}{1 + r_2} + \frac{D_3}{(1 + r_2)(1 + r_3)} + \ldots + \frac{D_n + P_n}{(1 + r_2)(1 + r_3)\ldots(1 + r_n)} \tag{2b}$$

$$P_{n-1} = \frac{D_n + P_n}{1 + r_n}, \tag{2c}$$

and,

$$r_n P_{n-1} = D_n + (P_n - P_{n-1}). \tag{2d}$$

Since an n-period investor does not realise any of his shares until end-year n, the sequence of periodic incomes corresponding to the n-year holding period is therefore:

$$D_1, D_2, \ldots, D_{n-1}, D_n + (P_n - P_{n-1}).\tag{2e)[6]}$$

Except for the terminal period, the (finite) multiperiod sequence of periodic returns corresponds to the sequence of periodic income components i.e. dividends, delivered directly to the shareholder by the company. In the multiperiod situation, it is much more obvious that the company cannot distribute the full amount of the Hicksian periodic income since, in effect, such a periodic payment would violate the assumptions whence all subsequent dividends emerge. That is to say, any higher level of distributions could only be made possible either by resort to debt financing which is effectively a trade-off of future dividends for higher current dividends, i.e. a mere change in the time-profile of a dividend stream.[7] Alternatively, a company which, in attempting to distribute the full Hicksian periodic income, gradually realised its assets would contravene the ground rules in that it would quickly erode itself out of existence. Such a strategy would *in general* be non-optimal for shareholders since they would receive a stream of cash flows having a lower present value than that which could be provided by maintaining their company as a going concern.

It is worth emphasising that, whereas the terminal periodic income in the (finite) multiperiod case is by definition realised in full, it is, like the fully realisable periodic income of any other period, partly delivered by the company and partly obtainable from capital market transactions.

For completeness, the sequence of periodic incomes obtained by shareholders who realise the full periodic income each year may be considered. It is represented by:

$$D_1 + (P_1 - P_0), P_0/P_1[D_2 + (P_2 - P_1)], P_0/P_2[D_3 + (P_3 - P_2)], \ldots \tag{3}$$

Thus, in all three of the cases represented by (1a), (2e), and (3) respectively, the total periodic income which may be realised or disposed of by shareholders is the sum of a component delivered directly by the company and a second component which may – or may not – be realised by the selling (or buying) of shares in the market place. Except for the limiting case of share prices which are constant in

6. In (2), (2b), (2c), (2d), (2e) and (3) new capital, B_j, contributed by shareholders is ignored.
7. This strategy would effectively force shareholders to realise the (indirect) share appreciation component of periodic income since it amounts to the substitution of debt for equity capital which, in turn, will cause a decline in the value of equity shares by precisely the amount of the debt-financed component of the total dividend.

perpetuity, a company in any of the three above situations cannot provide shareholders with the full Hicksian periodic income. Since a company can only deliver the dividend part of the disposable periodic income, the corporate income measurement process can, to the extent that it is proprietorship-oriented in the sense described above, report no more than the determinants of current and future periodic dividend payments or, in the case of zero dividend payments, the determinants of plough-back alone.

4. The determinants of dividend and retentions

The determinants of a company's dividend payments are by definition periodic cash inflows and periodic cash outflows. Ignoring the peculiarities of the advance corporation tax, which is a feature of the U.K. imputation tax system,[8] the determinants of a company's dividends may be expressed[9] as:

$$D_j = k_j - h_j - A_j - F_j - t_j - R_j \pm M_j \pm N_j \pm B_j \tag{4}$$

The R.H.S. of (4) represents a company specified as a total cash flow statement. The symbol $\pm B_j$ stands for new capital raised $(+)$ from shareholders or capital repaid $(-)$. The shareholders' periodic cash flow is therefore $D_j \pm B_j$ and, assuming the company continues in perpetuity, the (geometric mean) rate of return on the *original* equity investment is given by the value of r_e which satisfies the equation:

$$B_0 = P_0 = \sum_{j=1}^{\infty} \frac{D_j + B_j}{(1 + r_e)^j} \tag{5}$$

An examination of equation (4) readily suggests the manner in which it (or part of it) may be applied as a criterion of financial performance. If a company is financially viable, the following condition will 'on average' be satisfied:[10]

$$k_j - h_j - A_j - F_j - t_j > 0 \tag{6}$$

8. Cash grants for which particular categories of capital expenditure may qualify are also ignored.
9. A full glossary of symbols is given at the end of this chapter.
10. The expression 'on average' or, alternatively, 'taking one year with another' really means:

$$\sum_{j=1}^{\infty} \frac{k_j - h_j - A_j - F_j - t_j}{(1 + r_e)^j} > 0$$

However, financial performance *is* measured annually so the problem of annual performance must be

The L.H.S. of (6) can be regarded as post-tax earnings measured on cash flow basis.

To the extent that:

$$k_j - h_j - A_j - F_j - t_j - D_j > 0 \tag{7}$$

a company's directorate has exercised a discretion to reinvest some proportion of internally-generated funds (which might otherwise have been distributed as dividends) in growth capital projects. The L.H.S. of (7) therefore defines plough-back or *internally-financed* capital formation. Total new capital formation is represented by R_j in (4), and may be partly financed by net externally-raised finance: $\pm M_j \pm N_j \pm B_j$.

Whilst a company's directorate is, to the extent that annual cash flow earnings are positive, able to exercise some discretion over the allocation of $k_j - h_j - A_j - F_j - t_j$ between dividends, D_j, and new capital formation, R_j, care needs to be exercised in the interpretation of the annual cash flow *earnings* criterion. This point is valid regardless of the accounting basis on which annual earnings are to be measured. The fact of the matter is that annual earnings *are only of significance for an individual year examined in isolation.* Thus, denoting $k_j - h_j - A_j - F_j - t_j$ with CFE_j, the sequence of earnings CFE_j, CFE_{j+1}, CFE_{j+2}, ..., is, even aside from the impact of inflation, not amenable to inter-period comparison. It is only possible for shareholders to enjoy each of the periodic earnings CFE_j, CFE_{j+1}, CFE_{j+2}, ..., if those earnings are distributed in full.[11] If earnings are less than fully distributed, a time series of earnings data is a misleading series from a financial performance measurement standpoint. In other words, there is an interdependence between the level of plough-back, no matter how small, and future earnings which, as stated, means that each of a sequence of earnings cannot be enjoyed by shareholders in full. In fact, plough-back represents a sacrifice of current earnings in return for higher future dividends.

There is, thus, virtually no logical escape from the proposition that the dividend payment (or the determinants thereof) is the critical focal point in the corporate periodic income measurement process. However, since the plough-back level represents the measure of the amount that is currently sacrificed by shareholders in return for higher future dividends, it (the current plough-back level) is obviously a number of some considerable relevance to shareholder financial welfare. That is to say, the true current plough-back level is also, or at least

faced. Hence the attempt to measure annual earnings on a cash flow basis and the possible need of a little subjective judgement as implied by 'on average'.

11. A somewhat similar point has recently been cogently argued by A. J. Merrett (1975); it is considered at greater length by Lawson and Bean (n.d.).

arguably, an important piece of information in relation to the complex capitalisation process already mentioned, viz., the estimation and capitalisation of future dividends.

A cash flow system of accounting is the one and only method of disclosing accurate plough-back data. This is not to say that a cash flow earnings measure of plough-back will always be perfectly accurate. This is not so. The accuracy of the plough-back measure depends essentially upon the accuracy with which the dividing line between replacement investment, A_j, and growth investment, R_j, can be drawn. This may not always be easy. In defining plough-back as the funds that can be used to finance *new* capital formation, the pre-empted component of 'conventionally measured' earnings represented by periodic working capital investment must explicitly be allowed for. A genuine cash flow measure of earnings automatically includes the periodic working capital corrective.

5. Comparison with other accounting systems

The foregoing analysis represents at least part of the logical basis of a corporate accounting model which is consistent with observable reality and which has as its main aim the reporting of financial performance from a proprietorship standpoint. If this aim is accepted as the paramount objective of accounting, the cash flow earnings equation can be taken as a yardstick for evaluating other accounting models in that it can be used to indicate the extent to which the latter over- or understate the earnings which may truly be divided between plough-back and dividends in an individual year.[12]

5.1. CAAM versus CFA model

Earnings, $E_j^{(H)}$, measured in accordance with generally-accepted (historic cost-based) accounting principles are given by:

$$E_j^{(H)} = d_j - (a_{j-1} + b_j - a_j) - L_j - F_j - t_{j+1} - t_{j+1}^* \qquad (8)$$

12. An especially interesting aspect of this problem concerns the effect of overestimated earnings on the measure of plough-back and, in turn, the possible correlation between the latter and future earnings growth. For example, if earnings of 100 embody a 25 per cent overstatement, i.e. should be 80, a 40 per cent pay out ratio will cause plough-back to be overstated by 50 per cent. That is to say, plough-back would be stated as $100 - 40 = 60$ instead of $80 - 40 = 40$. As the writer has shown elsewhere (Lawson, 1974a; 1974b), this kind of overstatement can provide a complete explanation for the low to zero correlations between plough-back and future earnings growth which have been reported by a number of researchers during the last decade or more.

Cash flow earnings, CFE_j, have already been defined as:

$$CFE_j = k_j - h_j - A_j - F_j - t_j \tag{6}$$

Deducting (6) from (8) we obtain:

$$E_j^{(H)} - CFE_j = (d_j - k_j) - (b_j - h_j) + (a_j - a_{j-1}) +$$
$$+ (A_j - L_j) + (t_j - t_{j+1} - t_{j+1}^*) \tag{9}[13]$$

$$= l_j - i_j + f_j + \text{ditto} + \text{ditto}$$

$$= \varDelta \text{ debtors} - \varDelta \text{ creditors} + \varDelta \text{ inventories} + \text{ditto} + \text{ditto}$$

$$= p_j \text{ (periodic working capital investment)} + A_j - L_j \text{ (depreciation shortfall)} + t_j - t_{j+1} - t_{j+1}^* \text{ (difference between tax paid and total tax provided).}[14]$$

Thus, in order to convert *pre-tax* conventionally-calculated profits into earnings measured on a cash flow basis, the former needs to be adjusted by p_j and $A_j - L_j$. That is to say,

$$CFE_j(\text{pre-tax}) = d_j - (a_{j-1} + b_j - a_j) - L_j - F_j - p_j - (A_j - L_j) \tag{10}$$

Consequently, the implementation of a full-blooded system of external reporting on a cash flow basis in no way interferes with a company's internal accounting and data processing. It merely necessitates the application of two simple correctives to the profit and loss account.

5.2. CAAM versus Sandilands current cost accounting (CCA) model

The comparison in this case is equation (8) with equation (11), i.e.

$$E_j^{(H)} = d_j - (a_{j-1} + b_j - a_j) - L_j - F_j - t_{j+1} - t_{j+1}^* \tag{8}$$

$$E_j^{(S)} = d_j - (a_{j-1} + b_j - a_j) - \alpha_j - L_j^{(S)} - F_j - t_{j+1}^{(S)} - t_{j+1}^{*(S)} \tag{11}$$

$$E_j^{(H)} - E_j^{(S)} = \alpha_j + L_j^{(S)} - L_j + t_{j+1}^{(S)} + t_{j+1}^{*S} - t_{j+1} - t_{j+1}^* \tag{8)–(11}$$

13. The symbol t_{j+1}^* stands for a transfer to a tax equalisation account.
14. In recent years $E_j^{(H)}$ has, in the U.K., exceeded CFE_j by very substantial margins at the company sector level. Indeed, in 1974 a positive $E_j^{(H)}$ was associated with a negative CFE_j. This situation was

Equation (11) differs from (8) in two fundamental respects and in two further respects which are a consequence of the corporate tax implications of the Sandilands CCA prescriptions (Inflation Accounting Steering Group, 1976).

The term α_j in equation (11) represents the Sandilands cost of sales adjustment and is given by:

$$\alpha_j = \frac{(y_j - y_{j-1})(x_j + x_{j-1})}{2} \tag{12}$$

where, y_{j-1}, y_j are opening and closing unit inventory costs respectively (measured on a F.I.F.O. basis); and x_{j-1}, x_j are opening and closing inventory volumes respectively. (Thus, $x_{j-1}y_{j-1} = a_{j-1}$ and $x_j y_j = a_j$.)

The term $L_j^{(S)}$ stands for depreciation calculated in accordance with the indexation method proposed by the Sandilands Committee. Indexed depreciation, $L_j^{(S)}$, can readily be compared with the historic cost-based depreciation charge L_j in equation (8). For example, if a company has a stock of assets, each of which has a life expectancy of w years, acquired at prices of $A_{-z}, A_{-z+1}, \ldots, A_{-1}$, $z, z - 1, \ldots, 1$ year ago, L_0, is given by:

$$L_0 = \sum_{j=-z}^{-1} A_j/w \tag{13}$$

By contrast, the Sandilands indexed depreciation, $L_0^{(S)}$, at end-year 0 is given by:

$$L_0^{(S)} = I_0 \sum_{j=-z}^{-1} A_j/wI_j \tag{14}$$

where $I_{-z}, I_{-z+1}, \ldots, I_0$ is the sequence of values of the index of asset prices at end-years $-z, -z + 1, \ldots, 0$.

In conditions of endemic inflation, that is, in general, $L_j^{(S)} > L_j$. Similarly, in an inflationary world, α_j will usually be positive for the majority of companies and the cumulative cost of sales adjustment $\sum_{j=1977}^{j} \alpha_j$ will be positive for an even larger majority.

The corporation tax charge, t_{j+1}, under the existing U.K. corporation tax regime, included in equation (8) differs from the 'Sandilands' tax charge, $t_{j+1}^{(S)}$. If, as is often the case in the U.K., total capital expenditure, $A_j + R_j$, incurred in

mainly due to the high periodic working capital investment, p_j, the main determinants of which were relative price changes. (See Lawson, 1974b, page 6 et seq.)

period j qualifies for a 100% tax depreciation allowance,[15] t_{j+1} is given by:

$$t_{j+1} = T_j[d_j - (a_{j-1} + b_j - a_j) - F_j - A_j - R_j - STA_j] \tag{15}$$

where T_j stands for the nominal rate of corporation tax in period j. By comparison, the Sandilands tax charge, $t_{j+1}^{(S)}$, is given by:

$$t_{j+1}^{(S)} = T_j[d_j - (a_{j-1} + b_j - a_j) - F_j - A_j - R_j - \alpha_j] \tag{16}$$

The difference between t_{j+1} and $t_{j+1}^{(S)}$ is obviously given by:

$$t_{j+1} - t_{j+1}^{(S)} = T_j(\alpha_j - STA_j) \tag{17}$$

Whereas α_j is the previously-defined Sandilands cost of sales adjustment, STA_j represents the stock appreciation allowance for which companies are eligible under the existing U.K. corporation tax regime and is given by:

$$STA_j = (a_j - a_{j-1}) - 0.15\{d_j - (a_{j-1} + b_j - a_j) - F_j - A_j - R_j\}$$
$$= 0.85(a_j - a_{j-1}) - 0.15\{d_j - b_j - F_j - A_j - R_j\} \tag{18}$$

If unit inventory costs (measured on a FIFO-basis) tend to increase over time, the Sandilands cost of sales adjustment, α_j, will reasonably approximate the stock appreciation allowance, STA_j, taking one year with another.[16] If so, the Sandilands corporation tax charge, $t_{j+1}^{(S)}$, is a tolerable approximation of the tax, t_{j+1}, charged under the present tax system.

The transfer, t_{j+1}^*, to a tax equalisation account shown in equation (8) is intended to adjust the tax charge, t_{j+1}, such that the total tax provision, $t_{j+1} + t_{j+1}^*$, expressed as a percentage of pre-tax profit, $d_j - (a_{j-1} + b_j - a_j) - L_j - F_j$, is equal to the nominal rate of corporation tax, T_j. That is to say, t_{j+1}^* satisfies the equation:

$$\frac{t_{j+1} + t_{j+1}^*}{d_j - (a_{j-1} + b_j - a_j) - L_j - F_j} = T_j \tag{19}$$

15. For simplicity, possible tax depreciation allowances at lower rates on capital expenditure incurred in previous periods are ignored here.
16. This proposition is based upon results yield by a computer-based, multiperiod total financial model. Note, however, that if unit inventory costs fall, that is, if $y_{j-1} > y_j$, the Sandilands cost of sales adjustment will take on a negative value. (See section 5.3.1.).

Similarly, the 'Sandilands' tax equalisation account transfer is the value of $t_{j+1}^{*(S)}$ which satisfies the equation:

$$\frac{t_{j+1}^{(S)} + t_{j+1}^{*(S)}}{d_j - (a_{j-1} + b_j - a_j) - \alpha_j - L_j^{(S)} - F_j} = T_j \tag{20}$$

Since

$$\frac{t_{j+1} + t_{j+1}^*}{d_j - (a_{j-1} + b_j - a_j) - L_j - F_j} = \frac{t_{j+1}^{(S)} + t_{j+1}^{*(S)}}{d_j - (a_{j-1} + b_j - a_j) - \alpha_j - L_j^{(S)} - F_j} \tag{21}$$

and

$$d_j - (a_{j-1} + b_j - a_j) - L_j - F_j > d_j - (a_{j-1} + b_j - a_j) - \alpha_j - L_j^{(S)} - F_j \tag{22}$$

then

$$t_{j+1} + t_{j+1}^* > t_{j+1}^{(S)} + t_{j+1}^{*(S)} \tag{23}$$

But if, as seems to be the case,

$$t_{j+1} \simeq t_{j+1}^{(S)} \tag{24}$$

then

$$t_{j+1}^* > t_{j+1}^{*(S)} \tag{25}$$

The last four equations viz., (19), (20), (21) and (22), constitute a precise juxtaposition of the CAAM and CCA earnings measures and are worthy of emphasis. They may be summarised as follows. The pre-tax CAAM earnings measure will usually exceed its CCA counterpart. The CAAM total tax provision will usually exceed the corresponding CCA total tax provision. However, since the tax charge, $t_{j+1}^{(S)}$, implicit in the CCA earnings measure will approximate the tax charge, t_{j+1}, payable under the existing corporation tax regime, the Sandilands (profit) transfer, $t_{j+1}^{*(S)}$, to the tax equalisation account will be less than the corresponding transfer under the CAAM in conjunction with the existing tax regime. It also follows, as is the explicit intention of the Sandilands CCA proposals, that $E_j^{(S)} < E_j^{(H)}$. To that extent, the CCA earnings measure, $E_j^{(S)}$, can be regarded as an improvement on earnings, $E_j^{(H)}$, measured in accordance with generally-accepted historic cost principles. In the present context 'improvement' means superior proxy of the earnings which may truly be allocated between dividends and plough-back.

5.3. Sandilands CCA model versus CFA model

To determine whether the CCA earnings measure is a reasonable proxy for the cash flow earnings, CFE_j, which may truly be divided between plough-back and dividends *in an individual year*, it is merely necessary to compare equations (6) and (11), i.e.,

$$E_j^{(S)} = d_j - (a_{j-1} + b_j - a_j) - \alpha_j - L_j^{(S)} - F_j - t_{j+1}^{(S)} - t_{j+1}^{*(S)} \tag{11}$$

$$CFE_j = k_j - h_j - A_j - F_j - t_j \tag{6}$$

$$E_j^{(S)} - CFE_j = (p_j - \alpha_j) + [A_j - L_j^{(S)}] + [t_j - t_{j+1}^{(S)} - t_{j+1}^{*(S)}] \tag{11)–(6)}$$

If $E_j^{(S)} - CFE_j$ is positive, the CCA earnings measure overstates the amount which may truly be divided between plough-back and dividends in an individual year and *vice versa*. An examination of the three components of $E_j^{(S)} - CFE_j$, each of which is basically a different problem-area, facilitates inferences as to the conditions under which $E_j^{(S)} - CFE_j > 0$.

5.3.1. Periodic working capital investment, p_j, versus the cost of sales adjustment, α_j
As already indicated, periodic working capital investment, p_j, is given by:

$$p_j = l_j - i_j + f_j \text{ [i.e., periodic change in (debtors } minus \text{ creditors } plus \text{ inventories)]}$$

and

$$f_j = a_j - a_{j-1} \text{ [periodic change in inventories]}$$

$$= x_j y_j - x_{j-1} y_{j-1}.$$

But,

$$\alpha_j = \tfrac{1}{2}(y_j - y_{j-1})(x_j + x_{j-1}) \text{ [Sandilands cost of sales adjustment]}$$

$$\therefore f_j - \alpha_j = \tfrac{1}{2}(y_j + y_{j-1})(x_j - x_{j-1}). \tag{26}$$

In conditions of endemic inflation, both f_j and α_j will usually take on positive values because of rising unit inventory costs and/or increasing physical inventory volumes. However, if f_j and α_j are generally positive, then, as the above analysis shows, f_j will usually exceed α_j. Moreover, in inflationary conditions, the probability that f_j is positive must be higher than the probability of a positive α_j since an occasional decline in unit inventory costs i.e. a situation such that $y_{j-1} > y_j$, can be countervailed by rising inventory volumes (i.e. $x_j > x_{j-1}$) such that $a_j > a_{j-1}$ (that is $f_j > 0$). By contrast, α_j will take on negative values whenever $y_{j-1} > y_j$ regardless of the values of x_{j-1} and x_j. In sum, the Sandilands cost of sales adjustment, α_j, will, in inflationary conditions, generally fall short of the full 'stock appreciation' corrective, $f_j = a_j - a_{j-1}$, which must be applied to the CAAM if it is desired to express earnings as the amount which can truly be allocated between plough-back and dividends.

As already indicated, f_j is one of the three components of p_j. The CCA method takes no cognisance of the other two, namely, l_j and i_j. Although l_j and i_j may, to a large extent, cancel out for companies in aggregate, the ratio of l_j to i_j at the level of the individual firm is characterised by a significant degree of (observable) dispersion and should therefore be treated as a separate corrective to the CAAM. In that the CCA model takes no cognisance of l_j and i_j, it is deficient by comparison with the CFA model.

5.3.2. Capital investment and indexed depreciation, $L_j^{(S)}$

The computation of the Sandilands depreciation charge, $L_j^{(S)}$, is a rather crude exercise in the use of index numbers in that such a calculation will eliminate much of the dispersion about the average of asset costs. This dispersion across companies is precisely the kind of information that ought to be captured by the accounting process in order to reveal different degrees of company profitability.

Rather more to the point is the question of what the Sandilands indexed depreciation method actually achieves in relation to crucial distinction between the earnings of an individual period *viewed in isolation* and the earnings of a *sequence* of periods.

Consider a purely equity-financed company[17] which has acquired identical assets at prices of $C_{-z}, C_{-z}(1 + g), C_{-z}(1 + g)^2, ..., C_{-z}(1 + g)^{w-1}$ at end-years $-z, -z + 1, -z + 2, ..., -z + w - 1$. Assume that each of these assets has a life expectancy of w years and, that after end-year $-z + w - 1$, when asset prices continue to increase at the rate g, one asset is replaced annually. Hence, after end-year $-z + w - 1$ the company operates with an asset stock represented by w

---

17. The choice of a purely equity-financed company is a simplifying assumption which immediately obviates provisos concerned with such tangential matters as long term money gains, etc.

identical assets. The respective investment and Sandilands-type depreciation policies of the company are thus:

End-year j	$-z$	$-z+1$	$-z+2$	$\ldots$	$-z+w-1$	$-z+w$	$-z+w+1$
Investment, C_j	C_{-z}	$C_{-z}(1+g)$	$C_{-z}(1+g)^2$	$\ldots$	$C_{-z}(1+g)^{w-1}$	$C_{-z}(1+g)^w$	$C_{-z}(1+g)^{w+1}$
Depreciation, $L_j^{(S)}$	—	$\dfrac{C_{-z}(1+g)}{w}$	$\dfrac{2C_{-z}(1+g)^2}{w}$	$\ldots$	$\dfrac{(w-1)C_{-z}(1+g)^{w-1}}{w}$	$C_{-z}(1+g)^w$	$C_{-z}(1+g)^{w+1}$

As the above table shows, it is only in conditions of zero investment growth that Sandilands-type depreciation, $L_j^{(S)}$, will coincide with total investment, C_j. Given any degree of growth, the *present* value of a sequence of Sandilands depreciation charges will, assuming continuously rising asset prices, generally be lower than the present value of the corresponding sequence of investments. It is therefore only in continuing conditions of zero investment growth that Sandilands depreciation is correct from the standpoint (a) of periodic earnings measured in isolation; *and* (b) of a time-series of earnings. In these conditions, periodic earnings and periodic dividends will, or should, coincide and the CCA model will also give full effect, in terms of the purchasing power of the period in which it was incurred, to total capital expenditure, C_j.

Given any degree of investment growth, the Sandilands depreciation charge will, ignoring the indivisibility problem,[18] always be equal to the cost of replacing the number of plant years consumed in the previous period. Hence, the CCA model is, like most other methods of accounting, unsuitable for disclosing a sequence of annual earnings, since it generally fails fully to give effect to total capital expenditure, C_j. Unless the serial dependence between the growth capital expenditure, R_j, in any individual year and future earnings growth is recognised, the CCA model will therefore repeat the classic error of most other accounting models and, even in a world free of inflation, will rarely generate a time-series of earnings which are amenable to inter-period comparison.

---

18. For example, at end-year $-z+1$ in the above table, $C_{-z}(1+g)/w$ is an arbitrary allocation representing the current cost of one plant year. It is arbitrary in the sense that assets cannot be decomposed into plant years simply by dividing their current costs by their expected lives. Second-hand assets with one-year expected lives may however be available in the market place. By contrast, at end-year $-z+w$, $C_{-z}(1+g)^w$ is the current cost of replacing w plant years and in no sense constitutes an arbitrary allocation.

5.3.3. Taxes paid, t_j, versus total taxes provided, $t^{(S)}_{j+1} + t^{*(S)}_{j+1}$, under the Sandilands proposals

Given the present U.K. basis of corporation tax, and recalling the time-lag between tax charges and tax payments, actual taxes, t_j, *currently* paid in any year j will generally be less than the total tax, $t^{(S)}_{j+1} + t^{*(S)}_{j+1}$, which would be provided in accordance with the Sandilands proposals.[19] Hence, whereas in general *pre-tax* $E^{(S)}_j$ > *pre-tax* CFE_j, the relative post-tax position is much less obvious.

That is to say, if, in general

$$t_j < t^{(S)}_{j+1} + t^{*(S)}_{j+1},$$

and

$$k_j - h_j - A_j - F_j < d_j - (a_{j-1} + b_j - a_j) - \alpha_j - L^{(S)}_j - F_j,$$

it is not clear whether

$$k_j - h_j - A_j - F_j - t_j < d_j - (a_{j-1} + b_j - a_j) -$$
$$- \alpha_j - L^{(S)}_j - F_j - t^{(S)}_{j+1} - t^{*(S)}_{j+1}$$

i.e., whether $CFE_j < E^{(S)}_j$.

It can however be safely suggested that the absolute deviation between $E^{(S)}_j$ and CFE_j will, as a rule, be less than the absolute deviation between *pre-tax E_j* and *pre-tax CFE_j*. Thus, because the Sandilands post-tax measure of earnings, $E^{(S)}_j$ includes a transfer, $t^{*(S)}_{j+1}$, to a tax equalisation account, not to mention the possibility that $t^{(S)}_{j+1} > t^{(S)}_j$, earnings, $E^{(S)}_j$, may somewhat fortuitously turn out to be a reasonable proxy for CFE_j.

In concluding these comments on corporate taxation, two crucial qualifications must be made. Because U.K. corporate tax payments, tax charges and profit transfers to tax equalisation accounts are not based upon a pre-tax cash flow measure of earnings, both U.K. corporate tax policy and tax equalisation accounting are at odds with the principles of tax neutrality (Sumner, 1975). Moreover, since both the existing U.K. basis of taxation and the basis proposed in the Sandilands Report do not allow for the full tax deductibility of periodic working capital, p_j, both will inevitably cause the effective rate of tax

---

19. In the interests of clarity, it is emphasised that in this comparison CFE_j embodies the existing tax regime whereas $E^{(S)}_j$ includes the existing tax regime with I_j substituted for STA_j. However, as already explained in section 5.2, these two regimes closely approximate each other and therefore $t^{(S)}_{j+1} \simeq t_{j+1}$.

paid on cash flow earnings, CFE_j, to exceed the nominal rate of corporation tax (Lawson, 1974b).

5.3.4. Sandilands CCA model versus CFA model: conclusion

As the comparison of equations (6) and (11) shows, there are three significant differences between the bases of the Sandilands CCA model and the CFA model respectively. Viewing the earnings of an individual period in isolation, the first of these differences will generally result in an overstatement of the earnings truly available for allocation between plough-back and dividends. The third difference, namely, that between taxes paid and total taxes provided, will tend to countervail the first two. That is to say, *post-tax* cash flow earnings, CFE_j, will usually be more closely aligned with the *Sandilands post-tax* measure, $E_j^{(S)}$, than is the case with the corresponding pre-tax magnitudes.

Even though the Sandilands post-tax *periodic* earnings measure, $E_j^{(S)}$, should, by and large, prove to be a reasonable proxy for CFE_j – a testable assumption which must be subject to very considerable doubt – the Sandilands CCA model cannot be regarded as a theoretically satisfying basis for measuring the amount of earnings which are truly available for allocation between dividends and funds available for the financing of new capital formation. Any earnings measure which relies on a combination of the dubious logic of tax equalisation accounting and the time-lags between tax payments and total tax provided to countervail a failure fully to allow for the cost of periodic working capital investment and a depreciation shortfall must be suspect.

The inability of the CCA model to cope with the serial dependence problem is an even greater indictment of the method and probably resides in the failure on the part of the Sandilands Committee to understand the relevance of the Hicksian concept of personal income to the measurement of company financial performance.

Finally, it is interesting to ponder whether the inaccuracy of accounting earnings measures is correctly detected by markets and whether such inaccuracy has implications for resource allocation. I incline to the view that, whereas the U.K. stock market may be efficient, the process of resource allocation by managerial decision-making may be much less so; and, that the Government's management of the economy including its fiscal policy has been disastrously misled by accounting data in the past. Judging from what one hears at the moment, there seems every chance that the same thing could happen again, though perhaps in a much less acute form. I would however speculate that bank managers will not be caught out the next time round and that henceforth they will rightly do their accounting in cash flow terms.

List of symbols

a_j inventory at *end of year* j valued on a FIFO basis $(= x_j y_j)$

A_j replacement capital expenditure paid in year j

α_j Sandilands cost of sales adjustment for year j

b_j revenue expenditure incurred by a company in year j

B_j external equity finance received $(+)$ or repaid $(-)$ by a company in year j

c_j cost of sales in year j

C_j total capital expenditure incurred in year j $(= A_j + R_j)$

CFE_j post-tax earnings measured on a cash flow basis in year j

d_j sales recorded in year j (invoiced sales *plus* cash sales)

D_j dividend paid to shareholders in year j

$E_j^{(H)}$ net profit (i.e. less depreciation, interest and total tax provided) measured on an historic cost basis in year j

$E_j^{(S)}$ net profit (i.e. less depreciation, interest and total tax provided) measured on a CCA basis in year j

f_j *additional* inventory investment in year j $(= a_j - a_{j-1} = b_j - c_j)$

F_j interest charged (and paid) in year j

h_j cash paid to suppliers in year j on revenue accounts

i_j *additional* credit taken in year j $(= b_j - h_j)$

I_j index of asset acquisition costs at end-year j

j_j total credit taken at *end of year* j $(= \sum i_j)$

k_j cash collected from customers in year j on account of sales (including cash sales)

l_j *additional* credit given in year j $(= d_j - k_j)$

L_j accounting depreciation (historic-cost basis)

$L_j^{(S)}$ accounting depreciation calculated in accordance with the Sandilands indexation method

M_j year j increase in bank overdraft or reduction in bank balance $(+)$; or, decrease in bank overdraft or increase in bank balance $(-)$

N_j medium and/or long term debt raised $(+)$ or redeemed $(-)$ in year j

p_j additional working capital invested in year j $(= l_j + f_j - i_j)$

P_j share price at end-year j

r_e geometric mean cost of equity capital (shareholder rate of return)

$r_1, r_2, \ldots, r_n$ sequence of single period costs of equity capital

R_j growth investment in year j

STA_j stock appreciation allowance in year j

t_j corporation tax payment due in year j

t_{j+1} tax charge in year j payable in year $j+1$ (CAAM in conjunction with the existing tax regime)

$t_{j+1}^{(S)}$ tax charge in year j payable in year $j+1$ (Sandilands CCA proposals)

t_{j+1}^{*} profit transfer to tax equalisation account (CAAM in conjunction with the existing tax regime)

$t_{j+1}^{*(S)}$ profit transfer to tax equalisation account under the Sandilands CCA proposals

T_j nominal rate of corporation tax charged in year j

w	expected life of an asset
x_j	physical inventory volume at end-year j
y_j	unit inventory cost at end-year j
z	age of first asset acquired with expected life of w

References

Hicks, J. R., 1946, *Value and Capital*, (Oxford University Press), p. 172.

Inflation Accounting: Report of the Inflation Accounting Committee, Cmnd. 6225, H.M.S.O., 1975, September, pp. 28–30.

Inflation Accounting Steering Group, 1976, *Guidance Manual on Current Cost Accounting*, December.

Lawson, G. H., 1969, 'Profit Maximisation via Financial Management', First published in *Management Decision*, Winter. Revised version published in *Handbook for Managers* (Kluwer-Harrap Handbooks, Installment 4), 1972, London.

Lawson, G. H., 1974a, 'Memorandum Submitted to the Inflation Accounting Committee', Working Paper 12, Manchester Business School, July.

Lawson, G. H., 1974b, 'The Rationale for Measuring the Cost of Working Capital', Working Paper 15, Manchester Business School, July.

Lawson, G. H., 1975, 'Initial Reflections on Sandilands – I', *Certified Accountant*, November.

Lawson, G. H. and Bean, n.d., *Enterprise Valuation – a Cash Flow Approach*. Forthcoming.

Lawson, G. H. and Stark, A. W., 1975, 'The Concept of Profit for Fund Raising', *Accounting and Business Research*, no. 21, Winter.

Lee, T. A., 1972, 'A Case for Cash Flow Reporting', *Journal of Business Finance*, vol. 4, no. 2, Summer.

Merrett, A. J., 1975, 'Measuring Trends in Profitability', *Lloyds Bank Review*, October.

Sumner, M. T., 1975, 'Neutrality of Corporate Taxation, or on Not Accounting for Inflation', Manchester School of Economic and Social Studies, December.

VI. THE CAPITAL-INCOME STATEMENT AS A NEW TOOL FOR MANAGEMENT

Cees van Dam

1. Introduction

Studying accounting and finance literature, it is easy to note two totally different approaches: a retrospective one and a prospective one.

Among those who are studying the capital investment decision, many advocate the use of the net present value method. If this method is used in evaluating capital investment projects, future cash flow streams are taken into account. Estimated unrealized values are calculated. In financial reporting (even for internal purposes) none of these figures is reproduced. In every firm, balance sheets, profit and loss accounts and other statements are composed periodically. Together with the explanation added to these records, management of the firm can get from them summarized information, primarily from a retrospective point of view.

Sometimes these statements include ex ante elements, not even sufficient to be called ex ante or prospective statements.[1] As will be analysed in greater detail in volume 2 of this series,[2] we interviewed, with a team of researchers, many top managers from thirty-three of the largest companies in the Netherlands. Part of the questionnaire regarded ex ante balance sheets and ex ante profit and loss accounts. From the answers to the questions concerned, it could be concluded that 88 per cent of the visited firms composed ex ante balance sheets for *internal* purposes. Within all thirty-three firms, each year one or more ex ante profit and

1. An *ex ante* balance sheet is a balance sheet composed for a future point in time with the help of the same foundations as the traditional ex post balance sheet. A *prospective* balance sheet is a balance sheet, as of today, composed on the basis of expected (unrealized) figures from a series of future periods (using the present as the starting point). See for both categories: W. Lücke und U. Hautz, *Bilanzen aus Zukunftswerten* – ein theoretischer Beitrag zum Inhalt und Aufbau von Planbilanzen, Wiesbaden (Th. Gabler), 1973. See for a variant of a prospective balance sheet: K. Käfer, *Die Bilanz als Zukunftsrechnung* – eine Vorlesung über den Inhalt der Unternehmungsbilanz, Zürich (Schulthess and Co), 1962.
2. Cees van Dam, *Trends in financial decision-making:* planning and capital investment decisions, Leiden (Martinus Nijhoff Social Sciences Division), 1977.

loss accounts are composed for *internal* use. Within two thirds of the firms this is done, together with ex ante balance sheets, for three or more years hence.

In practice we did not discover any example of a prospective balance sheet or profit and loss account. Theory still has big problems with these statements.

The problem

All firms we visited in the Netherlands have a budgeting system for each time one year hence. Most of them have a long-term planning system. These long-term plans fulfil a useful function within the firm. From the composed budgets or long-term plans, ex ante balance sheets and profit and loss accounts are made up. The budgets and plans are regularly confronted with reality. This leads to a steady stream of information within the firm. In evaluating investment projects the horizon is five, ten or more years. Following the projects during their lifetime can lead to worthwhile information, altogether an enormous amount of information that has to be summarized in a convenient manner to be useful for management.

For management to remain informed about the 'economic position' of parts of the firm from a prospective point of view, in my opinion prospective balance sheets and profit and loss accounts are not the most suitable means. My thoughts lean towards a new statement that can be used supplementary to a 'traditional' balance sheet, a profit and loss account and (for example) a funds flow statement. In that statement, figures will have to appear with which management can get a clear perception of those parts of the firm it wants to follow.

Furthermore the expected consequences of decisions taken in the period of reporting and before would have to be interpretable from the statement, as well as the consequences of changed views, changed estimates and changed data. The size, type and structure of the firm determine how, and how far, these consequences have to be subdivided and specified.

The subdivision can be in e.g.:
- projects;
- portfolios of projects;
- decision units;
- divisions;
- working companies;
- departments;
- profit centers; or
- investment centers.

2. A new statement to serve specific purposes

Let us posit a firm where capital investment decisions are made on the basis of (among other factors) the net present value criterion, and where management wishes to be informed periodically about the 'economic position' of the investment centers of the firm (investment centers are parts of a firm where capital investment decisions are made by own initiative and which are responsible for their results). Suppose that management relates 'economic position' to present values. From the statement I am considering, differences between estimated and realized figures for each investment center can be read. Furthermore, present values of each investment center appear in the statement as at some base period, each time recalculated on the basis of the most recent information.

Investment centers that (seem to) evaluate systematically in a positive or negative direction can easily be pointed out. I have tried to develop such a statement (Table 1).

I have called it a 'capital-income statement'. To be clear, the statement in Table 1 is only one variant out of a large number of possible variants, meant to be used for the above-mentioned purpose. In a Dutch work, I presented a variant to be used by firms that are able, and want to follow capital investment projects or combinations (portfolios) of projects.[3]

Contents of the capital-income statement in symbols
The contents of the statement is first presented in symbols, being easier to relate some columns of the statement to each other later on. I therefore make use of the following symbols:

PV^x for (net) present value of investment center x as composed *at the moment of estimation*.
Five indices are attached to this symbol:
− the *first* to indicate the date to which discounting takes place;
− the *second* to indicate from which date the estimates and data have been used (the moment of estimation);
− the *third* to indicate the first period that has been included in the calculations;
− the *fourth* to indicate the length of the period that has been included in the calculations; and
− the *fifth* to indicate the discount rate at the moment of estimation.

3. See my *Waarde en winst in prospektief perspektief* − enige beschouwingen rond een 'waarde- en winstoverzicht', Leiden (H. E. Stenfert Kroese), 1976.

Table 1. A variant of a capital-income statement.

Capital-income statement for the period ....

(1) Code number and description	(2) Estimates and data as at end of base period (b)	(3) beginning of period of reporting (k*)	(4) end of period of reporting (k)	(5) (4)–(2)	(6) CF as estimated at beginning of period of reporting (k*)	(7) CF realized	(8) (7)–(6)	(9) Estimates and data as at beginning of period of reporting (k*)	(10) end of period of reporting (k)	(11) (10)–(9)	(12a) (12b)...
	1. Identification of investment centers	2. Present values at end of base period (b) with estimates and data as at three different dates			3. Estimated and realized cash flows in the period of reporting (k)			4. Present values at end of period of reporting (k) with estimates and data as at two different dates [+]			5. Subdivision of differences in present values

[+] Only cash flows after period of reporting.

CF^x for total cash flow of investment center x.

Two indices are attached to this symbol:
- the *first* to indicate the period to which the cash flow figure is related;
- the *second* to indicate the moment of which the figures have been used.

The following indices have been used:

b: for end of base period as well as for the period ending at time b (a period in the past that has been chosen to relate to the developments and changes that took place since that period; $k - b$ is the number of periods in the past that is still taken into consideration);

k: for end of period of reporting as well as for the period ending at time k;

n: for the length of the planning period, as determined *at the moment of estimation* (the planning period is the number of years into the future that is taken into consideration);

i: for the rate of discount as determined *at the moment of estimation*.

If an index is supplemented with an * that means that the indexing relates to one period earlier.

If we work with discrete discounting and make the assumption – for discounting purposes – that each period the total cash flow is generated at the end of that period, then the contents of columns (2) to (11) inclusive can be symbolized as follows:

(2): $PV^x_{b,b,b+1,n,i}$

(3): $PV^x_{b,k^*,b+1,k^*-b+n,i}$

(4): $PV^x_{b,k,b+1,k-b+n,i}$

(5): $PV^x_{b,k,b+1,k-b+n,i} - PV^x_{b,b,b+1,n,i}$

(6): CF^x_{k,k^*}

(7): $CF^x_{k,k}$

(8): $CF^x_{k,k} - CF^x_{k,k^*}$

(9): $PV^x_{k,k^*,k+1,n-1,i}$

(10): $PV^x_{k,k,k+1,n,i}$

(11): $PV^x_{k,k,k+1,n,i} - PV^x_{k,k^*,k+1,n-1,i}$

Explanation of the capital-income statement

A verbal explanation of the capital-income statement seems useful. The statement consists of five sections.

1. Identification of investment centers

In section 1 the investment centers are identified, e.g. by a code number and a short description.

2. Present values at end of base period (*b*) with estimates and data as at three different dates

In section 2 three present values are reproduced for each investment center. All values have been calculated at the end of the base period from newer and newer figures, with the discount rate to match that, *over a longer and longer period:*

a. With estimates and data as at the end of the base period: column (2). This figure remains constant as long as the base period does not move up. Changes in estimates, views or data do not have any influence on that figure.
b. With estimates and data as at the beginning of the period of reporting: column (3). This figure has already been calculated at the date the last statement has been prepared, using the estimates from that date and the realized cash flows (at that date the value has appeared in column (4)).
c. With estimates and data as at the end of the period of reporting: column (4). These figures are as at the end of the period of reporting: estimates for the period(s) still to come, realizations for the period(s) past.

In this section for each project three present values as at the same date are reproduced to get – at first glance – an idea of the influence on the value of the investment center of the changes that have taken place since the end of the base period.

In column (5) the differences between the values in column (4) and the values in column (2) are reproduced.

3. Estimated and realized cash flows in the period of reporting (*k*)

In section 3 differences between estimated and realized cash flows are calculated.

In column (6) the (positive or negative) cash flows of the investment centers in the period of reporting as estimated at the beginning of that period are reproduced. These (not discounted) figures correspond to the figures in the projected profit and loss account, prepared for the period of reporting as at the beginning of that period.

In column (7) the cash flows of the investment centers that are realized in the period of reporting are reproduced. These (not discounted) figures correspond to the figures in the profit and loss account of the period of reporting (prepared at the same date as the capital-income statement), if cash flow figures are in the profit and loss accounts. In column (8) the differences between the realized cash flows (7) and the estimated cash flows (6) are reproduced.

4. Present values at end of period of reporting (k) with estimates and data as at two different dates

Contrary to the calculations made for section 2, in this section only cash flows are taken into account that have not been realized at the end of the period of reporting. For each item a difference between two present values is calculated.

In columns (9) and (10) the present values of the cash flows, at the end of the period of reporting, are reproduced – in column (9) as estimated at the beginning of the period of reporting, in column (10) as estimated at the end of the period of reporting. The sum of all figures in column (9), as well as in column (10), is seen as (part of) a value of the firm at the end of the period of reporting.

In column (11) the differences between the figures in column (10) and (9) are reproduced. An analysis of these differences is given in section 5 of the capital-income statement.

5. Subdivision of differences in present values

Section 5 consists of several columns, the number and character of which depend on the character of the analysis to be carried out. With the help of the figures in these columns, differences in present values can be subdivided and analysed.

One can think of the differences in columns (5) and (11); these are differences in present values that could have been caused by changed views, changed estimates, changed data, a changed planning horizon (end of planning period), and/or the approval, modifications or accelerated completion of projects.

The values in column (5) can be seen as the present values at the end of the base period of the consequences of the changes arisen between the end of the base period and the end of the period of reporting (regarding past and future periods). The values in column (11) can be seen as the present values at the end of the period of reporting of the consequences of the changes arisen during the period of reporting (regarding only the future). Other differences that could be subdivided and analysed are the differences between the present values of the investment centers at the beginning of the period of reporting (with estimates and data at same date) and at the end of that period (with estimates and data at that date). The last values can be found in column (10), whereas the first ones appeared in column (10) one period earlier.

To subdivide and analyse the above-mentioned differences, the set up of section 5 of the capital-income statement as in Table 2 might be helpful.

The contents of those columns can be symbolized as well. Now an index is sometimes supplemented with **, which means that the indexing relates to the end of the *base* period; x^{**} refers to the composition of the portfolio of investment projects of the investment center at the end of the base period (the

Table 2. A variant of section 5 of a capital-income statement.

5. Subdivision of differences in present values

Differences because of changes arisen between end of base period (b) and beginning of period of reporting (k^*)					Differences because of changes arisen during period of reporting (k)				
(12a) Present values at *end of base period* (b) of consequences of	(12b) changes in estimates regarding figures in the period between b and $b+n^{**}$	(12c) different planning horizon	(12d) changes in the rate of discount	(12e) present value of investment centers at k^* minus present value at b	(13a) Present values at *end of period of reporting* (k) of consequences of	(13b) changes in estimates regarding figures in the period between k and k^*+n^*	(13c) different planning horizon	(13d) changes in the rate of discount	(13e) present value of investment centers at
approval, modifications and/or accelerated completion of projects					approval, modifications, and/or accelerated completion of projects				

addition ** to x is only needed if the second index to PV is *not* $b!^4$). The contents of the columns are:

(12a): $PV^x_{b,k^*,b+1,k^*-b+n,i} - PV^{x^{**}}_{b,k^*,b+1,k^*-b+n,i}$

(12b): $PV^{x^{**}}_{b,k^*,b+1,n^{**},i^{**}} - PV^x_{b,b,b+1,n,i}$

(12c): $PV^{x^{**}}_{b,k^*,b+1,k^*-b+n,i^{**}} - PV^{x^{**}}_{b,k^*,b+1,n^{**},i^{**}}$

(12d): $PV^{x^{**}}_{b,k^*,b+1,k^*-b+n,i} - PV^{x^{**}}_{b,k^*,b+1,k^*-b+n,i^{**}}$

(12e): $PV^x_{k^*,k^*,k,n,i} - PV^x_{b,b,b+1,n,i}$

(13a): $PV^x_{k,k,k+1,n,i} - PV^{x^*}_{k,k,k+1,n,i}$

(13b): $PV^{x^*}_{k,k,k+1,n^*-1,i^*} - PV^x_{k,k^*,k+1,n-1,i}$

(13c): $PV^{x^*}_{k,k,k+1,n,i^*} - PV^{x^*}_{k,k,k+1,n^*-1,i^*}$

(13d): $PV^{x^*}_{k,k,k+1,n,i} - PV^{x^*}_{k,k,k+1,n,i^*}$

(13e): $PV^x_{k,k,k+1,n,i} - PV^x_{k^*,k^*,k,n,i}$

Some explanation seems useful again. In the second half of section 5 differences that are the consequence of changes that have arisen during the period of reporting are calculated. In columns (13a) to (13d) inclusive these differences are expressed in present values at the end of the period of reporting. The values in columns (12e) and (13e) are differences between present values at different dates.

In the first half of section 5 corresponding values are calculated as in the second half, but of changes arisen between the end of the base period and the *beginning* of the period of reporting. The figures in columns (12a) to (12d) inclusive are expressed in present values at the end of the base period.

In columns (12a) and (13a) are reproduced the present values of the consequences of all approvals, modifications and/or accelerated completions of projects.

In columns (12b) and (13b) can be found the present values of the consequences of changed views, estimates and data. The values in column (12b) are also influenced by differences between estimated and realized cash flows.

In columns (12c) and (13c) are reproduced the present values of the consequences of having a different planning horizon at the end of the period under consideration than at the beginning of that period.

4. Because the index to x is defined in relation to the second index attached to PV (the moment of estimation); n and i are also defined in relation to the moment of estimation. To be clear: If the second index, k, is supplemented with an *, the moment of estimation is the beginning of the period of reporting. Then n and i relate to data as determined at the beginning of that period too, unless they are supplemented with **. If the second index is not supplemented with an *, n and i relate to data as determined at the end of the period of reporting, unless they are supplemented with * or **. E.g. in (12e) n and i relate to the length of a period and the rate of discount respectively as determined at k^* in the first term and at b in the second term.

In columns (12d) and (13d) can be found the consequences of changes in the rate of discount used in calculating present values.

In the last columns of each half of section 5 are reproduced differences between the present values of the investment centers at the end and at the beginning of the period under consideration.

In the appendix some columns are related to each other schematically.

Economic profit

If one takes into account the realized cash flows (including investments and disinvestments) of the periods under consideration, the figures in columns (12e) and (13e) can be seen as periodic income figures based on the *economic* concept of profit. According to Hansen:[5] 'the contents of profit based on fundamental principles of the theory of income and capital.' Traditional ex post as well as ex ante balance sheets and profit and loss accounts are composed on the basis of the accounting concept of profit. If capital-income statements are prepared, applying the net present value method, the basis is the economic concept of profit, as is the case when prospective balance sheets and profit and loss accounts are prepared. Connecting the application of the net present value method with the economic concept of profit does *not* mean that discounting ex ante profits is the same as calculating economic profits. It *does* mean that applying the net present value method, calculated profit amounts only deserve to be called profit amounts in an *economic* sense and not in an accounting sense.

In the literature, several authors do see practical problems in basing calculations on the economic concept of profit. Bedford[6], for example, sees big measuring problems because of 'management's inability to separate its realistic true estimation of future receipts from its emotional opinion regarding future receipts', but he concludes that, in spite of these limitations, a subjective concept of profit can also give useful information to the management of a firm, an opinion I can fully agree with. When Barton[7] reviews Edwards and Bell's conception, he has a just point of view by stating that 'a measurement problem should not be the reason for rejecting the conceptual merit of economic income'.

In the German literature, Lippmann[8] reported on his examination of the

5. P. Hansen, *The accounting concept of profit* – an analysis and evaluation in the light of the economic theory of income and capital, København/Amsterdam (Einar Harcks/North-Holland), 1966, p. 9. In his contribution to this book, Hansen replaced the term 'economic concept of profit' by 'the going concern concept of profit'.
6. N. M. Bedford, *Income determination theory:* an accounting framework, Reading, Mass. (Addison-Wesley), 1965, p. 27.
7. A. D. Barton, 'Expectations and achievements in income theory', *The Accounting Review*, vol. 49, October 1974, pp. 664–681 (citation is on p. 666).
8. K. Lippmann, *Der Beitrag des ökonomischen Gewinns zur Theorie und Praxis der Erfolgsermitt-*

proposition to replace the traditional annual accounts by a system of reporting that has been based on the economic concept of profit.[9] He concludes that 'Ein Verzicht auf das Instrument des herkömmliches Jahresabschlusses zugunsten des ökonomischen Gewinns lässt sich nicht vertreten'.[10] I can fully agree with this conclusion, which for many people is reassuring. Further, I feel that many imperfections in the present way of periodic reporting will disappear if the system of reporting is extended with data that are included in the capital-income statement. That will lead to the periodic calculation of profit amounts on the basis of the accounting concept of profit as well as on the basis of the economic concept of profit. In the Dutch literature, Traas[11] rejected the economic concept of profit by stating that the concept becomes silted in an extreme subjectivism. I cannot agree with that, because no profit calculation in a modern corporation can be done objectively. Leffson[12] speaks in this connection about 'intersubjective verifiability' that can be done to a greater extent when utilizing the accounting concept of profit instead of the economic concept of profit. Let it be, but to be clear:

When a firm bases most of its decisions on subjective estimates and then rejects a system of financial reporting for internal use, based on those very same estimates, it seems to me not only illogical, but also unjustified, and in principle wrong.

That means that the capital-income statement may not and cannot be rejected because of prevailing objections against the use of the economic concept of profit.

3. An application

By means of an application I will try to explain the meaning of the capital-income statement a little further.

In Table 3 the figures produced by three investment centers are given. These include (a) figures estimated at different dates and (b) realized figures. For discounting purposes all cash flows in a particular year are assumed to be generated at December 31 of that year. The cash flows not enclosed by a rectangle

lung, Düsseldorf (Institut der Wirtschaftsprüfer), 1970. Another valuable contribution with a broader scope is: Y. Ijiri, *Management goals and accounting for control*, Amsterdam/Chicago (North-Holland/Rand McNally), 1965.
9. Cf. P. Hansen's contribution to this book.
10. K. Lippmann, op. cit. p. 115; an analogous conclusion is reached by, among others, H. Münstermann, 'Dynamische Bilanz: Grundlagen, Weiterentwicklung und Bedeutung in der neuesten Bilanzdiskussion', *Schmalenbachs Zeitschrift für betriebswirtschaftliche Forschung*, NF, vol. 18, 1966, pp. 512–531; and H. Münstermann, 'Die Bedeutung des ökonomischen Gewinns für den externen Jahresabschluss der Aktiengesellschaft', *Die Wirtschaftsprüfung*, vol. 19, 1966, pp. 579–584.
11. L. Traas, *Het winstbegrip in de open naamloze vennootschap*, Haarlem (F. Bohn), 1970, p. 7.
12. See epilogue of U. Leffson in K. Lippmann, op. cit., p. 123.

Table 3. Figures of three investment centers.

	Cash flows of investment center 1 as per December 31,					Cash flows of investment center 2 as per December 31,					Cash flows of investment center 3 as per December 31,				
	1970	1971	1972	1973	1974	1970	1971	1972	1973	1974	1970	1971	1972	1973	1974
1971	−100	$\boxed{-105}$	$\boxed{-105}$	$\boxed{-105}$	$\boxed{-105}$	−100	$\boxed{-105}$	$\boxed{-105}$	$\boxed{-105}$	$\boxed{-105}$	−100	$\boxed{-105}$	$\boxed{-105}$	$\boxed{-105}$	$\boxed{-105}$
1972	−100	−100	$\boxed{-105}$	$\boxed{-105}$	$\boxed{-105}$	−100	−105	$\boxed{-105}$	$\boxed{-105}$	$\boxed{-105}$	−100	−100	$\boxed{-105}$	$\boxed{-105}$	$\boxed{-105}$
1973	+100	+100	+100	$\boxed{+95}$	$\boxed{+95}$	+100	+105	+105	$\boxed{+95}$	$\boxed{+95}$	+100	+100	+125	$\boxed{+95}$	$\boxed{+95}$
1974	+100	+100	+100	+110	$\boxed{+95}$	+100	+105	+105	+95	$\boxed{+95}$	+100	+100	+125	+100	$\boxed{+95}$
1975	+100	+100	+100	+110	+110	+100	+105	+105	+95	+95	+100	+100	+125	+100	+150
1976	+100	+100	+100	+110	+110		+105	+105	+95	+95		0	+25	+100	+50
1977			+100	0	0			+105	+95	+95			+25	+100	+50
1978					+110					+95					+50
i	10%	10%	12%	12%	10%	10%	10%	12%	12%	10%	10%	10%	12%	12%	10%

Base year: 1970.
Figures in rectangles are *realized* cash flows; the other cash flows are estimated values.

are estimated values, the figures inside a rectangle are realized cash flows (for simplicity, the length of each period is a full year).

The example incorporates changes in estimated cash flows, changes in the discount rate and in the planning period (*pp*). Note the differences between expectations and realizations. *All three investment centers show exactly the same realized cash flows.*

The investment centers are identified by the code numbers I_1, I_2 and I_3. 1970 has been chosen as the base year for all following analyses. Parts of four worked out capital-income statements are reproduced in Table 4.

Some calculations can be summarized as follows, given $(1 + i)^{-n} = r^n$:

For the first investment center

1. With estimates as *at same date as PV* calculations:

PV at	31/12/70 $pp =$ '71–'75 $i = .10$	31/12/71 $pp =$ '72–'76 $i = .10$	31/12/72 $pp =$ '73–'77 $i = .12$	31/12/73 $pp =$ '74–'77 $i = .12$	31/12/74 $pp =$ '75–'78 $i = .10$
	$-100r$ $-100r^2$ $+100r^3$ $+100r^4$ $+100r^5$	$-100r$ $+100r^2$ $+100r^3$ $+100r^4$ $+100r^5$	$+100r$ $+100r^2$ $+100r^3$ $+100r^4$ $+100r^5$	$+110r$ $+110r^2$ $+110r^3$ 0	$+110r$ $+110r^2$ 0 $+110r^4$
in column (2):	32				
in column (10):		197	360	264	266

2. With estimates as at *one period before PV* calculations:

PV at	31/12/71 $pp =$ '72–75 $i = .10$	31/12/72 $pp =$ '73–'76 $i = .10$	31/12/73 $pp =$ '74–'77 $i = .12$	31/12/74 $pp =$ '75–'77 $i = .12$
	$-100r$ $+100r^2$ $+100r^3$ $+100r^4$	$+100r$ $+100r^2$ $+100r^3$ $+100r^4$	$+100r$ $+100r^2$ $+100r^3$ $+100r^4$	$+110r$ $+110r^2$ 0
in column (9):	135	317	304	186

Table 4. Parts of four capital-income statements.

Capital-income statement for ...

1. Identification of investment centers	2. Present values at end of base period (b) with estimates and data as at three different dates				3. Estimated and realized cash flows in the period of reporting (k)			4. Present values at end of period of reporting (k) with estimates and data as at two different dates		
(1) Code number and description	(2)	(3) Estimated and data as at	(4)	(5) $(4)-(2)$	(6) CF as estimated at beginning of period of reporting (k^*)	(7) CF realized	(8) $(7)-(6)$	(9) Estimates and data as at	(10)	(11) $(10)-(9)$
	end of base period (b)	beginning of period of reporting (k^*)	end of period of reporting (k)					beginning of period of reporting (k^*)	end of period of reporting (k)	
I_1	32	32	84	52	-100	-105	-5	135	197	62
I_2	32	32	93	61	-100	-105	-5	135	207	72
I_3	32	32	27	-5	-100	-105	-5	135	135	0

Capital-income statement fo...

(1)	(2)	(3)	(4)	(5)	(6)	(7)	(8)	(9)	(10)	(11)
I_1	32	84	110	78	-100	-105	-5	317	360	43
I_2	32	93	124	92	-105	-105	0	333	379	46
I_3	32	27	86	54	-100	-105	-5	249	330	81

Capital-income statement fo...

(1)	(2)	(3)	(4)	(5)	(6)	(7)	(8)	(9)	(10)	(11)
I_2	32	110	78	46	100	95	-5	304	264	-40
I_2	32	124	96	64	105	95	-10	319	289	-30
I_3	32	86	106	74	125	95	-30	245	304	59

Capital-income statement fo...

(1)	(2)	(3)	(4)	(5)	(6)	(7)	(8)	(9)	(10)	(11)
I_1	32	78	136	104	110	95	-15	186	266	80
I_2	32	96	160	128	95	95	0	228	301	73
I_3	32	106	124	92	100	95	-5	240	249	9

Dec. 31, 1971 (base year: 1970)

5. Subdivision of differences in present values

fferences because of changes arisen between end of base period (b) and ginning of period of reporting (k*)   Differences because of changes arisen during period of reporting (k)

(12a)	(12b)	(12c)	(12d)	(12e)	(13a)	(13b)	(13c)	(13d)	(13e)
	Present values at *end of base period* (b) of consequences of			present value of		Present values at *end of period of reporting* (k) of consequences of			present value of
approval, modifications, and/or accelerated completion projects	changes in estimates regarding figures in the period between b and b+n**	different planning horizon	changes in the rate of discount	investment centers at k* minus present value at b	approval, modifications and/or accelerated completion of projects	changes in estimates regarding figures in the period between k and k*+n*	different planning horizon	changes in the rate of discount	investment centers at k minus present value at k*
—	—	—	—	—	—	—	62	—	165
—	—	—	—	—	—	7	65	—	175
—	—	—	—	—	—	—	0	—	103

Dec. 31, 1972 (base year: 1970)

(12a)	(12b)	(12c)	(12d)	(12e)	(13a)	(13b)	(13c)	(13d)	(13e)
	−5	56	—	165	—	—	62	−19	163
	2	59	—	175	—	—	65	−19	172
	−5	0	—	103	—	79	16	−13	195

Dec. 31, 1973 (base year: 1970)

(12a)	(12b)	(12c)	(12d)	(12e)	(13a)	(13b)	(13c)	(13d)	(13e)
	−9	108	−21	328	—	−40	—	—	−96
	2	113	−22	347	—	−30	—	—	−90
	43	27	−16	298	—	59	—	—	−26

Dec. 31, 1974 (base year: 1970)

(12a)	(12b)	(12c)	(12d)	(12e)	(13a)	(13b)	(13c)	(13d)	(13e)
	1	62	−16	232	—	—	70	10	2
	−19	102	−20	257	—	—	60	13	12
	−12	108	−21	272	—	−31	32	8	−55

For the second investment center

1. With estimates as *at same date as PV* calculations:

PV at	31/12/70 $pp = $'71–'75 $i = .10$	31/12/71 $pp = $'72–'76 $i = .10$	31/12/72 $pp = $'73–'77 $i = .12$	31/12/73 $pp = $'74–'77 $i = .12$	31/12/74 $pp = $'75–'78 $i = .10$
	$- 100r$				
	$- 100r^2$	$- 105r$			
	$+ 100r^3$	$+ 105r^2$	$+ 105r$		
	$+ 100r^4$	$+ 105r^3$	$+ 105r^2$	$+ 95r$	
	$+ 100r^5$	$+ 105r^4$	$+ 105r^3$	$+ 95r^2$	$+ 95r$
		$+ 105r^5$	$+ 105r^4$	$+ 95r^3$	$+ 95r^2$
			$+ 105r^5$	$+ 95r^4$	$+ 95r^3$
					$+ 95r^4$
in column (2):	32				
in column (10):		207	379	289	301

2. With estimates as at *one period before PV* calculations:

PV at	31/12/71 $pp = $'72–'75 $i = .10$	31/12/72 $pp = $'73–'76 $i = .10$	31/12/73 $pp = $'74–'77 $i = .12$	31/12/74 $pp = $'75–'77 $i = .12$
	$- 100r$			
	$+ 100r^2$	$+ 105r$		
	$+ 100r^3$	$+ 105r^2$	$+ 105r$	
	$+ 100r^4$	$+ 105r^3$	$+ 105r^2$	$+ 95r$
		$+ 105r^4$	$+ 105r^3$	$+ 95r^2$
			$+ 105r^4$	$+ 95r^3$
in column (9):	135	333	319	228

For the third investment center

1. With estimates as *at same date as PV* calculations:

PV at	31/12/70 $pp = $'71–'75 $i = .10$	31/12/71 $pp = $'72–'76 $i = .10$	31/12/72 $pp = $'73–'77 $i = .12$	31/12/73 $pp = $'74–'77 $i = .12$	31/12/74 $pp = $'75–'78 $i = .10$
	$- 100r$				
	$- 100r^2$	$- 100r$			
	$+ 100r^3$	$+ 100r^2$	$+ 125r$		
	$+ 100r^4$	$+ 100r^3$	$+ 125r^2$	$+ 100r$	
	$+ 100r^5$	$+ 100r^4$	$+ 125r^3$	$+ 100r^2$	$+ 150r$
		0	$+ 25r^4$	$+ 100r^3$	$+ 50r^2$
			$+ 25r^5$	$+ 100r^4$	$+ 50r^3$
					$+ 50r^4$
in column (2):	32				
in column (10):		135	330	304	249

2. With estimates as at *one period before PV* calculations:

	PV at 31/12/71 pp = '72–'75 i = .10	31/12/72 pp = '73–'76 i = .10	31/12/73 pp = '74–'77 i = .12	31/12/74 pp = '75–'77 i = .12
	$-100r$			
	$+100r^2$	$+100r$		
	$+100r^3$	$+100r^2$	$+125r$	
	$+100r^4$	$+100r^3$	$+125r^2$	$+100r$
		0	$+25r^3$	$+100r^2$
			$+25r^4$	$+100r^3$
in column (9):	135	249	245	240

The figures in column (4) of Table 4 have been calculated directly from Table 3, for instance the figure for investment center 1 as per 31 December 1973 (= 1 January 1974) can be found as follows:

$$-105r - 105r^2 + 95r^3 + 110r^4 + 110r^5 + 110r^6 \quad (\text{for } r^n = 1{,}12^{-n}) = 78$$

An analysis can be carried out on the basis of the figures in the statements. A summary of these analyses for 1971 and 1972 follows.

1971

The present value of *investment center 1* at the end of the period of reporting is 197, see column (10): this value is 32 one period earlier, and can be found in column (3) because end of base period = beginning of period of reporting. The difference between these two values is in column (13e). There are no changes in estimates. Because of a realized cash flow of -105 as compared to an estimated value of -100, -5 appears in column (8). The present value in column (4) is higher than in column (2), the difference is:

$$(-105 + 100) \times 1{,}10^{-1} + 100 \times 1{,}10^{-6} =$$
$$= -4 \text{ (concerning 1971)} + 56 \text{ (concerning 1976)} = 52.$$

The planning period at the end of 1971 includes 1976, so in column (13c) appears $+100 \times 1{,}10^{-5} = 62$. This figure is in column (11) too, because there are no values in columns (13a), (13b) and (13d).

The present value of *investment center 2* increases from 32 to 207, the difference is in column (13e). Because of changed figures for the years 1972, 1973, 1974 and 1975, a value appears in column (13b):

$$-5r + 5r^2 + 5r^3 + 5r^4 \quad (\text{for } r^n = 1{,}10^{-n}) = 7.$$

The consequence of a longer planning period is $+105 \times 1{,}10^{-5} = 65$, see column (13c). The sum of the values in columns (13a) to (13d) inclusive is in column (11). Because of a realized cash flow of -105 as compared to an estimated value of -100, -5 appears in column (8). The present value in column (4) is 61 higher than in column (2). This difference is the sum of:

$$
\begin{array}{lll}
(-105 + 100) \times 1{,}10^{-1} = - & 4{,}5 & \text{(regards 1971)} \\
(-105 + 100) \times 1{,}10^{-2} = - & 4{,}1 & \text{(regards 1972)} \\
(105 - 100) \times 1{,}10^{-3} = + & 3{,}8 & \text{(regards 1973)} \\
(105 - 100) \times 1{,}10^{-4} = + & 3{,}4 & \text{(regards 1974)} \\
(105 - 100) \times 1{,}10^{-5} = + & 3{,}1 & \text{(regards 1975)} \\
105 \times 1{,}10^{-6} = & +59{,}3 & \text{(regards 1976)} \\
\hline
& +61 &
\end{array}
$$

The present value of *investment center 3* increases from 32 to 135, and in column (13e) is 103. Again -5 appears in column (8). The consequence of a longer planning horizon is nil: in (13c) is zero.

The present value in column (4) is lower than in (2), because of the last two observations.

Since the end of the base period and the beginning of the period of reporting are the same, it is impossible that any value appears in columns (12a) to (12e) inclusive.

1972

In 1972 as well, there is no approval, modification or accelerated completion of a project. So again no values appear in column (13a). And because of the same situation in 1971, no values appear in (12a).

Again -5 appears in column (8) for investment center 1 as well as for I_3. The realized cash flow for I_2 is equal to the value as estimated at the beginning of 1972. For I_1 and I_2 the same values appear in column (13c) as in 1971. For investment center 3 the present value of the consequence of taking one year more (the year 1977) into consideration than in 1971 is

$$+25 \times 1{,}10^{-5} = 16$$

The estimates of I_3 for the years 1973 to 1976 inclusive changed drastically, resulting in the figure 79 appearing in column (13b):

$$+ (125 - 100)r + (125 - 100)r^2 + (125 - 100)r^3 + (25 - 0)r^4$$
$$(\text{for } r^n = 1{,}10^{-n}) = 79.$$

New are the figures in column (13d), differences in present values because of a higher rate of discount (12% instead of 10%). Using the cash flow figures as estimated at the end of 1972 for the ensuing five years leads to differences of -19, -19 and -13 respectively.

The present values at the end of the base period in column (5) are again higher than one year earlier, because of a combination of:

a. a realized cash flow of -105 (instead of -100 for I_1 and I_3);
b. changed estimates (only for I_3);
c. a positive estimated cash flow figure for 1977; and
d. a change in the discount rate.

The value 78 that appears in column (5) for investment center 1 is 26 higher than in 1971. The value 26 is the sum of

$$(-105 + 100) \times 1{,}10^{-2} + 100 \times 1{,}10^{-7} -$$
$$- 105(1{,}12^{-1} - 1{,}10^{-1}) - 105(1{,}12^{-2} - 1{,}10^{-2}) +$$
$$+ 100(1{,}12^{-3} - 1{,}10^{-3}) + \ldots + 100(1{,}12^{-7} - 1{,}10^{-7}).$$

Column (13e)

The values in column (13e) can be split as follows:

	1971			1972		
	I_1	I_2	I_3	I_1	I_2	I_3
+ the increase in present value in the period of reporting caused by the shift of the moment of discounting from beginning to end of period of reporting ($i \times$ value at beginning of period of reporting)	3	3	3	20	21	13
− the estimated value of the cash flow realized in the period of reporting = column (6)	100	100	100	100	105	100
+ the present value at k of the consequences of changes in estimates = column (13b)	−	7	−	−	−	79
+ the present value at k of the consequences of a different planning horizon = column (13c)	62	65	0	62	65	16
+ the present value at k of changes in the rate of discount = column (13d)	−	−	−	−19	−19	−13
Value in column (13e)	165	175	103	163	172	195

For 1972 only part one of section 5 has still to be explained, columns (12a) to (12e) inclusive. As no values have yet appeared in column (13a), column (12a) remains empty.

In *column* (*12b*) we can only find consequences of changes in estimates regarding figures for the years 1971 to 1975 inclusive (the planning period at the end of the base year).

The present value at the end of 1970 of the changes in the estimates for investment center 2 is:

$$-5r - 5r^2 + 5r^3 + 5r^4 + 5r^5 \text{ (for } r^n = 1,10^{-n}) = 2.$$

For I_1 and I_2:

$$-5r \text{ (for } r = 1,10^{-1}) = -5.$$

The values in *column* (*12c*) can be calculated as follows:

for I_1: $+100 \times 1,10^{-6}$ (regards 1976) $= 56$
for I_2: $+105 \times 1,10^{-6}$ (regards 1976) $= 59$
for I_3: 0 (regards 1976).

In column (12d) no values appear. In column (12e) the same values appear as in column (13e) one year before.

1973
At least two explanations seem useful for 1973.
1. The values in *column* (*12d*) have been calculated each time from the *seven 1972 figures* in table 3; firstly discounted to 1970 with 12%, secondly with 10%. The difference between the last two present values is -21, -22 and -16 respectively. The present values at 12% are 110, 124 and 86, figures that appear in column (3) of the capital-income statement.
2. The values in column (12e) are for each investment center the sum of the values in column (13e) in the years 1971 and 1972.

4. Epilogue

To avoid misunderstandings: the capital-income statement is a supplementary statement, *not* meant to replace the balance sheet or profit and loss account.

An advantage of preparing the statement (in the variant as developed in this paper) periodically for *internal* purposes is *periodically* getting worthwhile condensed information with which:
1. The 'economic position' of the investment centers can be judged;

2. The capitalized earnings value of (parts of) the firm can be calculated (to support some policy decisions);
3. The reliability of estimates can be judged;
4. The consequences of decisions made can be judged;
5. The consequences of changed views, changed estimates and changed data can be judged; and
6. The differences between estimates and realizations can be analysed.

The introduction into a firm of capital-income statements as developed in this paper will have as a consequence the introduction of an additional system of accounting: present value accounting.[13] The *meaning* of the capital-income statement depends neither on the use of the NPV method nor on the subdivision of a firm into investment centers. Many variants can be developed, e.g. to include the consequences of changing foreign exchange rates.

The next step is to incorporate some (simple) risk measures[14] in the capital-income statement. The meaning of portfolio theory in this context can hardly be overrated.

I am very reserved about the possibilities and desirability of composing capital-income statements for *external* use. Much study still has to be done.[15]

I hope to have given a contribution to a bridging of the gap between accounting and finance. Unfortunately what Edwards and Bell[16] wrote in 1961 is still true: 'Economics deals with the future and the decisions which will determine that future, while accounting is primarily concerned with historical description!'

13. Cf., e.g., M. Gordon and G. Shillinglaw, *Accounting – a management approach*, Homewood Ill. (R. D. Irwin), 5th edition, 1974, p. 250–260.
14. See my *Beslissen in onzekerheid*, Leiden (H. E. Stenfert Kroese), 1973.
15. Cf. M. Bromwich, 'The use of present value valuation models in published accounting reports', *The Accounting Review*, vol. 52, July 1977, pp. 587–596.
16. E. O. Edwards and Ph. W. Bell, *The theory and measurement of business income*, Berkeley and Los Angeles (University of California Press), 1961, p. 1.

Appendix

A relation between some columns of the capital-income statement in the variant presented.

For simplicity, the following contracted notations are used:

$$PV^x_{k,\ldots,n,i} \quad \text{for} \quad PV^x_{k,k,k+1,n,i}$$

$$PV^x_{b,\ldots,k^*-b+n,i} \quad \text{for} \quad PV^x_{b,k^*,b+1,k^*-b+n,i}$$

A. Part two of section 5

$$PV^x_{k,\ldots,n,i} - PV^{x^*}_{k,\ldots,n,i} = (13a)$$

$$(10) \quad PV^{x^*}_{k,\ldots,n,i} - PV^{x^*}_{k,\ldots,n,i^*} = (13d)$$

$$PV^{x^*}_{k,\ldots,n,i^*} - PV^{x^*}_{k,\ldots,n^*-1,i^*} = (13c)$$

$$PV^{x^*}_{k,\ldots,n^*-1,i^*} - PV^x_{k,k^*,k+1,n-1,i} = (13b)$$

$$(9)$$

$$(10) - (9) = (11) = (13a) + (13b) + (13c) + (13d)$$

N.B.: $k, \ldots$ is for $k, k, k+1$ (PV at k, estimates as at k, figures regard only the future).

B. Part one of section 5

$$PV^x_{b,\ldots,k^*-b+n,i} - PV^{x^{**}}_{b,\ldots,k^*-b+n,i} = (12a)$$

$$(3) \quad PV^{x^{**}}_{b,\ldots,k^*-b+n,i} - PV^{x^{**}}_{b,\ldots,k^*-b+n,i^{**}} = (12d)$$

$$PV^{x^{**}}_{b,\ldots,k^*-b+n,i^{**}} - PV^{x^{**}}_{b,\ldots,n^{**},i^{**}} = (12c)$$

$$PV^{x^{**}}_{b,\ldots,n^{**},i^{**}} - PV^x_{b,b,b+1,n,i} = (12b)$$

$$(2)$$

$$(3) - (2) = (12a) + (12b) + (12c) + (12d) =$$
$$= (5) \text{ one period earlier}$$

N.B.: $b, \ldots$ is for $b, k^*, b+1$ (PV at b, estimates as at k^*, figures from period $b+1$ on).

If all k^* in the schedule above would be replaced by k, the result would be a subdivision of $(4) - (2) = (5)$. That could lead to another part of section 5 of the capital-income statement. Then the period b to k inclusive would be catched in one analysis.

C. The columns (12e) and (13e)

$$PV^x_{k,k,k+1,n,i} - PV^x_{k^*,k^*,k,n,i} = (13e)$$

$$(10) \qquad PV^x_{k^*,k^*,k,n,i} - PV^x_{b,b,b+1,n,i} = (12e)$$

$$(2)$$

$$(10) - (2) = (12e) + (13e)$$

VII. THE ANNUAL STATEMENT NEEDS A THEORY

Palle Hansen

The annual statement and its information value is in the limelight at present.

The unrest apparently originates from the interest groups encompassing the company and appears to increase concurrently with the growing awareness and power of such groups.

Thus present and potential shareholders as well as lenders are doubtful of whether they can rely on the information when inflation is prevalent. But evidently they are even more worried about the information value of the statements when a company is in trouble.

In case after case where a company has gone bankrupt, readers have found that the annual statements previous to the collapse did not adequately reflect the progress of the crisis.

And in observing the 'new' interest groups – the employees and the public at large – one finds that they are not satisfied either. They press for information more in keeping with their information requirements. Mainly, they are looking for a figure of value added and how it is divided between the interest groups (so-called 'social accounting').

All things considered, it seems to me that we are on our way to an information crisis in the Western countries between the producers of annual statements (the corporations and their auditors) on the one hand and the information users (shareholders, employees, lenders, financial analysts and the public) on the other.

As in other situations where a crisis is impending, it pays to get to the root of the matter and to avoid 'patching up the outworks'.

In other words, to analyze and discuss the very theory of information on which the traditional annual statement is based.

1. What does the annual statement aim at?

Let us for a moment consider the question: What does a reader presumably experience when reading a traditional annual statement, certified by the auditor, stating that 'the statement presents a fair picture of the company's financial position'?

I think it is fairly realistic to assert that most readers (and very likely most producers too) are of the opinion that the annual statement provides them with the following main information:

1. The *income statement* presents a *realized profit*, although not correctly computed; in any case, a conservatively computed profit, the disposal of which will not detract from the company's financial position (so far interpreted as the accounting value of the owners' equity).

2. The *balance sheet* presents, although not correctly, in any case the conservatively estimated value of the company's possessions (wealth, assets) together with a fairly correctly computed statement of the company's obligations (liabilities) at balance-sheet date. The residual will, for this reason, be taken as a conservatively estimated net value of the owners' equity. In other words, the reader interprets the balance sheet as a statement – conservatively estimated – of the company's financial position as a *going concern*. Reading the balance sheet, he does not expect – at the one extreme – to find a statement of the company's *disposal value*, nor – at the other extreme – to find a statement of the *liquidation value*, but something in between.

Apparently an evaluation, though not guaranteeing the continuing existence of the company, at least claiming that owing to the 'generally accepted accounting principles' applied, the figure given for the owners' equity (whatever it amounts to) stands for an economic value, a kind of a conservatively estimated 'buffer'.

But is this really the information the reader receives from the income statement and the balance sheet? Is the *concept of profit* in the income statement really a statement of a conservatively computed, realized increase in capital value, the amount of which, after deduction of taxes, the owners can dispose of and the readers evaluate management performance with?

And what about the *concept of owners' equity (net capital value)*?

Is it realistic to take this concept as expressing a conservatively calculated value which, compared with the amount originally paid in by the owners for instance, indicates that this payment is still intact, or has increased or decreased in value?

If such questions are formulated, most members of the accounting profession as well as academics will undoubtedly answer: 'No, the accounting concepts of profit and net capital value are not identical with these descriptions, even when the accompanying notes and comments in the annual report are considered'.

But if this is the case, what then does the annual statement reflect? Is the annual statement as a whole in fact based on a realistic theory of information?

2. The annual statement lacks a theory of information

For analyzing and discussing more closely the accounting concepts of profit and net capital value, the examination of a practical case might disclose some important facts.

The concern in question was a joint-stock Danish wholesale company, founded on January 1, 1941, with a paid-in share capital of 44,000.[1]

At January 1, 1952, the company went into liquidation. The realization value paid out to the shareholders amounted to 72,000.

Table 1 shows in a concentrated form and with rounded-off figures, the economic development during the company's lifetime as reflected in the annual statements computed in accordance with generally accepted accounting principles.

The survey shows the development of the accounting net capital value (owners' equity) (line 3) and furthermore the periodic accounting profit (line 6) in accordance with the formula $(W + Eu \div Ep)$, i.e. as the sum of withdrawals (dividends) during the period and the change in net capital value.

Line 7 shows the yield, i.e. profit expressed as a percentage of net capital value. It appears that particularly during the first accounting years there were exceedingly high and widely fluctuating percentages.

As a whole, you will notice that during the company's lifetime there was a relatively favourable capital development. The net capital value increased from 44,000 originally to 126,000 at January 1, 1952. It was this 'value' which was 'sold' for 72,000, the consequence being a liquidation loss of 54,000.

Let us now ask: Did this information give a realistic (or at least a conservative) estimate of the company's financial position during the 11 years from 1941 to 1952?

In this case, with a definite knowledge of shareholders' withdrawals during the 11 years, we can answer the question by comparing each year's profit according to the accounts with the actual, realized internal interest (the real profit or real return on investment). And we can also compare the net capital value at each year's end according to the accounts with the company's actual (real) net capital value.

1. Hansen, Palle, *The Accounting Concept of Profit*, 2nd edition, Nyt Nordisk Forlag and North Holland Publishing Company, Copenhagen-Amsterdam 1972, pp. 122 ff.

Table 1. Summary survey of profit and value of net capital according to the accounts.

	1/1 1941	1/1 1942 (1941)	1/1 1943 (1942)	1/1 1944 (1943)	1/1 1945 (1944)	1/1 1946 (1945)	1/1 1947 (1946)	1/1 1948 (1947)	1/1 1949 (1948)	1/1 1950 (1949)	1/1 1951 (1950)	1/1 1952 (1951)
1 Assets	114,000	133,000	123,000	150,000	169,000	166,000	176,000	184,000	171,000	255,000	337,000	334,000
2 Liabilities	70,000	84,000	51,000	59,000	59,000	46,000	49,000	55,000	42,000	120,000	201,000	208,000
3 Net capital (1–2)	44,000	49,000	72,000	91,000	110,000	120,000	127,000	129,000	129,000	135,000	136,000	126,000
4 Change in capital		5,000	23,000	19,000	19,000	10,000	7,000	2,000	0	6,000	1,000	−10,000
5 Withdrawals		11,000	5,000	17,000	18,000	13,000	27,000	27,000	19,000	21,000	19,000	0
6 Profit (4 + 5)		16,000	28,000	36,000	37,000	23,000	34,000	29,000	19,000	27,000	20,000	−10,000
7 Profit as percent of net capital		36%	57%	50%	40%	20%	28%	23%	15%	21%	15%	− 7%

The two computations of actual, real profit and real capital value are made with the discounting formula and are based on withdrawals during the 11 years, including the liquidation value of 72,000 at the end.

The computations indicate that the shareholders' input ($+/-$ retained profit) carried an actual interest (profit) of 33% per annum during the company's lifetime.

Table 2 shows the development of the actual (real) net capital value during the years, equal to equity at the start plus actual profit (33% on net capital at the start) less withdrawals.

There is no more precise way of objective computation of a going concern's annual profit and net capital value than applying the discounting formula to actual withdrawals. Similarly to an investment calculation.[2]

Figure 1 is a graphical representation illustrating net capital value development according to the two computations mentioned: the accounting method based on the rule of 'generally accepted accounting principles' and the purely theoretical computation based on complete knowledge of future withdrawals.

As pointed out earlier, the accounting method of evaluating net capital value obviously does not aim at indicating the company's disposal value at balance-sheet date, nor the liquidation value, but something in between.

The aim is apparently a conservative valuation of the company as a going concern achieved by complying with the limitation rule involved in the philosophy of 'generally accepted accounting principles'. This rule, of course, does not allow assets to be taken into account unless paid for (before or after procurement), and furthermore it does not permit writing-ups.

The idea has apparently grown from this rule among members of the accounting profession that the annual statement reflects, conservatively estimated, a *going-concern computation* of profit and net capital value.

So the question requiring an answer is: Is this interpretation of the accounting concept of profit and net capital value as conservatively computed outcomes of the company considered as a going concern, in fact, tenable?

By studying table 3 (deviations in capital value) and table 4 (deviations in profit), the reader will find the answer. The statement compare the figures according to table 1 (survey of the accounting results) and table 2 (computation of the actual going-concern results).

It is quite obvious that there is no correlation whatsoever between the figures, and furthermore – in this case – the profit figures and also the net capital values

2. In the computation in fig. 2, the influence of inflation on the buying power of the withdrawals has been ignored. This effect could be taken into account by adjusting the withdrawals in accordance with the rate of inflation prior to carrying out the discounting computation. For further examination of this aspect see: *The Accounting Concept of Profit*, op. cit., pp. 129 ff.

Table 2. Computation of actual real capital value and change in capital based on 33% interest (real going-concern profit).

Discounting factor at 33%	1/1 1941	1/1 1942	1/1 1943	1/1 1944	1/1 1945	1/1 1946	1/1 1947	1/1 1948	1/1 1949	1/1 1950	1/1 1951	1/1 1952
0.75	8,250	3,750	12,750	13,500	9,750	20,250	20,250	14,250	15,750	14,250	54,000	72,000
0.57	2,850	9,690	10,260	7,410	15,390	15,390	10,830	11,970	10,830	41,040		
0.43	7,310	7,740	5,590	11,610	11,610	8,170	9,030	8,170	30,960			
0.33	5,940	4,290	8,910	8,910	6,270	6,930	6,270	23,760				
0.24	3,120	6,480	6,480	4,560	5,040	4,560	17,280					
0.18	4,860	4,860	3,420	3,780	3,420	12,960						
0.14	3,780	2,660	2,940	2,660	10,080							
0.11	2,090	2,310	2,090	7,920								
0.08	1,680	1,520	5,760									
0.06	1,140	4,320										
0.04	2,880											
Capital value	44,000	47,000	58,000	60,000	62,000	69,000	64,000	58,000	58,000	56,000	55,000	72,000
33% withdrawal	14,000	16,000	19,000	20,000	20,000	22,000	21,000	19,000	19,000	18,000	17,000	
	11,000	5,000	17,000	18,000	13,000	27,000	27,000	19,000	21,000	19,000	0	72,000
Change in capital	+3,000	+11,000	+2,000	+2,000	+7,000	−5,000	−6,000	0	−2,000	−1,000	+17,000	0

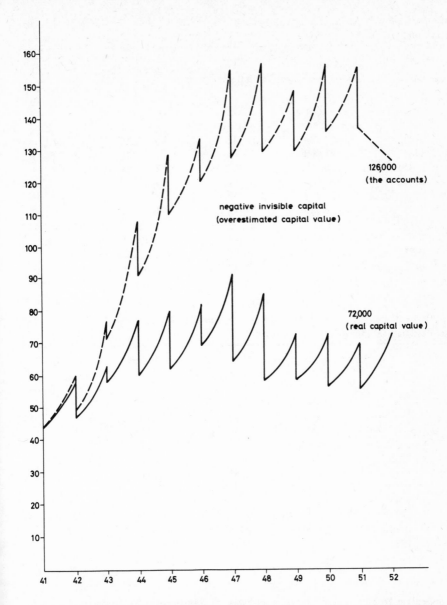

Fig. 1. Survey of capital development of the firm according to the accounts (-----) and according to actual capital development (33% interest) (——).

Table 3. 'Gap' between capital values according to the accounts and real capital value (33% R.O.I.).

	Accounting capital value	Real capital value	Overestimated	
			Amount	Per cent
1941	44,000	44,000		
1942	49,000	47,000	+ 2,000	4%
1943	72,000	58,000	+ 14,000	24%
1944	91,000	60,000	+ 31,000	50%
1945	110,000	62,000	+ 48,000	80%
1946	120,000	69,000	+ 51,000	73%
1947	127,000	64,000	+ 63,000	100%
1948	129,000	58,000	+ 71,000	122%
1949	129,000	58,000	+ 71,000	122%
1950	135,000	56,000	+ 79,000	141%
1951	136,000	55,000	+ 81,000	148%
1952	126,000	72,000	+ 54,000	77%

Table 4. 'Profit gap' between accounting statements of income and real profit (33% realized capital interest).

	Accounting profit	Real profit	Over/under-estimated	Percentage variance
1941	16,000	14,000	+ 2,000	+ 14%
1942	28,000	16,000	+ 12,000	+ 75%
1943	36,000	19,000	+ 17,000	+ 90%
1944	37,000	20,000	+ 17,000	+ 85%
1945	23,000	20,000	+ 3,000	+ 15%
1946	34,000	22,000	+ 12,000	+ 55%
1947	29,000	21,000	+ 8,000	+ 38%
1948	19,000	19,000	0	—
1949	27,000	19,000	+ 8,000	+ 42%
1950	20,000	18,000	+ 2,000	+ 11%
1951	− 10,000	17,000	− 27,000	− 160%
	259,000	205,000	+ 54,000	—

according to the accounts are markedly overestimated as compared with the actual figures.

They are not in any way conservatively computed. During the company's lifetime the balance sheets have in fact been characterized by including *negative* hidden reserves and certainly not by positive hidden reserves, as normally supposed, in adopting 'generally accepted accounting principles'.

The conclusion: One cannot attach any meaningful definition to the two basic accounting concepts of profit and net capital value.

3. Two major conclusions

Based upon the above analysis, two major conclusions can be drawn:
1. The accounting profession cannot – in the long run – continue operating with basic concepts of profit and net value so indefinable.
2. There is no likelihood of improving this situation by making the balance sheet contents more future-oriented.

This idea of making the balance sheet more future-oriented implies taking into consideration the effect of future impacts on the company's financial position when the annual statement is prepared.

It means that the accounting profession must abandon the traditional basic rule of 'generally accepted accounting principles' so that assets (positive or negative) not paid for could be accounted for in the balance sheet.

It is of course conceivable that the accounting profession and the legislature could be persuaded to make this radical change, though I have serious doubts about this.

But abandonment of this basic principle itself will not lead to more explicit conformity between the contents of the two main accounting concepts and the going-concern concepts of profit and net capital value.

Making allowance for the future confronts the accountant with the estimation of a multitude of coming events and circumstances outside and inside the company, the positive or negative effects of which are practically impossible to anticipate and point out and for this reason impossible to assess and embody in an annual statement.

Examples are: management creativity during present and future circumstances, competitors' future initiatives, future government encroachments, etc., etc.

For these reasons, therefore, we must reject present ideas such as: 'Human resources accounting', evaluation and depreciation on 'replacement value', the various suggestions for 'inflation accounting', the ideas of more specific 'accounting standards' etc. To the best of my knowledge, these recommendations will only make matters worse if the proposers think they will produce more realistic and informative annual statements.

4. A reliable theory of information

From the foregoing observations we must conclude that the traditional annual statement is useless in qualitative and quantitative content if the reader expects a realistic or in any event a conservative computation of profit and net capital value.

For this reason, it is suggested that the accounting profession seriously considers abandoning the traditional model of the annual statement and substituting an information theory more in keeping with reality.

Such a theory could be based on the same idea as that for *investment control*.

The fact is that every company is encompassed by several, so-called interest groups (as regards the annual statement: mainly the owners, the potential owners, the employees, the lenders and the public at large).

Fundamentally, these groups have the common feature that they consider the company as an investment project into which they put capital, work or service and from which they expect a satisfactory return. The *owners* contribute capital, expecting dividends and capital growth. The *employees* contribute their skill and work, in return for which they are paid salaries or wages but for which they also expect a return in the form of healthy progress of the company's profitability, ensuring security of employment, favourable working conditions and wage increases. In the long run perhaps even joint ownership.

The *lenders* advance capital against payment of interest. Risking their capital, the lenders are interested in checking up on the company's profitability and financial position.

And *society* (the public), so to speak, provides the company with the right to conduct business and with various public resources in return for which it expects taxes, and conduct in accordance with prevailing rules.

Thus, like investors, although associated differently with the company, all the interest groups have a common interest in verifying the company's ability to produce a satisfactory return.

Consequently, the information they need is basically similar to that which a company's management will require when verifying the economic effects of an investment in, say, a new plant, new machinery or a new subsidiary.

In calculating (using the discounting method), the data needed for estimating the return on investment (internal interest) are the *ex-ante* returns (expected revenues less expected expenditures).

During the verification phase, the company will periodically compute the ex-post returns (realized revenues less realized expenditures) and compare actual figures with the estimates.

To follow the discussion it is important to stress that depreciation figures will not be included in these computations (neither in the ex-ante calculation, nor in the ex-post computations). And furthermore, for verification purposes the management has no need of estimates – at certain intervals – of the economic value (real or conservatively estimated) of the investment, leading to the initial expenditure being written up or written down.

What is of interest, on the other hand, is periodical adjustment of the expected returns on the basis of which the decision to invest was made, owing to changing circumstances (budget revision of revenues and expenditures). But this will not require any adjustment of the value of the initial investment.

In my opinion, the same point of view applies in discussing a realistic model of the annual statement. The model suggested below is based on this investment control idea, informing the reader of the realized return excluding depreciation and for this reason excluding any adjustments of values in the balance sheet.

In other words, the concept of profit is similar to Irving Fisher's *realized income* (yield) and is not in line with the traditional accounting concept of profit, which Fisher described as *earned income* (or earnings), which includes the increase in net capital value (positive or negative).[3]

Thus, the model of an annual statement is based on two main statements:
1. The statement of income administration
2. The statement of capital administration.

5. The statement of income administration

As shown in table 5, the income administrative statement is divided into two statements, viz. *the realized income statement* and *the income distribution statement*.

The main items in the realized income statement have the following conceptual content:

Item A_1 *Revenues*. Signifies realized (invoiced) sales income in the period.

Item A_2 *Unit costs*. The unit costs matching the realized sales income.

Item A_3 *Contribution margin*. Signifies realized contribution margin.

Item A_4 *Capacity costs*. With the important exception that this item does not include depreciation of fixed assets, the conceptual content will be similar to the traditional concept of so-called 'fixed costs'. It means that the item includes (1) cost of capacity utilized for the purpose of incorporating the contribution margin (in other words matching the realized contribution, item A_3). But

3. *The Accounting Concept of Profit*, op. cit., p. 16.

Table 5. Statement of income administration.

A	*REALIZED INCOME*	
	1	REVENUES
	2	– UNIT COSTS
	3	CONTRIBUTION MARGIN (1–2)
	4	– CAPACITY COSTS
	5	REALIZED INCOME (3–4)
B	*INCOME DISTRIBUTION*	
	1	REFINANCING FIXED ASSETS
	2	TAXES
	3	DIVIDENDS
	4	SURPLUS
	5	TOTAL (= A5)

capacity costs also includes (2) the required capacity utilized during the period for the purpose of producing contribution margins in future periods (different types of development costs). The latter, in other words, does not match the realized contribution margin, but aims at 'maintaining' the continuing intake of future contribution margin.

In order to comply strictly with the 'investment control theory' stated herein, interest on loans ought not to be included among capacity costs – as is the case in the traditional income statement – but be included with the items in statement B: income distribution (see below).

Item A_5 *Realized income.* This concept is undoubtedly the most realistic (and operational) income concept that can be produced on the basis of available accounting data in a going concern.

Based on the *realized contribution margin*, the concept of income is clear of the influence of applying 'conservative' principles of inventory evaluation. Inventory evaluation according to this model will be based on evaluation at *unit cost*.

The item of capacity costs also includes the *realized expenditure*, which means that the item realized income is a fairly good (realistic) statement of the return on assets for the period.

As already stated, realized income is not affected by depreciation of fixed assets. In a traditional annual statement, this depreciation is an extremely dubious way of expressing wear and tear, but here, in this model, it is completely irrelevant.

6. The statement of income distribution

Following the present viewpoint, one might say that the statement of income distribution informs the reader to what extent the claims (expectations) of the interest groups have been fulfilled.

It holds good for the *owners* (dividends, item B_3 and retained surplus item B_4) and for the *employees* (the fact that the company has maintained and probably strengthened its financial position through the reservations for refinancing fixed assets (item B_1, (see below) and item B_4). Further, it holds good for the interest partner: *society* (item B_2 taxes). And, finally, if interest on loans is included in the statement of income distribution, this information along with the information of the amounts retained for refinancing and for surplus purposes presents the *lenders* with relevant information.

Item B_1 *Refinancing of fixed assets*. The aim of this reservation is to retain out of income funds for refinancing fixed assets at the time of replacement.

We are referring to *refinancing* not depreciation, to underline the important fact that the aim of this reservation is *not* to reflect a periodic decline in the value of fixed assets but to retain from the returns, during the period the fixed assets are operating, a total amount sufficient, at the time of replacement:

1. to balance those liabilities which have (partly) financed the now replaced fixed assets.

2. to finance, at *replacement cost*, that part of the investment financed from the company's own resources.

Owing to the fact that a company normally aims at continuous operation, i.e. as a going concern, this setting aside for refinancing fixed assets can be said to be *future directed*, whereas traditional depreciation is *turned towards the past* (aiming at distributing historic costs over the periods the assets are utilized).

In certain cases it is conceivable that the amount of depreciation calculated in accordance with generally accepted accounting principles will coincide with the amount it is necessary to retain for refinancing purpose. But the two estimates will most probably turn out differently because inflation and technological development will lead to higher replacement costs.

According to the idea on which traditional 'depreciation-as-cost' is based, there is no room for taking replacement value into account when estimating the depreciation figure.

Hence the depreciation based on replacement cost so widely recommended at present is, strictly speaking, completely at variance with the basic philosophy inherent in the traditional annual statement (quite apart from the difficulty of producing the necessary data for estimating replacement costs of fixed assets *still* in operation at balance-sheet date).

But this idea of retentions for future replacement financing fits clearly into the model now presented.

In principle, this reservation for refinancing applies to a replacement whose performance (capacity) is of the same dimension as the existing asset.

If the company finds it necessary, and possible, to set aside – for (partly) financing a fixed asset with a larger capacity at the time of replacement – the excess amount has to be reserved via item B_4 (surplus).

The remainder of the items included in the statement of income distribution do not give rise to any particular comments for the purposes of the present discussion. After reservation for income tax (in accordance with current law) the remainder of the realized income may be set aside for the purpose of dividends, bonuses and as surplus, taking into consideration prevailing laws and future conditions.

7. The statement of capital administration

With regard to ways of presenting this statement, different models may be mentioned. The two main concepts in the statement, however, will be:
1. Investment (capital applied)
2. Financed with (capital procured).

It is important to emphasize that the conceptual content of the statement is totally different from that of the traditional balance sheet.

As mentioned above, the *assets side* of the traditional balance sheet claims to present an (indefinable) evaluation of the company's possessions (wealth) and claims on the *liabilities side* to show the owners' part of that wealth and the debts.

As demonstrated, it is ipso facto impossible to put anything meaningful regarding evaluation of the company as a going concern into the figures of the traditional balance sheet.

The statement of capital administration does not aim at this unattainable objective. The purpose of the statement is, on the contrary, to provide realistic information on the sum of nominal capital administered by management at the balance-sheet date, from which sources the capital is derived and in which items the capital is invested.

Table 6 presents the main items in the statement.

Table 6. Statement of capital administration

Capital administration ('Balance sheet')	
Investments (capital employed)	Financed by (capital procured)
Contribution margin derived	Current liabilities (non-interest claiming)
	Loan (interest-claiming)
Capacity derived	Retained for refinancing
	Owners' equity (share capital surplus)

In the investment part of the statement the reader will find the various items divided into two main groups:
1. Contribution-derived investment
2. Capacity-derived investment.

This grouping is not exactly the same as the traditional grouping into current and fixed assets and certainly not as regards the principles of valuation. For instance, in the capital administration statement you will find liquid assets included in capacity-derived assets.

But, as stated, the important thing is that the statement does not claim to show any valuation of the investments.

The items of plant and machinery, for example, are entered at *initial cost* during the investment's lifetime; inventories at *unit cost* and accounts receivable either (as is the case in the traditional balance sheet) at *invoiced price* or – more in accordance with the 'pure' theory of the capital administrative statement – at *product unit cost*.

In the *financed by* part of the statement, the reader will find, besides the usual groups of current liabilities and loans, the item: 'Retained for refinancing'. This item includes the accumulated amount of income retained for financing future replacement of the present operating fixed assets including retained for repaying the liability-financed part of the investments.

At the time of replacement, the initial cost of the replaced assets will be set off against the reservation for refinancing.

Additional reservation owing to the anticipation of higher replacement cost is credited to the owners' equity (surplus).

8. The auditors' certificate

In certifying the income administrative statement and the statement of capital administration, the auditor is no longer in need of such vague and 'morally' determined phrases as: 'In conformity with generally accepted accounting principles' or 'the financial statement presents fairly the financial position of the enterprise' now so commonly used.

Based, as the items are in the *realized income statement*, on actual, realized activities, the auditor will have no real problems in certifying that the statement includes revenues realized and costs (expenditure) spent. And that the residue – realized income – is similar to the realized return, distributed as indicated in the income distribution statement, including reservation for refinancing future replacements of fixed assets.

Of course, estimating future replacement costs is no easy task and can give rise to disagreement between the auditor and the board. But as I see it, the problems involved are not really more complicated than those involved in accounting for the item depreciation of fixed assets in the traditional annual statement.

And certifying the *capital administrative statement* does not require the auditor to be answerable for a 'conservative' valuation of the assets and the owners' equity. His certificate merely states that, at the date of the statement, a certain amount of capital is administered, how it is invested and from which sources it is derived.

Considered realistically, this is what an income statement and a balance sheet statement of capital administration can account for and consequently what an auditor is able to certify.

VIII. ACCOUNTING FOR THE COST OF INTEREST

Robert N. Anthony

1. Accounting should adopt the concept of interest used in economics

In economics, the word *interest* refers to the cost of using capital. The definition of interest in financial accounting differs from its economics definition in two fundamental respects. First, in financial accounting, interest refers only to the charge for using *debt* capital; accountants do not record a charge for the use of *equity* capital. Second, in financial accounting, interest is not ordinarily treated as an element of cost in the sense that labour and material are so treated; rather, interest on debt capital is regarded as an expense that is deducted in full from the revenues of the period in which the interest is incurred.

My proposal is that accounting should adopt the concept of interest used in economics. Specifically, it is proposed that interest on the use of both debt and equity capital should be accounted for as an item of cost – the cost of using capital – and that it should be recorded in the same way as other items of cost are recorded.

This proposal is not new. In the early decades of the twentieth century a similar proposal was vigorously advocated and hotly debated. The debate subsided in the late 1920s, and although a few accounting theoreticians have discussed the possibility in more recent years, the business community has given practically no thought to the possibility of changing generally accepted accounting principles so as to incorporate such a proposal.

Although interest on total capital is not recorded as a cost in financial accounting – that is, in the accounting that governs the preparation of financial statements prepared for the use of investors and other external parties – the concept that the use of capital does have a cost and that this cost should be explicitly recognized is well accepted in the internal accounting that serves as an aid to management.

For example, in analyzing a proposed capital acquisition, a relatively new but widely accepted approach is to include among the relevant costs not only the cost of the asset itself, but also the cost of the capital used to acquire the asset. In arriving at selling prices, many companies take into account the cost of the capital employed in making the product. In measuring the profitability of a division or other profit centre, many companies used the residual income method, in which a capital charge is subtracted from profits computed in the conventional manner. The capital charge corresponds to interest as the term is used here.

2. Implications of the proposal

Recording interest as a cost would have a greater impact on the numbers reported in balance sheets and income statements than any change since the introduction of depreciation accounting. It also has implications for the use of accounting information in public policy discussions and in taxation, rate regulation, contract pricing, and other government activities. It will increase the harmonization of management accounting information with financial accounting information. Its implication in each of these areas is described briefly below.

Implications for financial accounting

If the economic facts of interest were recorded in the accounts, readers of financial statements would have a clearer understanding of the status and performance of a business.

Except in public utilities, a building constructed by a company's own personnel appears on the books at a lower cost than an identical building constructed by an outside contractor, because no interest cost is counted for a self-constructed building. There is no logical reason for omitting interest costs for self-constructed buildings and including them for purchased buildings, nor for treating buildings built for public utilities differently than buildings built for other companies.

The longer an item remains in inventory, the greater is its real cost to the company. The amount of this additional cost is immaterial in companies where inventory turns over frequently, but it is of considerable importance in companies that hold inventories for ·significantly long periods of time. Accounting does not recognize this cost, and accounting therefore understates the cost of inventories held for long periods of time.

The return that a company earns on its equity capital consists of two elements: interest and profit. In current practice, these elements are combined in the single number labelled 'net income.' Although all the production and marketing activities of a company contribute to the generation of income, accounting recognizes the return only as of the time when the product is sold. In effect, therefore, accounting reports that all the return on capital is earned by the marketing organization, and none of it by the production organization. If interest were recorded as a cost that is incurred throughout the operating cycle, the offsetting credit would show that a return on capital was correspondingly being earned throughout the cycle.

If the interest component of return on capital were accounted for separately, the amount reported on the 'bottom line' of the income statement would be smaller than it now is. Net income, on the proposed basis, would show how much a company earned over and above a minimum charge for the cost of the capital that it used. The amount would be a good measure of performance, for a company has not performed satisfactorily if it has not generated enough revenue to cover all its costs, including the cost of using capital. This net income amount would not be affected substantially by the relative amount of debt and equity in a company's capital structure; the debt/equity ratio has a great influence on the net income amount in current practice.

Additions to shareholders' equity during a period would come from two sources, the charge for equity interest and net income. The sum of these two amounts would differ somewhat from the present credit that corresponds to net income because of timing differences arising from the interest cost that is embedded in assets, but over a period of years the total of shareholders' equity would not be materially affected by the proposal.

Public policy implications

Many government agencies use accounting information they obtain from business firms. Including interest as an element of cost would facilitate the work of these agencies. The process of rate setting by regulatory agencies would be simpler and more straightforward. Price controls could be designed on the principle that prices should provide a fair return on capital employed. The Department of Defense and other government agencies, which now arrive at the price on cost-type contracts by using a profit margin that is essentially a percentage of estimated cost, could shift to the much more equitable basis that takes into account the amount of capital employed.

Although the proposal *per se* does not contemplate a change in the basis of calculating income for tax purposes, there are advantages in adopting a similar principle for income tax calculations. The fact that interest expense on debt is tax deductible, while no deduction is allowed for the corresponding cost of using equity capital, has some undesirable social consequences. These would be removed if a minimum interest cost on equity capital were allowed as a business expense.

It is difficult to convince people that a business must earn enough to cover the cost of its capital if it is to survive. This message would come through to the public more clearly if the cost of using capital were labelled for what it is – a real cost. Although a few people may claim that any amount of profit above the minimum cost of capital is unwarranted, the general public would undoubtedly regard the net income amount as a reward for good performance, which is essential in our economic system. In any event, the calculations that now 'prove' that profits are a large fraction of the sales dollar, or of the GNP, could no longer be made. As a related point, the consumer wonders why profit margins, expressed as a percentage of sales, vary so widely among companies of various types. Since one important reason for these differences is the difference in the amount of capital employed, the facts would be clearer if interest were counted as an element of cost.

3. Harmonizing financial accounting and management accounting

Although no law or principle requires that the internal accounting information used in managing a business be consistent with the financial accounting reports prepared for outside parties, such consistency has at least two advantages. First, it reduces the need for two sets of books. Second, there is a widespread belief that financial accounting numbers are 'real' numbers and that numbers constructed according to something other than financial accounting principles are 'soft' or even 'phony.' Many people, probably the majority, do not believe that equity interest is a real cost, despite what the economic books say and despite the fact that, when they stop to think about it, they know full well that equity capital cannot be obtained without cost. If financial accounting recognized equity interest as a real cost, this misconception would be overcome. Consequently, there would be an increasing acceptance within a business of measurements of profit-centre performance that incorporate a charge for capital employed and of the importance of recognizing interest costs in calculations of economic order quantity, in determining appropriate inventory levels, in optimizing working capital amounts, in pricing, and in other business decisions.

Conceptual foundations

Economists refer to the 'factors of production', usually listed as labour, natural resources, and capital. Each of these factors has a cost. The cost of using labour represents the amount necessary to induce employees to supply their personal services. The cost of using capital represents the amount necessary to induce investors to supply capital to the business. A company obtains capital from two sources: from lenders and from shareholders. Capital received from lenders is called debt capital or borrowed capital and capital received from shareholders is called equity capital. In economics, interest is the cost of using *both* debt capital and equity capital.

Profit is the difference between revenue and the sum of all costs; that is, no profit is earned until all costs, including interest, are covered. Economists differ about where to draw the line between interest and profits. Some maintain that interest cost should take into account the risks and uncertainties associated with a given investment, while others believe that risks and uncertainties are more properly considered as one of the factors that explain the amount of earned profit. This difference of opinion complicates the problem of measuring the cost of interest, but nevertheless, a satisfactory and practical solution to this problem does exist.

Financial accounting concepts

Financial accounting is supposed to measure and report the economic realities of a business: the assets controlled by a business, the sources of the capital used to acquire these assets, and the flow of resources into and out of the business. Accounting measurements cannot be completely consistent with the principles of economics, primarily because certain of these principles conflict with the fundamental requirement that accounting measurements be reasonably objective. Economics states, for example, that the value of a business is the present value of the stream of future earnings that the business will generate, but an estimate of this amount is so highly subjective that accountants do not attempt to record it for financial accounting purposes. Nevertheless, financial accounting should not be at variance with economics unless there is a compelling reason.

Financial accounting does not recognize the interest cost of equity capital at all, and in measuring the cost of manufactured products, financial accounting does not include the interest cost of either debt capital or of equity capital. Accountants give very little thought, however, to this difference between financial accounting and economics. They state flatly that their practices are 'in accordance with generally accepted accounting principles', and that the recording of interest (except for the interest on debt capital) is *not*. This conclusion is unwarranted. Two basic financial accounting concepts do support the recording of interest as a cost. They are the entity concept and the cost concept.

The entity concept

In the nineteenth century, accounting was governed by what is called the *proprietary concept*. Most businesses were managed by their proprietors; there were few public corporations, that is, companies whose equity capital was furnished by outside investors. Under the proprietary concept, assets are considered to be owned by the proprietors, and liabilities are considered the liabilities of the proprietors. This was legally the situation in unincorporated businesses, and it was considered the *de facto* situation in corporations owned by one person or one family. With such a concept, it was pointless to record as a separate number the cost of using equity capital. Rather, the important problem was to separate the interest of creditors, who were the only truly outside parties, from those of the proprietors. Profit was whatever remained after the claims of outsiders had been satisfied. Thus, it was important to measure the interest cost of debt capital, but not the interest cost of equity capital.

With the development of publicly owned corporations and, more recently, the development of the idea of corporate social responsibility, the basic thrust of accounting shifted from the proprietary concept to the entity concept. Under the entity concept, the corporation is viewed as an entity separated from its proprietors. The entity obtains its capital from two principal sources: it obtains debt capital from creditors and equity capital from shareholders. Management decides on the best mix between debt capital and equity capital. Equity capital, therefore, becomes just another source of funds. Both creditors and equity investors are viewed as outsiders. The decision on whether to raise additional capital from creditors or from shareholders (either from the sale of shares or by retaining earnings) turns essentially on the balance between the risk and cost characteristics of these two sources of capital.

Under these circumstances, it would seem appropriate to measure the cost of using equity capital, which is supplied by outside shareholders, just as it is appropriate to measure the cost of using debt capital, which is also furnished by outside parties. From the standpoint of the entity, each type of capital is a resource furnished by an outside party. This, however, is not now done in accounting.

The entity concept conceivably could be used to assert that neither debt interest nor equity interest should be recorded as a cost in accounting. In such an accounting system, income would be the total amount available to both creditors and equity investors, and debt interest and dividends on common stock would be viewed as a distribution of income to creditors and shareholders, respectively. Those who support such an approach argue that information on business operations should be reported separately from information on how those operations are financed. Whatever the merits of this theory in relation to the *entity* concept, it clearly is inconsistent with the *cost* concept. Implementation of such a theory would move accounting even further away from economics than it now is.

The cost concept

Financial accounting records costs. Assets are ordinarily recorded at their cost, and income is the difference between revenues and expenses, which are the costs associated with those revenues. Thus, interest should be recorded in the accounts if – but only if – interest is truly a cost.

Accounting terminology Bulletin No. 4 contains a widely used definition of cost: 'Cost is the amount, measured in money, of cash expended or other property transferred, capital stock issued, services performed or a liability incurred, in consideration of goods or services received or to be received.' This definition is satisfactory as far as it goes, but it does not make entirely clear that cost always refers to the cost of *something;* this 'something' is technically called a *cost objective.* For example, the cost of a building is the total amount of the resources used to acquire the building. This amount is represented by cash if the building is purchased, or by the sum of labour, material, and other resources if the building is constructed by the company itself. Similarly, the cost of a product is measured by the amount of cash expended or liability incurred if the product is purchased, and it is measured by the sum of labour, material, and other resources if the product is manufactured by the company.

Thus, cost measures the amount of resources used for a cost objective. In manufacturing a product, a company uses labour, measured by labour costs; it uses material, measured by material costs; and it uses services, measured by utility costs, rentals, and similar items. The appropriate amount of cost for each resource is not always easy to measure. The cost of personal services, for example, includes not only wages and salaries earned by employees, but the associated fringe benefits as well. One of these fringe benefits may be the right to a future pension, and it is difficult to estimate the current cost of providing for pensions that will be paid some years hence. Despite the difficulties, such estimates are made, and accounting principles set forth fairly detailed guidelines for making them.

A business also uses capital; that is, it obtains funds that it uses to acquire assets. It obtains this capital from two principal sources: lenders and shareholders. Lenders will not furnish debt capital to a company unless they expect to receive a reward for doing so. This reward, called interest, is the cost of the use of debt capital. The equity capital obtained from shareholders also has a cost. Investors will not furnish equity capital to a company unless they expect to receive a reward for doing so, and this reward is the cost of the use of equity capital. To the business entity, this cost is as real as the cost of the use of debt capital.

The amount of the expected reward for the use of equity capital is less clearly identifiable than that for the use of debt capital. Those who provide debt capital expect an amount that is labelled interest. Those who provide equity capital expect a reward that is the sum of two amounts: 1. dividends and 2. an appreciation in the market value of their shares. They do not expect that dividends alone will be an adequate reward; rather, they anticipate that some of the earnings that result from their investment will be retained by the corporation and that the profits generated by these retained earnings, as well as other factors, will cause an appreciation in market value. The fact that the reward expected by an equity investor takes these two separate forms does not alter the conclusion that equity capital does have a cost and that this cost is related to the reward that equity investors expect when they furnish their capital to the business.

Unfortunately, accounting has no generally agreed on term for the cost of using equity capital. This is part of the problem. *Dividends* is not the correct term because, as noted above, shareholders in most companies expect that their total return will be greater than the current dividend yield, and that they will receive this portion of the return in the form of a higher market value when they sell their shares. The fact that the average dividend yield is only about 3 per cent, as compared with rates for debt interest of 9 per cent or more, proves this fairly obvious point. The amount of current dividends is therefore an understatement of the cost of equity capital.

Profit and *net income* are also incorrect terms for the cost of using equity capital. Net income measures a company's performance; it is not itself a cost, but rather represents the difference between expired cost (i.e. expense) and revenue. In the present financial accounting structure, net income *includes* the cost of using equity capital, but it is not equated to that cost. Net income also includes the rewards for superior management, a superior product, a superior market position, and so on.

Although no specific term in accounting covers the cost of using equity capital, there is no need to invent one. Accountants can follow economists and use *interest* as the term for the cost of using either type of capital – debt capital or equity capital. This would emphasize the similarity of the *use* of both types of capital. Once capital has been acquired, a dollar of equity capital is the same as a dollar of debt capital. A business does not use debt capital to pay some of its bills and equity capital to pay the remainder. It pays its bills with cash; and each dollar of cash is like every other dollar.

When it is desirable to specify the source as being equity capital, we can use the phrase 'equity interest', just as we now use 'bond interest', 'debt interest', 'note interest', and similar terms.

Imputed costs

Although few would assert that equity interest is not a cost, some argue that it is an imputed cost and that accounting does not record imputed costs. This is a slippery point, because there is no precise meaning in accounting for the term imputed. Kohler defines it as 'a term often used to indicate the presence of arbitrary or subjective elements of product cost having more than usual significance; the worth of a factor of production joined with and inseparable from one or more other factors'.[1] This definition, however, fails to capture what is actually practised. Accountants do not record *some* 'arbitrary or subjective' elements of cost, but they do record others. They do not record 'opportunity costs', that is, the value of a resource as measured by its value in some alternative use; nor do they record those social costs that are not measured by actual company outlays, such as the cost to society of a company's pollution of the atmosphere or a river. These are imputed costs in the sense that no measurable transaction is associated with them.

On the other hand, accounting does record some types of cost for which no documented transaction exists. Under certain circumstances, a leased building or machine is recorded at its equivalent purchase cost although no record of this cost exists. If a company acquires a non-cash asset in exchange for a note that either does not stipulate an interest rate or stipulates a rate that is clearly unreasonable, APB *Opinion No. 21* requires that the true interest component be estimated. As already noted, labour cost includes an estimate of the present value of future pension benefits, and although this estimate is dignified with the word

1. Eric L. Kohler, *A Dictionary for Accountants*, 4th ed., Prentice-Hall, Englewood Cliffs, N.J., 1970.

'actuarial', neither the actuary nor anyone else knows what the correct amount is. Allowances for bad debts, for the future cost of warranty agreements, and for writedown of inventories to market are estimates, not based on documented transactions. In short, the argument that financial accounting deals only with 'transacted' costs is not supported by actual practice.

Imputed costs are not synonymous with non-cash costs. The depreciation expense in a given year is a non-cash cost. Although the cost of the depreciable asset itself is usually measured by a cash outlay, the amount of this cost assigned as a depreciation expense in a single year is an estimate, not substantiated by an arm's length, or any other kind of transaction. Fifty years ago, this was used as an argument against recording depreciation; today, everyone agrees that it is better to be 'approximately right than entirely wrong'. It is better to make an estimate of depreciation expense than to omit this cost on the grounds that the amount cannot be measured precisely. Similarly, most of the examples given in the preceding paragraph do not involve a determinable cash outlay as of the time the events occur. The amount of cash that eventually will be involved is an estimate. In the case of donated assets, even depreciation is not tied to a cash transaction.

In general, the argument that accounting does not record imputed costs is valid only if imputed costs are defined as those costs that accounting has decided not to record. This circular argument is not very useful.

A more accurate conclusion from the examples given above is that accounting records items of cost that can be measured or estimated in some reasonable way. Equity interest meets this criterion.

4. Measuring interest cost

Interest cost is determined by applying a rate to the amount of capital employed. The amount of capital employed is easily determined; it is the book value of the assets employed for a cost objective. (Book value, rather than market value or any other value, is relevant because of the cost concept which is basic to accounting.) The problem arises in attempting to find the rate. More specifically, the problem relates to equity interest, for it is well accepted that debt interest costs can be measured. As is the case with all accounting practices, the method must satisfy three criteria:

1. It must be reasonably objective. Its results must not be greatly influenced by subjective human judgment. The results must be verifiable. On the other hand, the method need not be absolutely objective; many accounting practices require estimates of what will happen in the future or have other subjective elements.

2. It must measure approximately what the interest cost actually is. It need not do this precisely because few accounting measurements are precise.
3. It must be feasible. It must not involve such elaborate computations or depend on such expensive data gathering that the cost of applying the method exceeds its value. It must use information that is available when the accounting entries are made.

Equity interest cost

The measurement of debt interest cost is reasonably straightforward. There is no precise way to measure the interest cost of equity capital, however. Although hundreds of books and articles have addressed the problem, no one has devised a practical solution, or at least no one has devised a solution that is accepted by a large number of knowledgeable people.

The nature of the problem is as follows: In an artificial world in which a company paid out all its earnings as dividends, and in which earnings per share were stable over time, the dividend yield would be the cost of equity capital. If investors were willing, for example, to pay $100 for the privilege of receiving $10 in dividends annually, the cost of equity capital would be 10 per cent. The real world, however, differs from this artificial world in two respects. First, most companies do not pay out all their earnings; instead, they retain a fraction of them (in some cases, all) with the expectation of putting these retained earnings to profitable use. Second, the stream of earnings is not stable; instead, it fluctuates from one year to the next for a number of reasons. Investors expect a higher return under conditions of relative uncertainty than under conditions of relative certainty, as demonstrated by the fact that interest rates on government bonds are lower than interest rates on more risky industrial bonds, taking into account tax and length of maturity differences. The market price of a stock is influenced by investors' appraisal of these facts, but there is no exact way to measure how much of the price of a share of stock reflects the cost of equity capital, and how much of it reflects the market's judgment about the value of retained earnings and the company's prospects for future earnings.

In the voluminous literature on measuring the cost of capital, many approaches are suggested. In the special case of regulated companies, there may be a determinate solution, because there is a causal connection between the prices that these companies are permitted to charge and the cost of capital. For unregulated companies, however, the equations usually contain a symbol, G which stands for the estimated future growth of the company's earnings, and there simply is no objective way of finding a number to use for G.

Despite these difficulties, businessmen do make judgments that involve, either explicitly or implicitly, a measurement of the cost of equity capital. Alternatively, they use a number that approximates the total interest cost for both debt and equity. Since the cost of debt interest is calculable, the cost of equity interest can be deduced if the total interest cost is known. The following questions need to be answered:

1. Should the equity interest rates vary depending on the risk characteristics of individual companies?
2. Should the Financial Accounting Standards Board set a rate directly, or should it prescribe a method that each company will use to arrive at its own rate?
3. How should the rate be derived?

An allowance for risk?

It is conceptually possible to regard equity interest cost either as 'normal' interest, that is, with the same rate applicable to all companies, or as a cost that reflects the risk characteristics of individual companies. The latter approach is much more difficult to make workable than the former.

There have been attempts to develop 'beta coefficients' that measure the risk of certain securities,[2] but these coefficients are not directly translatable into a risk component of interest rates, and they can be applied only to securities that are actively traded. Many individual companies estimate their own equity interest cost, for internal management purposes, and these estimates do reflect the company's risk characteristics. However, these estimates are quite subjective, and there is no general agreement about the proper approach for making them.

Further research would be worthwhile, but it does not seem likely, for the near future, that an operational technique can be developed to incorporate differences in risk characteristics into the equity interest rates. If no such technique can be found, the answer to the first question is clear: the equity interest rate should be a normal interest rate, one that reflects the cost of equity capital without an allowance for the risk characteristics of particular companies. Such a rate is similar to, but higher than, the prime lending rate for debt capital – that is, the rate at which banks will lend to their least risky industrial customers. It might by analogy be called the *prime equity rate*. The prime debt rate is approximately the

2. William Beaver, Paul Kettler, and Myron Scholes, 'The Association between Market Determined and Accounting Determined Risk Measures', *Accounting Review*, October 1970, pp. 654–82; and R. Hamada, 'Portfolio Analysis, Market Equilibrium, and Corporation Finance', *Journal of Finance*, March 1969.

same throughout the USA; at any moment of time, it does not vary by more than a small fraction of one per cent. Rates for other types of loans do differ from one another considerably at one moment of time, and the essential reason for these variations is that transactions have different risk characteristics.

If this approach to the determination of equity interest cost is adopted, the reward for risk will be included as part of net income, rather than as interest. In other words, each company has a specified cost for the equity capital it uses in a given year, and its net income reflects how well it has performed after covering that capital charge.

Prescribed rate or prescribed method?

If it is agreed that the measurement of risk is not feasible and that equity cost should be derived from a prime equity rate, then the question becomes whether the FASB should prescribe this rate directly or whether it should prescribe a principle that would guide a company in arriving at its own rate.

The first alternative has the advantage of simplicity. After appropriate analysis, along lines discussed in the next section, the FASB would state that, effective on a certain date, interest on equity capital shall be computed at a rate of x per cent. The rate would be changed in response to significant changes in interest rates in general. The difficult task of devising words that would clearly describe how each company should compute its own rate would be avoided. The conceptual justification for such an approach is that the rate intentionally excludes variations in risk characteristics among companies, and that these variations account for the differences in the cost of equity capital among companies. This being the case, it is appropriate that all companies use the same rate.

Such an approach, however, poses two problems. First, neither the FASB nor its predecessors have gone so far as to prescribe a number as the solution to any problem; the closest they have come to this is to prescribe limits, for example, for the maximum period over which goodwill should be amortized. With this precedent, the Board probably would be reluctant to prescribe a specific number. It might feel, with justification, that the business community would regard such a move as arbitrary. Second, it is not demonstrable that variations in equity interest rates are entirely associated with variations in a company's risk characteristics. This approach rests entirely on the plausibility of this assertion, since the reasoning is that the reward for risk can be treated as profit. Although the assertion *is* probably plausible, other forces may well be at work that can be identified and measured in a given company. More research on this point is desirable. If, for either of these reasons, the FASB decides that it should not prescribe a rate, then it must prescribe how companies should compute their own rate. Thus, this is one of the questions that, for the present, remains unanswered.

How should the rate be derived?

There are two possible approaches to the derivation of the equity interest rate; it can be related to some debt rate, or it can be derived independently.

Defliese suggests that the equity interest rate might be set equal to the debt interest rate, on the grounds that a company usually has the option either to borrow capital or to sell stock and that therefore the debt rate available at the time the equity investment is made is most appropriate.[3]

Arthur Andersen and Co. suggests that the cost of total capital to be allowed as a cost element on defense contracts might be calculated at a rate that is 150 per cent of the current New York prime rate 'to reflect prime borrowing rates plus allowances for compensating balances and prime rate premiums for the defense industry'.[4]

Linking the equity interest rate to the debt rate would permit the equity rate to fluctuate with movements of interest rates in general. If this approach is adopted, further study would be required to establish the most appropriate relationship between the equity interest rate and the prime borrowing rate.

Alternatively, the prime equity rate could be estimated directly. Several empirical studies of this subject already exist, and they can be used as a starting point.[5] Generally, these studies were made for the purpose of finding the discount rate appropriate for use by the Federal Government; this rate should approximate the rate that the average taxpayer uses, because government investments use funds that otherwise would be invested in the private sector. The studies tend to show that the average equity interest rate is relatively stable over time, and that it is in the neighbourhood of 10 per cent.

Although empirical studies do support a rate in the neighbourhood of 10 per cent, these studies deal with *average* equity costs and therefore include an

3. Philip L. Defliese, *Should Accountants Capitalize Leases?*, Coopers & Lybrand, New York, 1973, p. 18.
4. Arthur Andersen and Co., *Cost Accounting Standards for Defense Contracts*, Chicago, 1972, p. 53.
5. See, for example, Otto Eckstein, *Water Resources Development: The Economics of Project Evaluation*, Harvard University Press, Cambridge, Mass., 1961; Jacob A. Stockfish, 'The Interest Rate Applicable to Government Investment Projects', in Hinrichs and Taylor, *Program-Budgeting and Benefit-Cost Analysis*, Goodyear, Pacific Palisades, Calif., 1969; William J. Baumol, 'On the Appropriate Discount Rate for Evaluation of Public Projects', (also in Hinrichs and Taylor); George J. Stigler, *Capital and Rates of Return in Manufacturing Industries*, Princeton University Press, Princeton, N.J., 1963.

allowance for average risk. If the basic approach is that the equity interest rate is to be a *prime* equity rate, then the rate selected probably should be somewhat less than 10 per cent, perhaps 8 per cent.

Although no attempt is made here to arrive at a definitive answer to the question of how the rate should be derived, it seems clear that a feasible, objective way of arriving at an interest rate for equity capital can be developed. The range of acceptable rates is not wide. The rate selected within that range will be an approximation, of course, but accounting contains many approximations: the write-off of intangible assets of uncertain life, the methods of assigning overhead to products and to segments of a corporation, and, above all, depreciation. There is increasing acceptance of the principle that it is better to make a reasonable approximation than to neglect the problem entirely, a principle that is applicable to the present problem.

5. Accounting procedures

If one accepts the fundamental proposition that interest is a cost and that it should be treated similarly to the way other elements of cost are treated, most of the procedures for working interest cost into the financial accounting system are easy to determine by analogy. The general principles are:
1. An interest rate is determined annually by dividing total annual interest cost by the amount of capital employed.
2. In most circumstances, the interest cost assigned to a cost objective is found by multiplying the capital employed for the cost objective by this interest rate.
3. The interest cost of capital assets used in the manufacturing process is an element of product cost and is assigned to products in the same way that depreciation on plant and equipment is assigned.
4. Interest is an element of the cost of newly acquired plant and equipment. The cost includes the interest cost of the capital assets used in constructing plant and equipment, the interest cost of other capital tied up during the construction process, and the interest cost of advance payments or progress payments on purchased plant and equipment.
5. When assets are held in inventory for significantly long periods of time, interest cost is an element of the cost of these assets.
6. That portion of the interest cost for a year that is not assigned to cost objectives in accordance with the above principles is a general expense of the year.
7. The annual equity interest cost is credited to retained earnings.

Calculation of the interest rate

A company obtains capital from various sources, some from banks, some from bond issues, some from other creditors, some from equity investors, and some from retained earnings. In general, the capital obtained from each source is best thought of as flowing into a common pool. Although the right-hand side of the balance sheet shows the sources of capital, and the left-hand side shows the assets in which capital has been invested, there usually is no direct connection between an individual item on the right-hand side and an item on the left-hand side.

The interest cost is in the nature of an interest pool, similar to other overhead cost pools. The accounting entries can be similar to those used for collecting and allocating other overhead costs.

The debit to the interest pool for debt interest is calculated at the aftertax rate, since debt interest is a tax-deductible expense. The difference between this aftertax cost and the actual interest cost on debt would be debited to a tax adjustment account. The amount for equity interest should be at its calculated rate, since this cost is not tax deductible. The credit part of the entry for equity interest should be to retained earnings.

Depreciation on assets used in the manufacturing process becomes part of the cost of manufactured products. It therefore is part of the inventory cost of these products and appears on the income statement as part of cost of sales when the products are sold. Depreciation on assets used in marketing, administrative, and other non-manufacturing activities is charged as an expense of the current period.

Analogous procedures would be used for interest cost. Interest on the capital used in the manufacturing process becomes part of the cost of manufactured products; as such, it is included in the inventory cost of these products, and it appears on the income statement as part of the cost of sales when these products are sold. Interest on capital used in marketing and administrative and other non-manufacturing activities is charged as an expense of the current period. In short, the same mechanism used to assign depreciation to products could be used to assign interest to products.

The principles of cost accounting apply not only to products manufactured for sale but also to assets constructed by a company for its own use. Interest cost on the plant and equipment used in constructing such assets is an element of their cost. So, too, is the interest cost of capital tied up by the company during the construction process if it is a significant amount, which it is likely to be for major construction projects. By the same token, if the company uses its own capital on construction projects performed by outside contractors, as is the case when it makes advance payments to such contractors, the interest cost on such capital is an element of the cost of the project.

The general rule is that the cost of an asset includes all elements of cost that are involved in bringing the asset to the point in place and time where it is ready for productive use. Interest is one of the elements of such cost.

Conceptually, an interest cost is associated with holding assets in inventory. If the manufacturing cycle is short, the cost may not be significant enough to warrant the effort of assigning an interest carrying cost to products. When the passage of time is itself a significant part of the production process, however, interest cost is important enough to record. Examples include the accretion of lumber and fruit trees, tobacco, distilled liquor, and petroleum.

This procedure would not lead to inflated inventory amounts because the lower-of-cost-or-market rule sets a ceiling to inventory amounts, and this rule would remain in full force. The actual effect should be to bring inventory amounts for assets that are held for long periods of time up to levels that more closely approximate their cost to the company.

In summary, the total interest cost for a year, on both debt capital and equity capital, is debited to an 'interest pool' account. This account is credited for the interest cost that is assigned to cost objectives according to the procedures described above. The balance in the account represents unassigned interest cost. It represents a general expense for the year, just as do other elements of cost not assigned to specific cost objectives. As with these other elements of cost, the unassigned interest cost becomes part of the general and administrative expenses of the year and would be so reported on the income statement.

An illustration

Table 1 shows a condensed set of financial statements, structured so as to highlight the changes that would occur if the proposal were adopted. Each change will be discussed. Throughout, it is important to remember that the contrast depicted in table 1 is the situation in the year of transition. In subsequent years, the effect may be different, and these differences are also discussed briefly. Transactions affecting the Interest Pool are shown in table 2.

These entries should be interpreted in the following way: Debt interest and equity interest were added to the pool. The actual cost of debt interest was $20, and its aftertax cost was half this, or $10; the other $10 was debited to a tax adjustment account. The equity interest cost was $30, making the total interest cost $40. This $40 was disposed of by the following transactions: $31 was charged as a cost of products manufactured, and by the end of the year $23 of this

Table 1. Financial statements under current and proposed principles income statement.

	As currently reported		As proposed	
Sales revenue		1,000		1,000
Cost of sales	680		703	
Selling, general and administrative	220		205	
Tax adjustment	0	900	10	918
Income before taxes		100		82
Income tax expense		50		50
Net income		50		32
Total interest cost			40	
Less debt interest cost (after taxes)			10	
Equity interest cost				30
Addition to retained earnings				62

Ending balance sheet

Assets		
Inventory	150	158
Plant and equipment (net)	300	304
Other assets	300	300
Total assets	750	762
Liabilities and shareholders' equity		
Current liabilities	150	150
Long-term debt	250	250
Capital stock	100	100
Retained earnings	250	262
Total equities	750	762

Table 2. Interest pool transactions.

Debits		Credits	
From debt	10	To cost of sales	23
From equity	30	To inventory	8
		To plant	4
		To general expense	5
	40		40

cost had flowed through to cost of sales and $8 remained in product inventory; $4 was added to the cost of new plant; and $5 was not assigned to cost objectives and therefore became a general expense of the year.

The effects of these transactions on items in the income statement are:

1. *Cost of sales* increases by the interest component, $23, that was included as an element of cost. In future years, cost of sales would always be higher than under current practice because of the inclusion of interest.

2. *Selling, general, and administrative expenses* are reduced by the $20, which, under current practice, was the amount of debt interest expense, and it was increased by $5, the amount of interest expense that was not assigned to cost objectives – a net decrease of $15.

3. The *tax adjustment* item is shown separately here to account for the tax effect of debt interest. In practice, other ways of showing this item might be more informative.

4. *Income tax expense* has not been changed in the example. The effect of the proposal on income tax transactions depends on: whether or not the debt interest that is capitalized in asset amounts will nevertheless be allowed as a current tax-deductible expense; whether equity interest will be allowed as a deductible expense; and practice with respect to interperiod tax allocations. Because different assumptions would lead to different results, and in the interest of simplicity in exposition, no adjustment at all was made. If taxable income is increased by the capitalization of debt interest, there will be a corresponding increase in income tax expense. In the example, it would be $\frac{1}{4}$ of the capitalized interest cost of $12, multiplied by the income tax rate (assumed to be 50 per cent), which comes out to $1.50. The income tax effect is largest in the year of transition. Income tax expense will *not* be affected by the recognition of equity interest, unless the tax statutes are changed, because the difference between accounting income and taxable income that arises from equity interest is a permanent difference rather than a timing difference.

5. *Net income* decreases by $18. Essentially, this is because equity interest has been included as an element of cost, but the amount does not correspond to the $30 amount of equity interest cost, because $12 of equity interest cost has become lodged in asset accounts. In future years, net income will be lower under the proposed method than under the present method because of the inclusion of equity interest as an element of cost.

6. *Inventory*, on the balance sheet, increases by $8 which is the amount of interest included as an element of cost in products that have been manufactured but not sold. On future balance sheets, the same phenomenon will operate to make inventory amounts higher than they would have been under current practice.

7. *Plant and equipment* increases by $4 because of the inclusion of interest as an

element of cost in new plant assets. (The balance sheet does not reflect a revaluation of existing assets in order to avoid distorting the overall effect of the transition. In any event, such a revaluation is probably not worth the trouble of making it.)

8. *Retained earnings* increases by $12. This is the net effect of two changes, as follows:

	Present	Proposed	Difference
Net income	$50	$32	$−18
Equity interest	0	30	+30
Total additions	$50	$62	$+12

Net income is lower under the proposed method, but this is offset by the amount of equity interest. In the year of transition, these two changes do not offset one another, because of the addition of equity interest to inventory and plant accounts. This is essentially a one-time phenomenon. In future years, the total additions to retained earnings should be approximately the same under the proposed method as under the present method, subject only to fluctuations in the amount of capital employed in inventory and plant.

In summary, the changes are:

1. Cost of sales increases, because of the inclusion of interest as an element of cost.
2. Net income decreases, because of the recognition of equity interest, which, under current practice, does not appear as an element of cost or expense.
3. Certain asset amounts increase, because of the inclusion of interest as an element of cost.
4. After the year of transition, the total credit to retained earnings will be approximately unchanged, as compared with the present method, but the total will comprise two elements: equity interest and net income.

6. Effect on financial statements

Several studies of the effect of this proposal on published financial statements have been undertaken and two have been completed. The results of these are summarized briefly.

David W. Young studied the impact on three timber companies. He adjusted the published data for these companies over a long period of time (at least 17 years), so as to allow for the full impact of the interest cost that would be added annually to the book value of the timberland asset. (He used an equity interest cost of 9 per cent.) An article on this research is scheduled for publication in the *Accounting Review*. A summary of the results is given in table 3.

J. A. Hayes studied the impact on the financial statements of 22 American integrated oil companies for 1970, 1971, and 1972. (He also used an equity interest rate of 9 per cent.) Results for 1970 are summarized in table 4. It will be noted that although the effect is to decrease reported net income in all cases, the relative amount of decrease varies greatly among companies. It depends on individual variations in debt/equity ratios, the cost of debt, the relative amount of inventory and plant as a proportion of total assets, and the method used to finance new plant.

Table 3. Summary comparison of three timber companies.
(All figures except percentages in millions of dollars).

Item	Weyerhaeuser	Georgia Pacific	Boise Cascade
Period covered	1951–74	1955–74	1958–74
Balance sheet items			
Timberland as a percentage of total assets (prior to revisions), 1974	16	15	8
Initial value of timberland	80	8	2
Reported ending value of timberland	453	337	121
Revised ending value of timberland	831	493	182
Percentage increase	83	46	50
Beginning value of retained earnings	58	11	12
Reported ending value	1,260	255	363
Revised ending value	1,638	407	424
Percentage increase	30	60	17
Income statement items			
Reported total profits for period	2,128	1,101	262
Revised total profits for period	862	541	(199)
Difference	1,266	560	461
Percentage reduction	60	51	176

Table 4. Net income of integrated oil companies, 1970 (millions of dollars).

	#	Net income as reported	Net income as proposed	Percentage change
Amerada Hess Corp.	1	114.0	127.1*	+ 11
APCO Oil Corp.	2	9.6	5.8	− 40
Ashland Oil Co.	3	51.1	24.7	− 52
ARCO	4	205.6	32.0	− 52
Belco Petroleum Corp.	5	13.0	7.2	− 45
Cities Service Co.	6	118.6	18.4	− 84
Continental Oil Co.	7	160.5	51.5	− 68
Crown Central Petroleum Corp.	8	3.6	1.3	− 64
Crystal Oil Co.	9	−0.2	−0.7	−292
Getty Oil Co.	10	101.9	2.0	− 98
Kerr-McGee Corp.	11	35.9	10.7	− 70
Marathon Oil Co.	12	84.6	29.0	− 66
Murphy Oil Co.	13	9.3	−0.3	−103
Phillips Petroleum Co.	14	117.1	− 16.2	−114
Quaker State Oil Refining	15	10.8	6.8	− 7
Reserve Oil and Gas	16	3.6	−0.7	−119
Shell Oil Co.	17	237.2	38.5	− 84
Skelly Oil Co.	18	36.2	−2.7	−107
Standard Oil Co. (Indiana)	19	314.0	56.8	− 82
Standard Oil Co. (Ohio)	20	64.4	−8.6	−113
Sun Oil Co.	21	139.1	51.9	− 63
Union Oil Co. of California	22	114.5	19.5	− 83

*Note:
For 1970, Amerada Hess Corp. (# 1) presents an unusual case of negative common equity. The effect of equity capital cost calculations based on negative common equity is to increase net income over what it would otherwise be, when the interest cost of negative common equity is greater than the sum of preferred dividends and one-half of the fixed charges. Consequently adjustments to the income statement deflate costs rather than increase them, leading to an increase in net income.

7. Conclusion

The proposal has advanced to the point where it has been placed on the agenda of the Financial Accounting Standards Board. It has also served as the basis of proposed Standard 414 of the Cost Accounting Standards Board, which is exposed for public comment as this is written. It has been put forth as a desirable change for income tax purposes, in order to stimulate the flow of equity capital. All these developments have taken place much more quickly than I had anticipated. They indicate that further discussion and research would not be a waste of time, and my hope is that readers of this paper will become interested in exploring the question.

Research in two principal areas is needed:

1. further studies along the lines of those mentioned above, to explore the effect on the financial statements of other industries and on companies generally of including interest as an element of cost;
2. research that will suggest the best practical solution to the problem of arriving at the equity interest rate, which is the only practical problem of any consequence.

References

American Institute of Accountants, 'Report of the Special Committee on Interest in Relation to Cost', *1918 Yearbook*, pp. 110–12.
Anthony, Robert N., *Accounting for the Cost of Interest*, D. C. Heath & Co., Lexington, Mass., 1975.
Arthur Andersen & Co., *Cost Accounting Standards for Defense Contracts*, Chicago, 1972, p. 53
Bradley, Albert, 'Financial Control Policies of General Motors Corporation and Their Relationship to Cost Accounting', *N.A.C.A. Bulletin*, January 1, 1927.
Cole, William Morse, 'Interest on Investment in Equipment', *Journal of Accountancy*, April 1913.
Defliese, Philip L., *Should Accountants Capitalize Leases?* Coopers & Lybrand, New York, 1973.
Hilton, W. P., 'Interest on Capital', *Journal of Accountancy*, October 1916.
Jeynes, Paul H., *Profitability and Economic Choice*, Iowa State University Press, 1968.
Mey, Abram, 'Theodore Limperg and His Theory of Values and Costs', from *Abacus*, Sidney University Press, September 1966, p. 5.
Mey, Abram, and Kenneth S. Most, 'Replacement Value Accounting', *The Accountant*, September 7, 1963, pp. 275–80.
Pierce, G. J., *The Measurement of Capital Employed*, Business Books, Ltd., London, 1970.
Scovell, C. H., *Interest as a Cost*, Ronald Press, New York, 1924.
Scovell, C. H., 'Interest on Investment', *American Economic Review*, March 1919.
Silvern, David Harold, 'Enterprise Income: Measuring Financial Management', *Financial Executive*, April 1975, p. 56.
Welsch, Glenn A., and Lewis F. Davidson, 'Issues in Accounting for Interest Costs', Working Paper 73–15, University of Texas, Graduate School of Business, Austin, Texas, 1973.

IX. ACCOUNTING PRINCIPLES THAT SERVE THE INFORMATION NEEDS OF CORPORATE INVESTORS

Myron J. Gordon

1. Introduction

It has been said that corporate financial statements serve a variety of purposes. This paper, however, is concerned with only one of them, providing information that is useful to investors for deciding whether to buy, sell or hold the common shares of a corporation.

We, therefore, are concerned with two questions. One is what do investors want to know for the purpose of making such investment decisions? The other question is how useful are the alternative bases of income determination and asset valuation that are or may be used in financial statement preparation for obtaining the desired information. More precisely, we will compare the usefulness of net present value, historical cost, replacement cost, and general price level adjusted cost as bases for income determination and asset valuation in providing information for investment decisions.

2. Valuation of an investor's share

In finance we represent an investor as maximizing the utility of his wealth one period hence. This depends on his personality and on the mean, variance and perhaps other parameters of his wealth one period hence. The variation in an investor's utility with his investment in a share depends on the risk return attributes of the share. Nonetheless for our purposes we may look on the investor as being concerned only with the price and value of the share. The price he knows and the value is the expected value of the dividend for the coming period plus the price at the end of the period discounted at a rate appropriate to the risk of the sum. Visualizing the repetition of this valuation process one period hence, it can be seen that the value of a share is the expected values of the future stream of dividends discounted at a rate appropriate to their risk, or:

$$V = \sum_{t=1}^{\infty} D_t/(1 + k)^t$$

where D_t is the expected value of the dividend in period t and k is the discount rate.

3. Estimating net present value

One solution to the information problem open to the accountant is to give the investor exactly what he wants to know – the value of the firm's common stock. The post World War Two literature on this subject began with a monograph by Sidney Alexander which had the limited objective of contrasting what accountants do in measuring income and wealth with what economists do or at least write about with regard to the measurement of these variables.[1] This monograph was followed by a number of articles and books which proposed and to some extent discussed the implementation of net present value as a basis of measurement in preparing financial statements.

The formidable problems in estimating net present value have led some writers to qualify the objective and propose that value in some limited purpose be the basis of measurement, e.g., value in liquidation or 'exit value.'[2] However, the value figure that investors want is the net present value of the expected future cash flows in the expected employment of the firm's assets and not in one of the numerous alternative uses that are not contemplated or at best are most unlikely to take place.

Such efforts at avoiding the problem of estimating value are understandable. What is required is the estimation of the firm's dividends over all future time and arriving at a discount rate appropriate to their risk. Given the value of the firm at each point in time, the measurement of income is a simple task: it is the change in value plus the dividends paid over the period. The expected value of the income for the coming year is also easy to measure. It is the product Vk, the net present value of the common stock multiplied by the discount rate used to arrive at the net present value. However, as the author has pointed out elsewhere, realized income for the last year under this basis of valuation is determined by the change in the expected future dividends and the change in the discount rate over the year plus the dividend paid during the year. In other words, realized income is the

1. In practice economists commonly use a cost basis of measurement as in the national income and wealth accounts, (see S. S. Alexander 1950).
2. Recently the leading advocates of some variation on value as a basis of measurement in accounting have been R. J. Chambers (1966) and R. R. Sterling (1970).

change in the present value of expected future income (cf. Gordon 1967; and Gordon and Shillinglaw 1974).

It is indeed fortunate for accountants that the last thing anyone would want them to do, is to use net present value as a basis of measurement in financial statements. Perhaps the academics who advocate the use of net present value as a basis of accounting should be exempted from this statement, but I am not sure that even they would like to have accountants use net present value as the basis of measurement.

It remains true that the investment decision of every investor reflects in some form or another a comparison of a share's price and his estimate of its value. Investors and the security analysts who advise them use an extraordinarily wide range of sources of information in reaching judgments on a share's value. Practically all of them make some use – for better or worse – of the financial statements prepared by accountants, and they would not look with favour on the substitution of one more judgment, particularly that of an accountant, for the information accountants provide under a cost basis of valuation.

Furthermore, given the penchant for objectivity and accuracy for which accountants are justly famous, the figure he would arrive at should be obvious. The finance literature on security valuation and capital market efficiency has found evidence to support the conclusion that all the publicly available information with regard to the value of a share is fully reflected in its price with little or no lag.[3] Accordingly, in the absence of inside information the best estimate of the value of a share is its price. I will not go into the problems an accountant would face, if his estimate of a corporation's value were based on inside information that the management had not itself made public. Therefore, accountants required to use net present value as the basis of measurement in financial reporting might be well advised and would be reasonably expected to use market price for the value of a company.

4. Corporate financial statements and share prices

I hope it can be agreed that the accountant should not abandon what he is now providing investors through corporate financial statements and provide instead a piece of information that the investor can obtain more rapidly by buying the morning newspaper.

However, recent developments in the theory of finance pose a more serious threat to the traditional practice of accountants than the proposal that cost

3. For a review of this literature on the subject see David Downes and T. R. Dyckman (1973).

should be replaced with value as the basis of measurement. If capital markets are efficient and share prices fully reflect all publicly available information what need do investors have for corporate financial statements? Whatever information about corporate performance is contained in financial statements is fully reflected in share prices before the statements are made public and the publication of the financial statements has little or no impact on share prices.[4]

If capital markets are efficient, all shares are fairly priced, and an investor need not search out and analyze the publicly available information for the purpose of discovering over- or under-priced shares. He need not even concern himself with the risk return attributes of individual shares for the purpose of putting together a portfolio that efficiently satisfies his risk return preferences. All that he need do is put together a well-diversified portfolio of shares and lever up or down on it depending on his attitude towards risk.

Does it follow that the investor need not concern himself with corporate financial statements and this paper can be brought to a close right now? I believe that the answer is no. Any investor may safely proceed on the assumption that security analysis is not worth the effort, because a large enough number of analysts do a good enough job analyzing the publicly available information to keep the markets efficient. However, we can be sure that if everyone turned to throwing darts in order to pick stocks, capital markets would become inefficient and the analysis of available information would become quite profitable. We can also be sure that our busy analysts are able to make share prices fully reflect the information in financial statements by the time the statements are published because the statements are prepared. How share prices would behave if financial statements were not even prepared is an interesting subject for speculation.

Furthermore, capital market efficiency as the term is used may have a serious limitation that is not adequately recognized in the literature. A game may be fair without being interesting or socially useful. Whether or not financial statements and their 'quality' make the work of security analysts more interesting need not concern us. On the social usefulness of financial statements, assume that earnings and other financial statement information were not even determined by the accountant so that the only information available to investors was dividend and price data. Capital markets might still be efficient in the sense that analysis of this information would be of no benefit in finding over- and under-priced shares. In fact, capital markets would be more efficient without financial statements insofar as there is any likelihood that the analysis of the data contained therein aids in the discovery or prevention of over- or under-priced shares.

4. Although the evidence examined in the previously cited paper is not uniform, some of the evidence not cited there is particularly disturbing with regard to the usefulness of financial statements under this criterion. See in particular George Benston (1967; 1973).

However, it might well be true that the behaviour of stock prices over time is more desirable, say fluctuate less, when the analysis of financial statement information enters into the determination of stock prices. The investigation of whether or not this proposition is true is beyond the scope of the present paper. Assuming it is true, however, enables us to proceed. In that event we may presume further that improving the financial statement information made available to security analysts improves the behaviour of stock prices.

5. Forecasting and the use of historical data

Based on the assumptions that a share's value is the expected values of the future cash flows or dividends that the share will pay discounted at a rate appropriate to their risk, and that the discount rate should vary with the uncertainty as to the future dividends, the questions we face may be posed as follows. Do financial statements based on cost provide information that is useful in forecasting the expected values and variability of a share's future dividends? Can we compare and choose among the alternative cost bases of valuation for this purpose?

Assume that for the last five years a corporation's financial structure has been constant, it has earned a return of r on its common equity, and it has retained the fraction b of its income. If these relations are expected to hold in the future and if last year's earnings per share were Y, next year's dividend is expected to be $(1 - b)Y(1 + br)$ and the dividend is expected to grow thereafter at the rate br.

In fact, few if any firms present the orderly stable picture just described. Assume instead we have a firm with a history over the last five years described in Table 1. For our purposes it will be adequate to only consider the return on common data. Should we characterize the firm as having a return on common equal to the 12 per cent average over the five years? Do the last two years represent an aberration that should be ignored or at least heavily discounted? Do these two years represent a new level of performance or points on an upward trend? The accountant who prepared the statements from which this data was derived has no special qualifications for answering these questions and he should not attempt to do so. Each analyst must find his own answer, using whatever additional sources of information he considers useful, including the judgments of other analysts and additional financial statement information. The answer to the question just posed, however, is the analysts' prediction of the firm's future earnings, given its dividend and other elements of financial policy.

It is of course true that the past record of dividends, earnings and financial structure do not tell us what the future holds for a company. However, it is the starting point in predicting the future. Regardless of how bold or cautious the

Table 1. Selected five year historical data for a hypothetical company.

	1971	1972	1973	1974	1975
Earnings	$ 2.40	$ .92	$ 3.69	$ 6.68	$ 6.54
Dividend	1.60	1.00	1.00	1.60	1.80
SOYCEBV[1]	30.00	30.80	30.72	33.41	38.49
Return on common	8%	3%	12%	20%	17%
Retention rate	33%	−9%	73%	74%	72%

1. Start of year book value of the common equity.

prediction is, regardless of how much or little confidence we place in it, we would be most unhappy about undertaking the effort without the information contained in the corporation's financial statements.

In examining the historical data the analyst is confronted with three reasons for the fluctuations in the company's return on common. One is changes in financial policy. Another is changes in sales volume and cost price relations for the firm's products. The third may be called noise. It is illustrated by extraordinary gains or losses from the liquidation of a capital asset or the write up or write down of inventory due to a change in prices. The analyst would like to have the noise, that is the income attributed to these non-recurring events, filtered out if they are strictly non-recurring and have no information content for predicting the future. If these events may not be purely random, the analyst would prefer to have the gain or loss associated with them shown separately and reach his own judgment on their predictive value.

6. Historical and replacement costs in an inflationary environment

This section compares the merits of historical and replacement cost as bases of income determination and asset valuation. The difference between them may be stated both briefly and roughly as follows.[5] Replacement cost charges against revenue the current cost of the inventory and depreciable assets consumed in generating the revenue. Historical cost charges against revenue the actual cost of the assets consumed, and it thereby recognizes as profit the difference between actual and current cost. Under replacement cost inventory and net plant accounts are written up or down to replacement cost with the offsetting credit made directly to a sub-account of net worth. Under historical cost the

5. For a more precise comparison see M. J. Gordon (1953).

replacement cost of the assets appear in the accounts as the assets are replaced, and the difference between actual and replacement cost of the assets consumed may be said to go to net worth through the income account.

Assume now an economy in which the prices of various products and the price level in general fluctuate from one period to the next. They are uncertain, but the best estimate of any price or the price level one, two, ... and n periods hence is the current price or price level. In short, we do not have an inflationary environment.

In this uncertain but non-inflationary environment, the inventory profit (difference between actual and current cost of goods sold) included in earnings may well be considered noise. The best estimate of its amount in any future period is zero, and the informational content of the earnings record for predicting future earnings is improved if the noise is suppressed or if the inventory profit is so identified in the accounts.

Dealing with the depreciation charge is not as easy. First, the replacement cost of the depreciable assets consumed is quite difficult to measure. Second, the 'plant profit', analogue to the inventory profit, is usually considerably smaller in amount. Third, the plant profit is a complex function of the cumulative movement in prices over many past years and not just the change in price over the current year. Fourth, future plant profits are correlated with their past values, and the plant profit will go to zero very gradually over time as the existing plant becomes fully depreciated. It follows that eliminating from the income account or separately reporting the gain or loss from the difference between the replacement and historical cost of the depreciable assets will have little or no informational content. Doing so may add more problems than it eliminates.

The conclusion I reach is that in a non-inflationary environment historical cost is to be preferred to replacement cost. The benefits of the latter are provided by separately reporting inventory profit. Historical cost also avoids the problems of measuring the depreciation charge at replacement cost, problems which provide little if any compensating benefits.

Let us now recognize the world in which we are currently living. There has been positive inflation on average over a considerable period of time, so that there is a large gap between the historical and current cost of the depreciable assets of most firms. Furthermore, the best estimate of a product's price and the general price level one, two, ..., n periods hence would incorporate price growth at some rate.

Under historical cost past earnings figures include inventory profits which are on average positive and fluctuate over a wide range.[6] Separately reporting this

6. It appears that average rate of change and the variability of the change in the price level are positively correlated. Hence, the higher the rate of inflation, the greater its variability, and the greater the noise due to inventory profits in historical cost statements. See M. J. Gordon and Paul Halpern (forthcoming).

element of profit allows the determination of how operating profit and the operating return on common have varied with inflation over time. It also allows the determination of how the company has fared with regard to inventory profits. For those who believe that inventory profits in an inflationary environment are not a component of true profits, replacement cost accounting for inventory is preferable. However, either course of action provides the analyst with the information he requires to forecast a firm's future profits without inventory profits, or with inventory profits assuming some rate of growth in the price level.[7]

The difference between the actual and replacement cost depreciation charge will depend materially on the extent of the inflation over the past ten to twenty-five years. If the inflation has been great, the difference between historical and replacement cost depreciation will be large. In his projections for the future the security analyst may well be interested in the difference between the two figures. Both figures cannot be obtained when the accounts are kept at historical cost, while they can be obtained under replacement cost accounting. Although the replacement cost determination of the depreciation charge and the net plant account is subject to a considerable margin of error, the error may well be small enough in relation to the amount involved to make the data useful.

The conclusion which follows from these observations is that when there has been considerable inflation and the inflation is expected to continue in the future, there is some advantage in using replacement cost as the basis of income determination and asset valuation. This advantage is eliminated or at least substantially reduced, however, if historical cost statements present as supplementary information the replacement cost of the depreciation charge and net plant account and the amount of inventory profit in earnings.[8]

7. General price level adjusted historical cost (GPLAC)

The departure from historical cost financial statements that has received the greatest attention from both academic accountants and organizations of practicing accountants in North America has been general price level adjusted historical cost (GPLAC). The considerable attention devoted to specifying exact rules for implementing the principle makes any summary description of it extremely difficult. What follows will ignore the problems posed by intra-period price level changes.[9]

7. This appears also to be the position taken in E. O. Edwards and P. W. Bell (1961). It is restated in E. O. Edwards (1975).
8. Therefore, the United States Securities Exchange Commission (1976) should be commended for requiring the supplementary reporting of replacement cost inventories and plant assets.
9. For a detailed and precise description of the practice recommended see Financial Accounting Standards Board (1974).

Assume that the inventory at the start of the year and the inventory at the end of the year were both acquired on those dates. The start of year inventory is multiplied by the ratio of the end of year to start of year values for a general price level index and the adjustment is carried to cost of goods sold. This basis of measurement therefore departs from current or replacement cost in eliminating inventory profit from the income statement insofar as the prices of the items in inventory do not move proportionately with the general price level.

With regard to the plant account, assume that at the start of the year the historical cost of each item has been multiplied by the ratio of general price index for the start of year to the price index at the time the item of plant was acquired. The account is then multiplied by the ratio of the end of year to start of year values for the general price index. This figure is then allocated between the depreciation charge for the year and the end of year balance of the plant on the basis of the fraction of the plant consumed during the year. Hence, both the charge and the balance in the account represent the general price level adjusted historical cost instead of the historical or replacement cost of the respective quantities.

The same procedure is applied to the ownership equity account. That is, the amount invested and retained in each past year is multiplied by the ratio of the general price index at the start of the year to the year of the addition to the net worth account. The ownership equity at the end of the year is the income (less dividends) as calculated above plus the start of year equity price level adjusted to the end of the year. For a corporation with monetary assets equal to its liabilities, the GPLAC assets sum to the GPLAC net worth with each calculated independently.

Turning to the monetary accounts, there is no price level adjustment to the net monetary or net debt position. The consequence is that the GPLAC adjustment to the net worth account is greater than the GPLAC adjustment to the real assets if the company has a net monetary position and the opposite if the company has a net debt position. This difference is eliminated by carrying the gain or loss on the net debt or monetary position due to the change in the price level to the current period's income statement.

The distinguishing feature and chief argument advanced in favour of GPLAC statements is that the consequences of relative price movements are recognized as income and the consequences of changes in the general price level are excluded from income. Under replacement cost the distinction is between operating income and capital gains due to changes in the level of asset prices. GPLAC like historical cost makes no such distinction. Income includes capital gains as realized through sale as well as operating income, but the capital gains attributed to the change in the general price level are eliminated.

GPLAC also has the great practical advantage over replacement cost of eliminating the problem of measuring the replacement cost of the plant assets, since the adjustment to all accounts is on the basis of a general price index. Under replacement cost measurement it would be theoretically wrong to use a general price index on the plant account, but for all practical purposes the error would not be serious in an inflationary environment.

Perhaps the most serious theoretical and practical problem associated with GPLAC statements is the treatment of gains or losses on the firms net monetary or debt position. Under replacement cost measurement they are carried to the net worth account directly. Under GPLAC they reach the net worth account via the income statement. The realization principle of historical cost is violated notwithstanding the fact that GPLAC is supposed to be an extension of historical cost to deal with inflation. The practical consequences are even more serious. At first glance the GPLAC statements that result are incomprehensible, and after some analysis they prove to be ridiculous (see Davidson and Weil 1975; and Gordon 1976).

The previous discussion of GPLAC statements is all by way of background. Our interest in them here is not for the purpose of 'correctly' measuring income and balance sheet quantities: our interest is for the prediction of future income. I have made some effort at interpreting such statements for the prediction of future income in the hope that I could report the comparative advantages and disadvantages of the GPLAC measurement rules. However, these efforts collapsed in utter chaos. My conclusion, perhaps an unscientific conclusion, therefore, is that GPLAC statements are materially inferior to their historical and replacement cost alternatives for the prediction of future income by security analysts.

8. Conclusions

The conclusions reached in the preceding pages contrast sharply with much of the literature on the comparative merits of alternative measurement rules for financial statements in an inflationary environment. It may therefore be advisable to make clear the differences and provide an explanation for them.

The major conclusions are that in an inflationary environment: (1) the security analyst is better served by replacement or current cost financial statements than by historical cost statements; and (2) this information advantage largely disappears if replacement cost data is provided as supplementary information to historical cost statements.

By contrast the literature on financial statements in an inflationary environment can be characterized as follows. First, the dominant idea raised is that the continued use of historical cost in financial accounting seriously threatens the satisfactory functioning of the economic system. Second, apart from occasional academic works on the subject (such as my paper and the Bell and Edwards book) there has been little interest in replacement cost statements or information prior to the pronouncement on the subject by the US Securities Exchange Commission.

Third, public accountants as represented by the American Institute of Certified Public Accountants and the Canadian Institute of Chartered Accountants have devoted practically all their efforts to exploring the use of general price level adjusted historical cost statements. Finally, corporate financial officers who represent the views of the managements of their corporations are simply unhappy. Their views as reflected in the pronouncements of the officers and committees of the Financial Executives Institute are: (1) historical cost statements in an inflationary environment are intolerable; and (2) any of the proposed alternatives to historical cost including GPLAC are unsatisfactory.

My explanation for the contrast between the conclusions reached here and the sharply different positions just stated is quite simple. This paper has been concerned with the informational content of financial statements for security analysis. The concern expressed in the literature referred to above has been with the distribution of income consequences of the statements. The dire consequences of historical cost statements that are complained about are paying taxes, dividends, and wages on the basis of historical cost income. The concern is with inadequate after-tax earnings from the viewpoint of meeting the capital requirements of industry and protecting investors from expropriation through inflation.[10] The legitimacy of these fears and the effectiveness of income measurement as a means of influencing income determination and avoiding the calamities feared are beyond the scope of this paper.

It may nonetheless be noted that this literature on the income distribution consequences of historical cost statements has not been successful in providing evidence to support the conclusions reached. It has not been shown that the measurement of income influences the distribution of income or that the inflation-historical cost caused reduction in corporate income that is alleged to have taken place is socially undesirable.

This concern with the distribution of income is an explanation for the unhappiness expressed by financial executives in response to any concrete proposal for changing the rules of measurement. Financial executives may well want the freedom to adjust for inflation when profits are high and not do so when profits are low. Any precise set of rules which denies them this freedom is

10. See Jan Klaassen (n.d.) for interview derived support for this conclusion.

unsatisfactory, particularly if the rules do not at least reduce taxable income. The continuing examination of GPLAC statements by the public accounting organizations in North America and their failure to take any action may be the most sensible way for them to deal with the conflicting forces which operate on them.

References

Alexander, Sidney S., (1950), 'Income Measurement in a Dynamic Economy', in *Five Monographs on Business Income*, American Institute of Accountants, New York.

Benston, George (1967), 'Published Corporate Accounting Data and Stock Prices', in *Journal of Accounting Research, Empirical Research in Accounting: Selected Studies*, pp. 1–54.

Benston, George (1973), 'Required Disclosure and the Stock Market: an Evaluation of the Securities Exchange Act of 1974', in *American Economic Review*.

Chambers, R. J. (1966), *Accounting Evaluation and Economic Behavior*, Prentice-Hall, New Jersey.

Davidson, S., and R. L. Weil (1975), 'Inflation Accounting for Utilities', in *Financial Analysts Journal*, May/June.

Downes, David, and T. R. Dyckman (1973), 'Efficient Market Research and Accounting Information', in *Accounting Review*, April, pp. 300–317.

Edwards, E. O. (1975), 'The State of Current Value Accounting', in *Accounting Review*, April, pp. 235–245.

Edwards, E. O., and P. W. Bell (1961), *The Theory and Measurement of Business Income*, University of California Press.

Financial Accounting Standards Board (1974), *Financial Reporting in Units of General Purchasing Power*, Exposure Draft, December 31, 1974, Stanford, Connecticut.

Gordon, M. J. (1953), 'The Valuation of Accounts at Current Cost', in *Accounting Review*, July, pp. 373–384.

Gordon, M. J. (1967), 'An Economist's View of Profit Measurement', in H. W. Stevenson and J. R. Nelson, eds., *Profits in the Modern Economy*, University of Minnesota Press, Minneapolis.

Gordon, M. J. (1976), 'Comparison of Historical Costs and General Price Level Adjusted Cost Rate Base Regulation'. Working paper, Faculty of Management Studies, University of Toronto.

Gordon, M. J. and Paul Halpern (forthcoming), 'Bond Share Yield Spreads under Uncertain Inflation', in *American Economic Review*.

Gordon, M. J. and G. Shillinglaw (1974), *Accounting, a Management Approach*, R. D. Irwin, Illinois.

Klaassen, Jan (n.d.), 'Current Replacement Value Accounting in Western Europe'. Free University, Amsterdam.

Sterling, R. R. (1970), *Theory of the Measurement of Enterprise Income*, University Press of Kansas, Kansas City.

United States Securities Exchange Commission (1976), S. E. C. Amendment to Regulation S-X, adapted March 24, 1976.

X. STOCK MARKET EFFICIENCY AND THE INFORMATION CONTENT OF FINANCIAL REPORTS

Hans G. Eijgenhuijsen and Jan Klaassen

1. Introduction: problem setting

Firms' financial statements or accounting reports are supposed to be of importance to the investment decisions of (potential) shareholders. This does not exhaust the significance of the accounting report figures because there are other groups for whom these figures may contain important information. Besides this, the figures may help shareholders to form an opinion concerning management policies, with a view to exercising their voting rights. At present we do not know enough about the question of what the importance of accounting reports is for shareholders' investment decisions. Yet a knowledge of this is important, because it would shed light on the problem of the extent to which firms can influence stockprices by means of their accounting reports. In the effort to improve accounting reports it would be possible – if information on this problem were available – to pay specific attention to the effects of certain proposals for the improvement of stock valuation.

Some studies regarding the valuation methods used in accounting reports assume a certain shareholder behavior. For instance Van der Zijpp stated that profits based on historic cost lead to higher stock prices than profits based on replacement values.[1] Furthermore, an enquiry[2] among a number of Dutch firms and a literature research concerning published reports show that some Dutch managers think that the profit figures based on certain valuation methods may influence stock prices. Wilschut writes in this connection:

In comparing company profits, the financial press does not generally eliminate the effects of whether replacement values have been applied or not, arguing that the public ultimately bases its opinions on the profit figure supplied by the company. In the first instance, this profit figure influences the way stock prices develop.[3]

1. Zijpp, I. v. d., 'Financieel beleid en jaarverslag', *E.S.B.* 12–8–1970, p. 770.
2. Klaassen, J., *De Vervangingswaarde, Theorie en toepassing in de jaarrekening*, Alphen aan den Rijn 1975, from p. 127.
3. Wilschut, K. P. G., 'Het stelsel van waardering en winstbepaling toegepast door de Akzo-groep', *Maandblad voor Accountancy en Bedrijfshuishoudkunde*, May 1975, p. 243.

Extensive literature has recently been published on the question of how the stock market values company shares. Among other questions, the problem was raised of whether shares can be permanently overvalued or undervalued, as compared with other shares, owing to differences in disclosed results consequent upon different valuation methods applied by the firm in question. Empirical research into stock price behavior generally indicates that the world's biggest stock exchange (New York) is close to the ideal type of an efficient stock market. An interesting and important question is whether such a market produces correct stock prices at all times.

So far the efficient market concept has hardly received any attention in the Netherlands at all.

At the same time – and this also applies to the United States – these problems have had little influence on the discussions as to how accounting reports should be drawn up. The purpose of this paper is to make a modest contribution towards filling this gap. Firstly, we shall deal with the efficient market concept. Secondly, we shall discuss the question of whether this concept has any relationship with reality. Thirdly, we shall ask whether market efficiency implies market transparency, in the sense that investors are able to form a correct opinion of stock values. Such an opinion can only be formed on the basis of information supplied by accounting reports. The different concepts of profit and valuation methods used in accounting reports can produce different results. Only if the market were able to appreciate these differences fully would it be true to describe the market as transparent. Lastly, we will deal with the question of the extent to which the market perceives these differences and to what extent this affects the discussions regarding the optimal content of accounting reports.

2. The efficient market concept

In the mid-sixties, extensive empirical research in the United States into the behavior of stock prices led to the conclusion that time/series of subsequent stock price changes (returns) form a close approximation of a random walk. The degree of interdependence between the successive returns usually appeared to be so small that information on this would not enable investors to improve their returns. It was not yet known, however, how the stockmarket produced this phenomenon: '... there existed a large body of empirical results in search of a rigorous theory'.[4] This is a remarkable thing, with which economic science is not

4. Fama, E. F., 'Efficient capital markets: a review of theory and empirical work', *The Journal of Finance*, May 1970, p. 389.

often confronted! Samuelson filled this theoretical gap by developing the efficient market model.[5]

A popular formulation of the efficient market concept is that stock prices at all times reflect all available relevant information. Though it is an important property of this market constellation that subsequent returns follow a random walk, the hypothesis goes even further. Present stock prices would reflect not only all the implications of past price behavior, but also everything that is known about the firms in question. In an efficient market, the return expected for 'tomorrow' is reduced to zero.

The conditions originally formulated for an efficient market are very restrictive: no transaction costs, free information and homogeneous expectations. This third condition implies that investors are in agreement regarding the implications of the available information for the level of stock prices. These conditions are not realistic, but this does not necessarily imply that the hypothesis must be abandoned *a priori*. A major argument is that non-fulfillment of all three conditions only implies the existence of as many *potential* sources preventing the efficient adjustment of stock prices to new information. Fama, one of the leading proponents of the efficient market concept, has formulated less stringent conditions.[6] He points out that as long as investors acting in the stockmarket take into account all available information, even high transaction costs as such need not imply that whenever transactions take place stock prices do not fully reflect this information. We might point out that stock prices have considerable freedom to adjust themselves to minor changes in investor expectations if transaction costs are low compared to stock values. The prompt reflection of all available information does not demand that new, relevant information should quickly reach *all* investors. This is necessary only for a sufficient number of investors. Besides this, the lack of agreement between investors in assessing new information does not impair market efficiency, unless certain (groups of) investors systematically arrive at better assessments based on available information than that reflected in stock prices.

Given this last assumption – not elaborated by Fama – it is of importance to delve deeper into the interpretation of information. An important question prompted by the assertion that 'stock prices always fully reflect all relevant available information' is, what do the words *'fully reflect'* mean? The problem becomes clear if one realises that even the discounting of all available information in stock prices does not necessarily imply that this leads to unbiased estimates of stock prices.

5. Samuelson, P. A., 'Proof that properly anticipated prices fluctuate randomly', *Industrial Management Review*, Spring 1965, pp. 41–49.
6. Fama, op. cit. pp. 387/8.

The type of market being considered is usually associated with the idea of efficient allocation of resources.[7] Assuming that investors behave rationally, this will be the case only if stock prices not only react promptly to new information, but also without being biased.

When investors have the same information and, given their divergent stock price estimates, do not agree on the assessment of this information, differences of opinion may be due to various misconceptions such as the errors in interpretation. The market price of stock at a given moment can be regarded as a consensus of the valuations by the investors trading in the market but, as already stated, this implies '. . . a consensus of their mistakes'.[8] The market price does reflect an unbiased stock-value estimate, if many investors contribute to this market consensus and if the mistakes they make are individual ones. In this case, by the law of averages, an error in the equilibrium value of stocks will probably be quite small as compared with individual mistakes.

However, if the postulate of mutual independence is undermined – and this will happen as soon as a large number of investors systematically make the same mistake in interpreting information – we can no longer count on stock prices not having been significantly influenced by these errors. In that case, the market stops being efficient, because new information is no longer reflected in stock prices without being biased.[9]

Having regard to the above, it may be useful to formulate the efficient market hypothesis more precisely, for example as follows: In an efficient market stock prices will at all times adjust quickly, and without being biased, to new relevant information.

3. How realistic is the concept?

The question poses itself, how far the stock market really conforms to this ideal picture. Especially in the case of shares quoted on the N.Y.S.E., efforts have been made to find out how quickly the market reacts to investor-relevant information, and to find out to what extent stock price estimates are (un)biased. As the hypothesis cannot be tested in its general form, research had to be split up on the basis of some interesting and well-defined categories of new information released to the market. This implies that the hypothesis regarding efficient adjustment to

7. Assuming that transactions are carried out at the lowest rates possible, see West, R. R., and Tinic, S. H., 'Corporate finance and the changing stock market', *Financial Management*, Autumn 1974, p. 15.
8. Bagehot, W., 'The only game in town', *Financial Analysts Journal*, March/April 1971, p. 14.
9. See Treynor, J. L., 'Efficient markets and fundamental analysis', *Financial Analysts Journal*, March/April 1974, p. 14.

new information can only be accepted or rejected in certain respects, depending upon the kind of information to which the investigation relates. Moreover, the possibility always remains that stock prices react slowly and/or in a biased way to a single type or several types of less material information. In spite of this, the overall results of the research provide an important indication of the degree of efficiency in the formation of stock prices.

In recent years, the impact on stock prices of the following types of information has been studied: stock splits, stock dividends, earning announcements, new stock issues and secondary offerings, discount-rate changes.[10] In these studies attention was focused on the effects of the announcements on stock prices, other factors (the markets' movements) being constant.

When the results of the investigations are considered, it seems justifiable to conclude that on the whole the types of new information covered by the research were incorporated in stock prices with a fairly high degree of efficiency. Usually, the process of stock price adjustment was characterized by a series of erratic, but rather unbiased movements towards a new equilibrium. This fits in well with situations in which future events were anticipated to a substantial extent. As regards the speed at which new information was incorporated in stock prices, the market has sometimes undoubtedly reacted to relevant news with a certain time-lag. Though most of the stock-price adjustment usually took place on the first trading day after the announcement, the rest of the adjustment process was spread over the next few days. Where there is such a delayed response, transaction costs usually preclude investors from any considerable benefit. Hence there are good reasons to assume that investing in the world's biggest stock market is very much like taking part in a 'fair game' in the sense that all investors (with the possible exception of those having a monopoly in access to new information) '. . . are on an equal footing when it comes to buying and selling stock in the markets . . .'.[11] Professional investors quite understandably have difficulty in conforming to this 'fair game' approach. Quite a few of them think that empirical results point towards quick adjustment of stock prices to public information, but only as regards the traditional, unsophisticated types of interpretation to which most investors confine themselves. Among professional

10. Fama, E., Fisher, L., Jensen, M., Roll, R., 'The adjustment of stock prices to new information', *International Economic Review*, February 1969, pp. 1–21; Ball, R. and Brown, P., 'An empirical evaluation of accounting income numbers', *Journal of Accounting Research*, Autumn 1968, pp. 159–178; Brown, P. and Kennelly, J. W., 'The informational content of quarterly earnings: an extension and some further evidence', *Journal of Business*, July 1972, pp. 403–415; Scholes, M. S., 'The market for securities: substitution versus price pressure and the effects of information on share prices', *Journal of Business*, April 1972, pp. 179–211; Waud, R. N., 'Public interpretation of discount rate changes: Evidence on the 'announcement effect', *Econometrica*, 1971 No. 2, pp. 231–250.
11. Sprecher, C. R., *Introduction to investment management*, Boston, 1975, p. 467.

investors, however, there should be sufficient capacity to produce systematically better evaluations of publicly available information than is implicit in stock prices. Professional investment research would be oriented towards developing fresh ideas and would lead to qualitatively superior judgments.[12]

Supporters of this view are clearly of the opinion that many investors often systematically commit the same errors in interpreting publicly available information. As a result, stock prices would not invariably be an unbiased reflection of inherent values. By careful analysis of publicly available information professional investors would be able to trace these discrepancies and benefit accordingly. Consequently, in the 'longer run' the performance of professionally-managed stock portfolios would be consistently better than results achieved by non-professional portfolio management, given the same level of risk.

It goes without saying that if professional fund-managers consistently produce better returns, on the basis of this supposed possession of 'inside information of the higher type' (Morgenstern's expression)[13] this would essentially impair the efficient market hypothesis.[14] This in itself is sufficient reason to test the question empirically.

With few exceptions, the necessary data are only available for investment funds and consequently empirical testing has had to be limited mainly to this group of professional portfolio managers, which is probably sufficiently representative. The proper procedure is to evaluate professional portfolio performance against an investment strategy in which portfolios are composed 'naïvely' and remain unchanged, whatever new information becomes available. For a sound judgment, we must consider both return and risk as relevant portfolio characteristics, and compare portfolios for a period long enough to eliminate random factors.

The insight obtained from trustworthy empirical research can be summarized as follows.[15] In general, there is no evidence at all that professional portfolio

12. Valentine, J. L., *Investment analysis and capital market theory*, Financial Analysts Research Foundation, Charlottesville, 1975, pp. 10/11.

13. Morgenstern, O., 'Information flow and stock-market price changes', In: Bicksler, J. L., ed., *Methodology in Finance-Investments*, Lexington, Mass., 1972, p. 121.

14. This also applies to benefiting from 'inside information' in its more common meaning. There is evidence that the specialists on the organized stock exchanges who have a market-making function in securities, have valuable inside information. See Niederhofer, V. V. and Osborne, M. F. M., 'Market making and reversal on the stock exchange', *Journal of the American Statistical Association*, December 1966, pp. 897–916. For another potential group, the 'corporate insiders', recent empirical research hardly supports the view that this has lucrative possibilities. See Jaffe, J. F., 'Special information and insider trading', *Journal of Business*, July 1974, pp. 410–428. As the text indicates, there is no need to fear that this imperfection will penetrate any further into the market.

15. See, for instance, Joy, O. M., and Porter, R. B., 'Stochastic dominance and mutual fund performance', *Journal of Financial and Quantitative Analysis*, January 1974, pp. 25–31; McDonald, J. G., 'Objectives and performance of mutual funds 1960–1969', *Journal of Financial and Quantitative*

management can produce consistently superior returns. On the contrary, there are strong indications that portfolio managers as a group, following a naïve buy-and-hold strategy, would produce – at least as a rule – the same results as they did in fact. Neither does presently available evidence generally support the view that there are significantly more professional portfolio managers with consistently superior returns than there would be as a matter of chance: merely a negligible percentage.

The viewpoint that the stock market would offer prospects of extremely favourable returns to capable and active people has great intuitive appeal. Consequently, it is easy to understand that the efficient market concept has been received in the first instance as a bizarre proposition. No one will deny the existence of stock market disequilibria, but no adequate proof has ever been forthcoming that it is at all possible to benefit systematically from these disequilibria in practice. This inevitably means that the initial viewpoint must be revised. Samuelson observes, about ten years after the theorem was first developed, that 'the only honest conclusion is to agree that a loose version of the "efficient market" . . . hypothesis accords with the facts of life'.[16]

4. A transparent stock market

A perusal of investment literature indicates that a number of authors are of the opinion that, roughly speaking, the market form of 'perfect competition' is the basis of the efficient market hypothesis.[17] One of the conditions for perfect competition is the existence of market transparency. Whether this premise is found in reality is a complicated and far-reaching problem. This becomes clear when one realizes that the meaning of market transparency is that investors are able to form a *correct value judgment* regarding the stocks traded in the market. *A correct value judgment comprises more than an unbiased value-estimate which is at the centre of the efficient market concept.*

Analysis, June 1974, pp. 311–333; Williamson, J. P., 'Performance measurement and investment objectives for educational endowment funds', New York 1972; Jensen, M. C., 'The performance of mutual funds in the period 1945–1964', *The Journal of Finance*, May 1968, pp. 389–416; Securities and Exchange Commission, *Institutional Investor Study Report*, Vol. 2, Washington 1971; Schlarbaum, G. G., 'The investment performance of the common stock portfolios of property-liability insurance companies', *Journal of Financial and Quantitative Analysis*, January 1974, pp. 89–105.

16. Samuelson, P. A., 'Challenge to judgment', *The Journal of Portfolio Management*, Fall 1974, p. 17.

17. See, for instance, Brealey, R. A., *An introduction to risk and return from common stocks*, Cambridge 1969, especially p. 5; Philippatos, G. C., *Financial management, Theory and Techniques*, San Francisco 1973, p. 377.

Given this statement, one can discern a considerable number of aspects to the problem of a transparent stock market. We may mention the following: the amount of new information supplied, problems relating to the accounting methods employed and, in connection with this, the relevance of the financial data supplied. Besides this, the problem of interpretation will probably have to be considered as well. The following are some introductory remarks on these points. The stream of information reaching the stock market is largely based on financial publications by quoted firms. Firstly, these are annual reports and annual accounting numbers, but also interim financial news supplied by the firm. Among the information assumed to have a significant impact on stock values, the relevance of earnings announcements looms large. Empirical research has proved that changes in earnings and in stock prices are positively correlated.[18]

Considering the criticism that has been levelled at the degree of realism of reported financial data, one wonders whether earnings information supplied by firms is such that it is optimally useful for making investment decisions.[19]

The ideal picture of a transparent market is liable to be jeopardized when calculations and reports on the firm's financial position contain ambiguities, broadly defined. There is clear risk of investor judgment being influenced as a result, in the sense that major errors are introduced into the market consensus. The way financial information is presented might mislead investors in various ways. Irresponsible comprimation of essential accounting data in the financial press is a clear example. By using different valuation methods or depreciation systems from one year to another, firms can moreover hinder investors from obtaining correct insight into the financial position, to say the least. Thus the problem is whether (professional) investors are affected with a functional fixation, so that in interpreting externally reported accounting numbers they are clearly misled by changes introduced in reporting methods. We will discuss these problems in the next section.

5. Market efficiency, market transparency and the informational content of financial reports

The finding that the stock market is highly efficient refers to the way prices are formed on the stock exchange. This implies that market efficiency only has

---

18. See Brealey, R. A., op.cit. Chapter 7; Niederhofer, V. and Regan, P. J., 'Earnings changes, Analysts' forecasts and stock prices', *Financial Analysts Journal*, May/June 1972, pp. 65–72.
19. See, for example, Treynor, J. L., 'The trouble with earnings', *Financial Analysts Journal*, September/October 1972, pp. 41–43.

significance for the supply of information for investment decisions by shareholders holding shares quoted on the stock exchange. In addition, these shareholders need information relevant to the exercise of their voting rights. Finally, financial reports may have significance for the decisions and assessments of other groups such as creditors and employees. To supply information for investment decisions is therefore only one of the objectives of financial statements. It is important to mention this because information needed for these decisions might not coincide with information for other decisions and assessments.

Some people conclude from the fact that the market reacts efficiently that shareholders base their behavior on the information supplied to them *only insofar as this information agrees with the underlying economic reality*. In other words they assume that the stock market is transparent. In our opinion, however, this conclusion is not fully justified. One cannot rule out the possibility that the present practice of financial reporting does not present all the aspects of economic reality. Some authors stress the competitive character of information supplied by the financial reports because the market also has other sources of information at its disposal.[20] Secondly, firms present the same type of transactions in different ways in their financial reports. In the Netherlands, the diversity in reporting economic events is probably greater than in the U.S.A., because U.S. regulations are directed much more towards uniform reporting than are those in Holland.

It is important to distinguish between two groups of methods that can be used to report on a transaction or a group of transactions.
A. Alternative reporting methods so closely related that the effects of using one method instead of the other can easily be appraised if they are not explicitly disclosed in the financial reports.
B. Reporting methods that do not allow the analyst to find out the outcome of alternative methods, unless the firm itself supplies additional information.

The information presently supplied by financial reports will partly belong to category A and partly to category B. New reporting proposals will also partly belong to category A and partly to category B.

As to A. Transparent alternative reporting methods
Empirical research in the U.S.A. into the influence of reporting methods – or changes in these methods – on the behavior of stock prices is limited in scope. It is related mainly to the treatment of depreciation, inventory valuation (lifo versus fifo) and taxes *both in balance sheets and income statements*. The researchers tried

20. Gonedes, N. J., 'Efficient Capital Markets and External Accounting', *The Accounting Review*, January 1972, from p. 14.

to find out to what extent the choice of a particular method of reporting these items influenced prices.[21] The research almost invariably related to the methods in A because in each case data were available concerning the results in alternative methods.

The conclusions of most research indicated that changes in reporting methods had no significant long-run effect on the level of stock prices. The market turned out to be able to gauge the changes in accounting methods correctly and quickly. One can therefore say that information in category A generally does not significantly prevent the market from being transparent. In addition, one may conclude that the *market as a whole* is not affected by functional fixation.

This research would further warrant the conclusion that from the companies' viewpoint there is not much point in reporting the same economic events in different ways. The contemplated effects on stock prices did not materialize while investors (and their advisers) had to incur expense to make the divergent information comparable to the information supplied by other firms. A number of investors may have been misled, however, while the market as a whole reacted in an unbiased way. It would seem that Wilschut's ideas, mentioned in the introduction, are not confirmed by this research. Especially the assumption that 'the public ultimately bases its opinions on the profit figure supplied by the company' does not agree with it.

On the basis of the foregoing it might be argued that the policy-making institutions should prescribe uniform valuation and presentation methods. However, by adopting this policy, these authorities would have to solve the problem of which valuation method (or presentation method) must be chosen as the best way of reporting a certain economic event.

To see whether this policy is justified, one can make the following distinction:

(a) The fact that alternative valuation methods have no significant long-term effect on stock prices may be due to shareholders not paying attention to the items concerned in their decision-making process, for instance because the influence of the alternatives on earnings is too small. In that event there would be no reason for uniformity, but no case against it either.

(b) The lack of influence on stock prices can be caused by shareholders' ability to correct data supplied by the firm in such a way as to make them relevant to their decisions.

These corrections can be based on:
- additional information supplied by the firm itself;
- information supplied by other firms employing an alternative valuation system.

21. See Lev, B., *Financial Statement Analysis: a new approach;* Englewood Cliffs N.J., 1974, from p. 237; this author gives an extensive review of empirical research.

In case (b) the choice of a 'correct' valuation method is important if one wishes to achieve uniform valuation methods. Uniformity is especially important for investors if they incur considerable cost in making different firms' figures comparable. If, moreover, the cost to the firms is hardly, if at all, affected by providing uniform information, this would be an additional argument for uniformity.

So far, empirical research has not substantiated the choice of a correct valuation method, because it has not been shown *which reporting methods* investors use for their decisions, and which methods they convert to other information. We can also assume that in some cases the market has only produced an unbiased reaction to information supplied by firms because other firms – in the same industry – reported on the same events using different methods.

If, for example, in two comparable firms, x and y, firm x applies lifo and firm y fifo in inventory valuation, the difference in reported earnings can only be traced because there is a diversity in reporting. If both firms apply fifo, there would probably be insufficient information to base stock prices on lifo, and vice versa.

The decision to demand uniformity might therefore lead to:
- greater conformity between reporting practice and the information so far used by investors; *or*
- a reduction in the volume of information to such an extent that it would have a negative impact on the pricing process.

It is not always possible to say in advance, however, what the consequences would be. There is not enough insight into the factors determining stock prices. We therefore think it advisable for the supply of information not to be needlessly limited by the requirement of uniformity. Lev has advocated uniformity in cases in which the results of different reporting methods cannot easily be reduced to each other.[22] But in these particular cases there is a risk of the formation of stock prices being influenced by such uniformity. These consequences (which can hardly be quantified however) would have to be considered in discussing the pros and cons of uniformity.

Our view is (especially when there is not enough insight into the impact of uniformity on stock prices) that it would be advisable to demand – an admittedly arbitrary – uniformity, but at the same time to demand explicit disclosure of the effects of alternative accounting methods in footnotes.

22. Lev, op. cit., p. 251.

There would then be no risk of the information stockholders believe they need becoming unavailable.[23]

As to B. *The supply of new information*

New information is defined as all the information which cannot be deduced at a reasonable cost from available data and which *a priori* can be considered of value to investor decision-making. There is always a possibility, however, that this information, if disclosed, would not be used. Potential users will only act on the new information if they think it will influence the level of stock prices.

Information relevant to stock prices flows from two sources:
- General information on economic trends (for instance in a particular industry or country);
- Data supplied by firms (a substantial part of this information is given in the form of quarterly or annual financial reports).

Both sources can produce new information. In the following discussion we shall deal only with information supplied by firms. Each of the present proposals and suggestions for the improvement of financial reporting could be verified and it could be examined whether its introduction would lead to the production of new information. If so, it could be assumed that the disclosure of the new information influences the stock-pricing process. This would imply that the volume and nature of the information affects the level of stock prices. The conclusion can then be drawn that investors are not capable of making a *correct* valuation of a particular share if they are not fully acquainted with all the relevant aspects of the firm.

Presently available empirical tests relating to the efficiency of the stock market do not sufficiently support the assumption that the market is transparent, since firms presumably have information (as yet) unpublished. This new information if made available to the market would lead to price changes, even though the market is efficient both before and after its presentation.

The problem arises of whether market efficiency affects the question of whether new information should be made available. Ronen[24] distinguishes between *descriptive research* into market behavior on the one hand and a *process of setting norms* on the other.

In the latter process a choice is made between supplying (new) information or not. Research into market efficiency shows in our opinion that this normative process should only be applied to new information. The idea behind Ronen's

23. This is also argued by Beaver, W. H., 'What should the FASB's Objectives be', *The Journal of Accountancy*, August 1973, p. 52.
24. Ronen, J., 'The Need for Accounting Objectives in an Efficient Market, Objectives of Financial Statements', New York, *A.I.C.P.A.* 1974, Volume II, from p. 36.

distinction is that, given certain objectives of financial reporting (for instance efficient allocation of capital), there is a related optimal price structure in the stock market at a certain moment. The normative process should therefore show what information should be supplied to achieve this price structure. It is beyond the scope of this paper to deal with the process of establishing reporting standards. But this process can obviously function as described by Ronen only if the consequences of disclosing new information on stock prices are clear in advance.[25]

Current research, however, does not enable us to forecast whether a certain type of new information will influence stock prices and, if so, to what extent. Consequently, the efficiency or lack of efficiency of the stock market has no decisive meaning for a process of establishing standards relating the advisability of disclosing new information to the influence of this disclosure on the level of stock prices. This also implies that other considerations should determine the desirability of supplying certain types of new information.

6. Conclusions

The efficient market concept implies that there is no point in investors looking for relatively undervalued or overvalued stocks with the aid of conventional stock analysis. Investors and their advisers should, therefore, realign their investment strategy.

The efficient market concept is not inconsistent with the fact that stock prices are formed, for instance, on the basis of earnings figures supplied by firms. As far as the market is able to do this, published profits are adjusted for differences resulting from alternative reporting methods.

Suppliers of information should realize that – given the characteristics of the stock market – it is generally impossible to induce any significant long-term effect on stock prices by simple changes in reporting methods.

It cannot be concluded from the foregoing that the stock market is transparent in the sense that the investor or the market can obtain a correct insight into stock values.

For the policy-making authorities, there is little point in seeking 'correct' reporting methods for items for which the market can assess the impact of the mode of reporting them.

25. Anderson and Meyers rightly state that another condition is that one should be able to define and measure the concept of optimality unambiguously. As this is impossible, they come to the same conclusion: Market efficiency as such does not provide an unambiguous basis for information selection. See Anderson, James A., and Meyers, Stephen L., 'Some Limitations of Efficient Market Research for determining Financial Reporting Standards', *Abacus*, volume 11 (June 1975), pp. 18–36.

For shareholders, these authorities should impose such a disclosure level that the impact of alternative reporting methods is made clear.

The efficient market concept is meaningless as regards the question of whether new information should be supplied.

References

Anderson, James A., and Stephen L. Meyers, 'Some Limitations of Efficient Markets, Research for the Determination of Financial Reporting Standards', *Abacus*, Vol. 11. June 1975.

Bagehot, W., 'The only game in town', *Financial Analysts Journal*, March/April 1971.

Ball, R., and P. Brown, 'An empirical evaluation of accounting income numbers', *Journal of Accounting Research*, Autumn 1968.

Beaver, W. H., 'What should the FASB's Objectives be', *The Journal of Accountancy*, August 1973.

Brealey, R. A., *An introduction to risk and return from common stocks*, Cambridge 1969.

Brown, P. and J. W. Kennelly, 'The informational content of quarterly earnings: an extension and some further evidence', *Journal of Business*, July 1972.

Fama, E. F., 'Efficient capital markets: a review of theory and empirical work', *The Journal of Finance*, May 1970.

Fama, E. F., L. Fisher, M. Jensen, R. Roll, 'The adjustment of stock prices to new information', *International Economic Review*, February 1969.

Gonedes, N. J., 'Efficient Capital Markets and External Accounting', *The Accounting Review*, January 1972.

Jaffe, J. F., 'Special information and insider trading', *Journal of Business*, July 1974.

Jensen, M. C., 'The performance of mutual funds in the period 1945–1964', *The Journal of Finance*, May 1968.

Joy, O. M., and R. B. Porter, 'Stochastic dominance and mutual fund performance', *Journal of Financial and Quantitative Analysis*, January 1974.

Klaassen, J., *De Vervangingswaarde, Theorie en Toepassing in de Jaarrekening*, Alphen aan den Rijn 1975.

Lev, B., *Financial Statement Analysis: a new approach*, Englewood Cliffs N.J., 1974.

McDonald, J. G., 'Objectives and performance of mutual funds 1960–1969', *Journal of Financial and Quantitative Analysis*, June 1974.

Morgenstern, O., 'Information flow and stock market price changes', in: J. L. Bicksler, ed., *Methodology in Finance-Investments*, Lexington, Mass., 1972.

Niederhofer, V., and P. J. Regan, 'Earnings changes, Analysts' forecasts and stock prices', *Financial Analysts Journal*, May/June 1972.

Niederhofer, V. and M. F. M. Osborne, 'Market making and reversal on the stock exchange', *Journal of the American Statistical Association*, December 1966.

Philippatos, G. C., *Financial management, Theory and Techniques*, San Francisco, 1973.

Samuelson, P. A., 'Challenge to judgment', *The Journal of Portfolio Management*, Fall 1974.

Samuelson, P. A., 'Proof that properly anticipated prices fluctuate random', *Industrial Management Review*, Spring 1965.

Ronen, J., 'The Need for Accounting Objectives in an Efficient Market', *Objectives of Financial Statements*, New York, A.I.C.P.A. 1974, Volume II.

Schlarbaum, G. G., 'The investment performance of the common stock portfolios of property-liability insurance companies', *Journal of Financial and Quantitative Analysis*, January 1974.

Scholes, M. S., 'The market for securities: substitution versus price pressure and the effects of information on share prices', *Journal of Business*, April 1972.

Securities and Exchange Commission, *Institutional Investor Study Report*, Vol. 2, Washington 1971.

Sprecher, C. R., *Introduction to investment management*, Boston 1975.

Treynor, J. L., 'Efficient markets and fundamental analysis', *Financial Analysts Journal*, March/April 1974.

Treynor, J. L., 'The trouble with earnings', *Financial Analysts Journal*, September/October 1972.

Valentine, J. L., 'Investment analysis and capital market theory', *Financial Analysts Research Foundation*, Charlottesville, 1975.

Waud, R. N., 'Public interpretations of discount-rate changes: Evidence on the 'announcement effect'', *Econometrica*, 1971, No. 2.

West, R. R. and S. H. Tinic, 'Corporate finance and the changing stock market', *Financial Management*, Autumn 1974.

Williamson, J. P., *Performance measurement and investment objectives for educational endowment funds*, New York 1972.

Wilschut, K. P. G., 'Het stelsel van waardering en winstbepaling toegepast door de Akzo-groep', *Maandblad voor Accountancy en Bedrijfshuishoudkunde*, May 1975.

Zijpp, I. v. d., 'Financieel beleid en jaarverslag', *E.S.B.*, 12–8–1970.

XI. TECHNICAL ASSUMPTIONS AND REVIEW OF FINANCIAL FORECASTS

Richard H. Haase and John J. Clark

1. Introduction

Bindenga and Bak have properly underscored the inadequacy of the cost model in recording economic transactions. The alternatives to cost, whether described as 'inflation accounting', 'replacement value accounting', or 'current value accounting' involve some kind of projective data. Edwards forthrightly examined *expected* accounting income as a basis for decision making. We also, are concerned with projected performance, i.e. the publication of short term (eighteen months or less) accounting earnings forecasts. In this, we shall assume – or at least beg the question – that security markets respond to changes in accounting income. A respectable body of opinion holds the contrary: that security markets pierce the veil of accounting earnings to discount the underlying cash flow.

In this respect, academicians have come to think of security markets as 'efficient'; that is, the stock market 'instantaneously' discounts all the information that is known or knowable concerning a particular security. The notion further presumes a linear relationship between risk and return: that the market consistently and rationally rewards for risk. Consequently, historical information embodied in annual reports to shareholders or to regulatory authorities is not relevant to the investment process. Shareholders are concerned with future earnings and quality of those earnings, i.e., the risk posture of the firm. The tradeoff of future risk and return marks the essence of the investment decision.

The efficient market concept was one factor contributing to the widespread interest of the past half decade in the publication by business firms of financial forecasts. Granted the market will still 'instantaneously' discount the projections before they become general knowledge and leave the average investor in the same relative position of impotence. Yet if the financial forecast serves to reduce the uncertainties surrounding future earnings, this should – the theory goes – improve the P/E ratio of the stock and the market value of the shares. Therefore, if the publication of financial forecasts is ultimately to constitute a significant advance in disclosure requirements, it must rest upon the impact of the projections on the valuation process. In turn, this depends upon the extent to which the uncertainties inevitably surrounding any forecast are faithfully delineated by the reviewing 'auditor'.

In their survey of business attitudes on the publication of financial forecasts, Asebrook and Carmichael (1973) noted the concerns of managers regarding possible legal liability, disclosure of confidential information to competitors, and the inability of investors to appreciate the uncertainties of forecasting. Each of these issues touches on the format and content of the published projections as keyed to a statement of assumptions. However, substantial ambiguities surround the nature and function of assumptions in the interpretation of financial forecasts.

2. Regulatory pronouncements on publication of financial forecasts

UK and American authorities specify that forecasts should be accompanied by a statement of assumptions to assist the investor in appraising the reasonableness of the forecast and the main uncertainties attached to it (Issuing Houses Association, 1972; Securities and Exchange Commission, 1973, 1975). In particular, the City Code of Take-overs and Mergers states that when profit forecasts appear in a document addressed to shareholders '. . . the assumptions, including the commercial assumptions, upon which the directors have based their profit forecasts, must be stated in the document' (Issuing Houses Association, 1972). Referring to this requirement, The Institute of Chartered Accountants in England and Wales (1969) stipulates 'chartered accountants should report whether or not the forecasts are consistent with the given assumptions, economic, commercial, marketing and financial, which underlie them'. The SEC merely provides that management's estimates:

. . . of a company's future performance is information of significant importance to the investor, that such assessment should be able to be understood in light of the assumptions made . . . (Securities and Exchange Commission 1973, 1975).

However, the rules do not (a) define an assumption; (b) state the relationship between the format of the projections and the assumptions, (e.g. a financial projection can take the form of a point estimate, probability distribution, or range; if the latter, the assumptions should be cast so as to allow assessment of the range interval); (c) establish criteria to determine which assumptions are material and should be disclosed.

Implicit in these omissions is a lack of clarity regarding the extent to which a statement of assumptions can assist investors in evaluating the reasonableness of the projections. Should the assumptions accompanying a financial forecast:

a. Merely alert the investor to the tentative nature of all forecasting?
   or
b. Enable the investor to translate a change in an assumption into the direction of change in the estimates?
   or
c. Permit the investor to substitute his own judgment on specific assumptions and trace the effects on the projection?
   or
d All of these?

This paper examines the role of assumptions in financial forecasting with particular reference to the assumptions implicit in the use of quantitative forecasting models. It is perilous to suggest (in the City Code) that assumptions be 'framed so as to be a maximum assistance to the reader' without comprehension of the limits to this assistance (Issuing Houses Association, 1972).

3. What is an assumption?

All forecasting rests upon hypotheses; that is, conditions assumed to be true or expected to occur in order to validate the forecast. A set of hypotheses, expressed or implied, constitutes the assumptions which support the forecast. Examination reveals, for firms of even modest size, any given set may comprise an extensive list of assumptions grouped under:

Planning assumptions relating to market and production strategies as well as erratic events (e.g. outcome of litigation) and perhaps the intuitive adjustments of top officers. This suggests an important *conceptual* distinction between a 'forecast' and a 'budget'. The sales forecast makes a *prediction* linking quantities to price levels while the budget describes a plan of *operation*. Major variables controlling total sales and elasticity of demand lie beyond direct intervention of the enterprise and represent constraints on the forecasting process. The budget, while derived from a sales projection, is primarily an instrument of control. Management establishes budget quotas to elicit feedback effects, fix organizational goals, and to reflect asymmetrical costs of over-or-under estimation. For example, if management found that either overestimation or underestimation was more costly in budget formulation, it might appropriately 'adjust' the most probable level of sales. Hence, full explanation of failure to achieve budget objectives may have to separate out poor predictive ability from poor operating control. Yet, it is difficult to disentangle, for statement presentation, assumptions *per se* from management plans (which, of course, depend upon assumptions).

Production strategies merit special comment. The bridge that leads from sales to net-income is distinct from the external link of sales to the market. Sales projections only initiate the design of a comprehensive operating plan, for management has considerable latitude in responding to the market environment. It may, for example, alter the product mix, adjust production schedules, modify inventory policies, regulate discretionary expenditures, etc. Consequently, *any single projected (or most probable) sales level can translate into a broad range of net-income estimates.*

Prime cost projections assume reliable estimates of factor prices and efficiencies in production; variable overheads may be allocated to product lines by statistical formulae and management judgment; discretionary fixed costs may actually be revised throughout the budget period; programmed fixed costs (such as, supervisory salaries or financial charges) share the uncertainties of interest rate changes and similar variations in specific price levels. Other illustrations could be introduced but the list is sufficient to emphasize the uncertainties of projecting business earnings and stresses the variety of assumptions, environmental and internal, buttressing net-income estimates.

There exists a group of *standard assumptions*, akin to the 'going concern' principle in financial accounting, which are vital to appraisal of the forecast yet merit explicit mention only by exception. Unless alerted to the contrary, the reader of a financial forecast properly assumes the projections are prepared in a manner consistent with the applicable accounting principles adopted by the firm in the annual report. Likewise the composition of top corporate management, the continuing availability of normal sources of supply, reasonable stability of the tax environment, and so on, are implied unless the reader is informed to the contrary.

Technical Assumptions relating to the forecast model. Few companies employ a purely quantitative model to forecast sales and net-income, but a growing number of companies make some use of quantitative projection methods. The choice of methodology is decidedly a matter of judgment and involves assumptions concerning the relevant variables and their interrelation. Different statistical techniques, applied to the same data base, can yield different forecasts. The same technique may yield divergent results for different time spans or if other explanatory variables are included. Naturally, management will modify its forecasting procedures to obtain estimates with a reliability appropriate to the circumstances of the business.

Statistical models are not perfect predictors and the variance from actual sales will in part be attributable to the particular assumptions of the model. Too often these assumptions lack explicit statement. However, the SEC requires that variances be explained. Specifically, the US Commission in its second set of provisional guidelines defines a reasonable range on sales and net-income projections as ± 10 percent from the mid-point of the sales or net-income range. Variances beyond the 10 percent criterion need to be explained, although there is no presumption of impropriety.

Clearly, a full array of assumptions would constitute a sizeable document. Moreover, since the underlying events may each assume a variety of different outcomes and these may occur in diverse combinations, a large number of projections can result from very few assumptions. The complexity obscures the impact on estimated net-income of changes in a single assumption, and underscores the difficulty in deciding which assumptions merit publication.

Businessmen, of course, are familiar with the Planning and Standard Assumption; and the professional literature on financial forecasting amply alerts 'auditors' of the need to identify these assumptions in assessing the reasonableness of the projections. By contrast, the literature contains few references to the Technical Assumptions supporting sales and expense item projections. Accordingly, we shall concentrate on the role of Technical Assumptions in accounting for variances in projections of sales and net-income.

4. Scope of the study

Basically, forecasting techniques divide into two broad categories: *Noncausal Methods* which, from an historical time series, identify a pattern of change that may be extended into the future with some assurance; and *Causal Methods* which identify and measure over a given time frame the relationship between a dependent variable (sales or cost) and some independent variable(s). The independent variable(s) is said to 'explain' the behavior of the dependent variable and thus permits the analyst to forecast sales or cost items. The models under each group vary greatly in sophistication, i.e. in the number of independent variables; in the weight given to recent data as opposed to earlier periods; in the introduction of lead and lag effects; and so forth. Models range all the way from simple weighted averages to econometric and simulation constructions. The latter are obviously more costly to install and maintain. *In this respect, we must bear in mind that business firms do not simply opt for the most theoretically satisfying technique. Rather, the firm will pay for a degree of precision appropriate to its circumstances: the nature of the market; the mix of fixed and variable costs; operational flexibility; penalties of over or underestimation of sales; etc.* Some firms are content to know the direction of change rather than a specific sales range; others strive to project sales and costs within a specified variance.

Whether causal or noncausal, forecasting models rest upon assumptions that constitute one set of uncertainties surrounding the projections.

These include:

a. The conditions in the past which generated the observed data will persist into the future. In the concept of stationarity, the future becomes an extension of the past and historical simulation is the standard method for validation of the model. Yet many of the changes affecting business activity spring from discontinuities and by definition are either unpredicted or unpredictable.

b. As a corollary, models generally respond to novel circumstances slowly. Rates of change are often too rapid for models to accommodate – the reaction time of the model is too slow. However, even in a stable situation, the time required to collect data, process data, and provide output to the decision-maker may conflict with the time schedule of budget formulation.

c. A further corollary, if the data base is flawed – if it contains inadequate, inaccurate, or irrelevant historical information – the past may be as obscure as the future. The model cannot rise above the quality of the input data.

d. In the case of noncausal methods, the variable is a function of time.

e. The evolution of the variables is completely systematic and hence predictable.

f. Except where qualified by the introduction of weights, all previous observations yield the same amount of information about the likely value of the next observation.

g. Causal models assume the average relationship calculated between the dependent and independent variable(s) will hold for the future. The task of defining these relationships is a formidable one during periods of accelerated change. Models of simple static systems are easy to construct but their naïveté will likely trap the user. On the other hand, models of complex and dynamic systems require painstaking efforts and *may* improve the precision of the projections – albeit with a higher price tag for the information.

h. Unless sales and cost data are considered to be random and normally distributed, the models do not provide a statistical basis for establishing the probability of error or confidence interval estimates.

i. In the absence of the above normality presumption, practice resorts to establishing ranges based upon past deviations between actual and projected results such that one can be reasonably certain the next period's projection will fall within the established limits. Statistically speaking, however, the assumption that future deviations will fall within the defined range is at best tenuous (Lippitt, 1969; Nelson, 1972).

In short, each model applied to economic data has an inherent 'error' factor or variance and this increases at the turning points between expansion and contraction in economic activity.

5. Impact of technical assumptions on the bottom line

The authors applied five common noncausal techniques to nine-year sales data
of General Electric (1966–1974) and Armstrong Cork (1965–1973). The parameters derived were used to project sales for the tenth period. A Mean Absolute
Deviation (MAD) and Standard Deviation (SD) accompanies each estimate. In
keeping with present practice, these were used to establish a range within which
actual sales may be expected to fall. This is not to say that GE or Armstrong
Cork employ any of the above techniques in sales forecasting or that they would
accept uncritically the output of any quantitative model. Managerial judgment
remains the final arbiter in fixing sales projections for budgetary purposes. The
data are useful, however, in illustrating the potential impact of deviations in sales
projections on earnings before taxes (EBT). Table 1 summarizes the projected
results by the selected noncausal techniques. Supporting calculations are
presented in Appendix A.

Generally, an operating budget contains a mix of fixed (overhead) and variable
costs. The presence of the former creates a leverage effect on EBT: deviations
from forecasted sales will, *all other things equal*, result in a greater proportionate
change in EBT. We calculated for both companies over the same period an
average leverage factor based upon: Percent Change in EBT/Percent Change in
Sales. The resultant factor thus reflects both operating and financial leverage.

Leverage calculations excluded periods of abnormally high leverage as well as
negative leverage. At this point, the reader should bear in mind the method of
measurement assumes a linear relationship between unit sales price and unit
variable costs. Hence, the calculated leverage factors for GE of 2.67 and
Armstrong Cork of 3.4 represent rough approximations. More precise estimates
would depend upon access to confidential information relating to the covariance
of sales and costs among separate product lines. However, the approximations
behave as one would expect in theory. The leverage factor tends to increase as
EBT falls toward the breakeven profit. The results presented in table 2
demonstrate the impact on EBT of variations in sales as described by MAD and
SD.

6. Interpretation of results

Except in the unusual case of an all variable cost company, an operating budget
will have a built-in leverage factor. The established range for the sales
projections – for example, the projected sales, plus/minus one standard

Table 1. Sales forecasts and dispersion by non-causal techniques General Electric and Armstrong Cork.

General Electric: 1975 actual and projected results.

Forecast Method*	Actual Sales (000,000)	Actual EBT** (000,000)	Projected sales	MAD***	MAD as percent of projected sales	Standard deviation****	Standard deviation as percent of projected sales
	$13,399	$949.6					
1			$13.11	.723	5.5	.871	6.6
2			13.37	.664	5.0	.764	6.0
3			13.97	.420	3.0	.567	4.0
4			12.89	.525	4.1	.612	4.7
5			13.19	.408	3.0	.251	1.9

Armstrong Cork: 1974 Actual and projected results.

	(000)	(000)					
	$889.3	$66.4					
1			$732.4	$77.5	10.6	$67.7	9.2
2			755.3	116.9	15.5	74.2	9.8
3			811.2	52.2	6.4	64.3	7.9
4			710.9	49.6	7.0	63.1	8.9
5			705.4	47.4	6.7	61.5	8.7

* Forecast methods:
1. Three-Year Moving Average with Trend Adjustment.
2. Exponentially weighted moving average with trend adjustment (weight = .5).
3. Exponentially weighted moving average with trend adjustment (weight = .9).
4. Linear curve fitting: $Y_F = a + bt$.
5. Exponential (logarithmic) curve fitting: $Y_F = ab^t$.
** Earnings before taxes.
*** Mean absolute deviation.
**** Standard deviation.

Table 2. Impact of sales forecast variations on earnings before taxes.

General Electric: Projected variation in sales and EBT, 1975.

Forecast method	MAD as percent of projected sales	×	Combined leverage factor	=	Percent change in EBT		SD as percent of projected sales	×	Combined leverage factor	=	Percent change in EBT
1	5.5	×	2.67	=	14.7		6.6	×	2.67	=	17.6
2	5.0	×	2.67	=	13.4		6.0	×	2.67	=	16.0
3	3.0	×	2.67	=	8.0		4.0	×	2.67	=	10.7
4	4.1	×	2.67	=	10.9		4.7	×	2.67	=	12.5
5	3.0	×	2.67	=	8.0		1.9	×	2.67	=	5.0

Armstrong Cork: Projected variation in sales and EBT, 1974.

Forecast method	MAD as percent of projected sales	×	Combined leverage factor	=	Percent change in EBT		SD as percent of projected sales	×	Combined leverage factor	=	Percent change in EBT
1	10.6	×	3.4	=	36.0		9.2	×	3.4	=	31.3
2	15.5	×	3.4	=	52.7		9.8	×	3.4	=	33.3
3	6.4	×	3.4	=	21.9		7.9	×	3.4	=	26.9
4	7.0	×	3.4	=	23.7		8.9	×	3.4	=	29.6
5	6.7	×	3.4	=	22.8		8.7	×	3.4	=	29.6

deviation – has significance only in relation to the leverage factor. Since the leverage factor approaches infinity as earnings before taxes fall toward the breakeven point, small variations in the sales projections can have explosive effects on the bottom line. From table 2, if General Electric sales projections stayed within a range defined by plus/minus one MAD or SD (and there is no assurance that past history will repeat) in only three cases would EBT vary by less than 10 percent. In these instances, the sales projections could not vary by more than 3 percent. Yet in 1974, the combined leverage factor for GE actually rose to 51. In the case of Armstrong Cork, in each instance, the variation in EBT amply exceeded the SEC's 10 percent criterion.

The financial pages of the daily newspaper confirm this phenomenon. In 1963, United Air Lines reported a 4.8 percent increase in operating revenues and a 121 percent increase in earnings after taxes; in 1963, the same company reported operating revenues up 7.5 percent and earnings after taxes up 86.8 percent, as the company moved up from breakeven. For the first quarter of 1976, RCA reported increases in sales of 15 percent and in earnings after taxes of 100 percent. Similar figures for Union Camp were 29 and 55 percent respectively.

The leverage effect is intensified or mitigated by the covariances of revenues and costs among the company's product lines. Since the company will likely forecast both sales and expense items, the auditor must be aware of the range of variation in the sales and cost estimates and their degree of correlation. Consider, for example, three possible (by no means exhaustive) alternative assumptions regarding vertical and horizontal covariance relations among the separate product lines:

Assumption I. Sales distributions are independent; variable costs are perfectly correlated to sales; fixed costs are independent.
Assumption II. Sales distributions are perfectly, positively correlated; variable costs remain perfectly correlated to sales; fixed costs are independent.
Assumption III. Sales distributions are perfectly, negatively correlated; variable costs, perfectly correlated to sales; fixed costs, independent.

The data in table 3 are interpreted under these assumptions. Table 4 summarizes the impact of each assumption on total sales and operating profit. Table 5 displays the results of applying the covariance assumptions of table 4 to the aggregate company budget and individual product lines. (Detailed calculations appear in Appendix B). Not unexpectedly, the deviation in operating profit increases with the degree of positive correlation among the sales and expense components (Clark and Elgers, 1972, 1973, 1974).

The problem of assessing Technical Assumptions in the publication of

Table 3. Budgeted income statement.

	Total	Product A			Product B		
		X	S	S/X	X	S	S/X
Sales	$300	$200	20	0.10	$100	5	0.05
Variable cost	150	110	11	.10	40	2	.05
Gross margin	$150	$ 90			$ 60		
Margin percentage	50%	45%			60%		
Fixed costs	100	60	12	.20	40	5	.125
Operating profit	$ 50	$ 30			$ 20		

X = Expected value of the variable
S = Standard deviation or $\sqrt{S^2}$

Table 4. Correlation assumptions. Total sales and operating profit.

	Assumptions		
	1	2	3
Variance of total sales	$425	$625	$225
Standard deviation of total sales	20.6	25	15
Variance of operating profit	259	313	205
Standard deviation of operating profit	16.09	17.69	14.32

Table 5. Profit confidence intervals.

	Mean values	95% Confidence interval ($\bar{x} \pm 2S$)		
		Assumption 1	Assumption 2	Assumption 3
Part 1: Aggregate company budget:				
Sales	$300	$258–342	$250–350	$270–330
Variable cost	150	128–172	124–176	132–168
Margin	$150	$130–170	$126–174	$138–162
Margin percentage	50%			
Fixed costs	100	74–126	74–126	74–126
Operating profit	$ 50	$17.8–82.2	$14.6–85.4	$21.4–78.6

Part 2: Operating profit by product line:

	Product A	Product B
Mean profit	$30	$20
Upper limit (+2S)	60	30
Lower limit (−2S)	0	10

Note:
The profit distributions for the product lines are identical under each of the assumptions (1), (2), and (3).

financial forecasts grows more complex when we consider the too frequent shortcomings of present practice. Assume the familiar two variable linear regression, $Y_c = a + bX$; where Y_c is the estimated expected sales given a specified value of X; where $a = \$50,000$, $b = 1.5$, $\bar{X} = \$100,000$, S_x (standard deviation of X) = \$40,000, $\bar{Y} = \$200,000$, S_y (standard deviation of Y) = \$60,000, $S_{y.x}$ (conditional standard deviation of Y given X) = \$20,000, n (number of paired observation) = 15, r^2 (coefficient of determination) = .897, and r (coefficient of correlation) = .947. Hence, given an estimated value of X at \$200,000:

$$Y_c = 50,000 + (1.5)\ (200,000) \tag{1}$$
$$= \$350,000$$

As we have seen, the \$350,000 forecast might fall wide of the mark for numerous reasons:

a. the assumption of stationarity may prove false;

b. internal events within the company can alter the sales picture;

c. the value of the parameters, a and b, may be incorrect due to faulty data;

d. the value of X, itself a forecast, carries a weight of similar uncertainties; errors in X will be transmitted Y_c;

e. the functional form may not be linear. Mathematical techniques are available to evaluate the 'goodness-of-fit' of functional equations but the final selection from among a number of plausible types allows for the judgment of the analyst;

f. the company's annual sales are influenced by random disturbances. This raises the issue of defining a range of variation in forecasted sales and assigning a level of confidence to that range.

By assuming these random disturbances are identically and independently normally distributed with zero mean and some variance, the standard linear regression model is developed. Corresponding to each value of X, Y_c is normally distributed with a mean that is a function of X, such that the function is linear as regards to the coefficients and with a variance that is constant for all values of X. Given these postulates, the analyst can estimate the magnitude of the random disturbances and define interval estimates for Y_c with related confidence levels.

Returning to the numerical illustration, the practice typically establishes a 95 percent confidence interval for the projection as being 1.96 times the standard deviation of the errors: 1.96 $(S_{y.x})$. The calculation yields the interval \$310,800 to \$389,200. *But this does not mean that next year sales stand a 95 percent chance of falling within the interval.* Such an interpretation is erroneous for the following reasons:

a. Under the regression model of normally distributed random errors, the equation yields an *estimate* of the expected value of Y, (i.e. the *mean* of the population of all Y values for the given value of X); it does *not* estimate a particular value of Y.

b. The value $ 350,000, about which the interval is established, is only an *estimate* of the location of the mean of the population of Y values; therefore, the location of the 95 percent interval may be incorrect.

c. The standard deviation of the errors, (i.e. 20,000) is only an *estimate* of the true standard deviation of the assumed normally distributed disturbances; therefore the width of the interval may be incorrect.

d. Under the regression model, the observed irregularities in the historical data make the coefficients in the estimating equation uncertain, and errors in the values of the coefficients introduce additional errors into the forecast; errors which increase as the forecast is made farther away from the average value of the causal variable, X; or, in the case of a time series, further into the future. In other words, the farther into the future we are forecasting, the less confident we can be of our estimate.

Consistent with the above four considerations, the corrected 95 percent confidence interval estimate for the next value of Y, i.e., sales, for the given X is determined by the expression:

$$Y_c - tS_y^* \leqslant Y_{next} \leqslant Y_c + tS_y^* \tag{2}$$

where: (a) Y_c is the estimate for the mean of Y for a given X determined by the least squares estimating equation: $Y = a + bX$; (b) S_y^* is the estimate of the standard deviation for the next value of Y and is determined by the expression:

$$\sqrt{S_y^2 + S_{y.x}^2}\,{}^1 \tag{3}$$

1. S_y^* incorporates two components: S_y^2, the sampling error in using $\bar{Y}$ for a given X; $S_{y.x}^2$, the estimate of the inherent variation in the random variable Y (i.e. the variance of the residuals). These two components are independent under the assumptions of the regression model, hence the variances are additive. Furthermore, S_y^2 is calculated by:

$$S_y^2 = S_{y.x}^2 \left[\frac{1}{n} + \frac{(X_0 - \bar{X})^2}{\sum(X - \bar{X})^2} \right]$$

where: n is the sample size (i.e. total number of data points used to estimate the least squares equation). The larger the sample size, the smaller will be the width of the interval because of the contribution of the $1/n$ term. The second term in the brackets adjusts for the fact that X_0 (the particular value of X used to estimate Y) is distant from $\bar{X}$ (the average value of the observed X's). This term underscores the fact that the farther away from the average value one is attempting to forecast (or the farther into the future) the less accurate are the forecasts.

and (c) t refers to the appropriate value from the student t distribution rather than the often incorrectly used value of the standard normal distribution as the multiplier. The t distribution must be used because $S^2_{y.x}$ is only an estimate of the true variance which introduces an additional error in making forecasts. The value of t depends on the sample size, and as the sample size becomes larger, the value of t approaches the corresponding standard normal value. The discrepancy between the two values generally is negligible for values of n greater than 100.

For the numerical example, the statistically correct 95 percent confidence interval for the forecasted next value of sales becomes:

$$\sum (X - \bar{X})^2 = (n - 1)S^2_X = (14) \ (40,000)^2$$

$$(X_0 - \bar{X})^2 = (200,000 - 100,000)^2 = (100,000)^2$$

$$S^2_y = (20,000)^2 \left[\frac{1}{14} + \frac{(100,000)^2}{14(40,000)^2} \right] = (20,000)^2 \ (.5179)$$

$$S^*_y = \sqrt{(20,000)^2(.5179) + (20,000)^2}$$

$$S^*_y = 20,000\sqrt{1.5179} = \$ \ 24,640$$

$$t \ \ = 2.145 \ \ (14 \text{ degrees of freedom and 95 percent interval})$$

$$Y_c = 50,000 + (1.5)(200,000) = \$ \ 350,000$$

with a 95 percent confidence interval of:

$$\$ \ 350,000 \pm (2.145)(\$ \ 24,640)$$

or

$$\$ \ 297,150 \leqslant Y_{next} \leqslant \$ \ 402,850 \tag{4}$$

The interpretation for this confidence interval is: 'For a large number of repeated independent samples of size 15, it is reasonable to assume that about 95 percent of the intervals constructed in the above manner, will contain the next independently selected value of Y, provided the population from which the Y value is selected is stationary, i.e. has not changed since the original data was generated.'

Note, the appropriate interpretation *does not* refer at all to the probability (likelihood) that the next Y value will fall within the interval. Herein lies the crux of the forecasting problem. In the case of published financial forecasts, managers and investors look for a set of limits coupled with the stipulation that one can be reasonably sure only a small proportion of the randomly generated data will fall outside of these limits. Such a pair of limits, L_1 and L_2, are called 'tolerance limits'.

The theory and mathematical solution for the tolerance limits is an accepted procedure and tabled values are readily available. For example, if one wants to be 99 percent sure that 95 percent of data randomly selected from a normal population will fall within a pair of limits, L_1 and L_2, the tolerance limits are defined as

$$L_1 \text{ to } L_2 = Y_c \pm (k) (S_Y) \tag{5}$$

The table value for k in the example is 3.62. Therefore, the tolerance limits become:

$$350,000 \pm (3.62) (24,640) = \$ 260,800 \text{ to } \$ 439,200$$

The analyst may now assert with 99 percent confidence that at least 95 percent of the data are included between these tolerance limits in repeated samplings. Given the structure of statistical inference, the original range of $ 310,800 to $ 389,200 is much too small and misleading to users of the forecast.

We have said enough to make the point that the Technical Assumptions underlying a published financial forecast merit a careful review by chartered accountants in assessing the reasonableness of the projections. This holds even conceding the paramount role of managerial judgment in fixing the level of budgeted sales. As we have seen, in the presence of high leverage factors, small variations in projected sales may have substantial effect on planned earnings before taxes. The reviewing accountant, in summary, needs to examine the appropriateness of the forecast range, the degree of covariance among sales and cost items, and the relation of these to the leverage built into the budget.

7. Which assumptions merit disclosure?

Neither the UK nor US guidelines set out standards for selection. Table 6 displays a selection of assumptions which the UK administrative body (The Panel) criticize for stating no more 'than the estimates used [in making the forecast] will prove to be right'. Consequently, The Panel revised the rules to guide the drafting of assumptions. The criteria now stipulate:

a. the reader should be able to understand the implications of assumptions and so help in forming a judgement as to the reasonableness of the forecast and to the main uncertainties attached to it;

b. the assumptions should be, wherever possible, specific rather than general, definite rather than vague;

Table 6. Examples of assumptions criticized by The Panel.

a.	'Sales and profits for the year will not differ materially from those budgeted for.'
b.	'There will be no increase in costs other than those anticipated and provided for.'
c.	'The book record of stocks and work in progress will be confirmed at the end of the financial year.'
d.	'The estimate of stocks on hand at 31 December 1971 will prove substantially accurate.'
e.	'The profits anticipated will not be unduly affected by any unforeseen factors.'
f.	'There will be no significant unforeseen circumstances.'
g.	'No abnormal liabilities will arise under guarantees.'
h.	'Provisions for outstanding legal claims will prove adequate.'

Source: The City Code on Take-overs and Mergers, Practice Note 4, February 16, 1972.

Table 7. Examples of assumptions which follow The Panel rules.

a.	'The company's present management and accounting policies will not be changed.' (For a company being acquired.)
b.	'Interest rates and the bases and rates of taxation, both direct and indirect, will not change materially.'
c.	'There will be no material change in international exchange rates or import duties and regulations.'
d.	'Percentage of time lost in building sites, due to adverse weather conditions, will be average for the time of the year.'
e.	'Turnover for the year will be £ 1m. on the basis that sales will continue in line with levels and trends experienced to date, adjusted for normal seasonal factors; a reduction of £ 100,000 in turnover would result in a reduction of approximately £ 10,000 in the profit forecast.'
f.	'Beer sales will increase in line with the trend established in the previous year, which corresponds to the national average rate of increase.'
g.	'An increase of about 10 percent in subscriptions will be achieved as a result of increases in the prices of certain journals and an increase in the number of subscribers.'
h.	'Trading results will not be affected by industrial disputes in the company's factories or in those of its principal suppliers.'
i.	'The current national dock strike will not last longer than six weeks.'
j.	'The new factory at Inverness will be in full production by the end of the first quarter. A delay of one month would cause the profit forecast to be reduced by £ 5,000.'
k.	'Increases in labour costs will be restricted to those recently agreed with the trades unions.'
l.	'Increases in the level of manufacturing costs for the remainder of the year will be kept within the margin of 2 percent allowed for in the estimates.'
m.	'The conversion rights attaching to all the convertible loan stock will be exercised on the next conversion date.'

Source: The City Code on Take-overs and Mergers, Practice Note 4, February 16, 1972.

c. all-embracing assumptions and those relating to the general accuracy of the estimates should be avoided;

d. the assumptions should relate only to matters which have a material bearing on the forecast (Issuing Houses Association, 1972).

Table 7 records assumptions judged to meet the revised criteria. While obviously more precise, they disclose little information, not otherwise available, to knowledgeable competitors and investment advisors. Moreover, the classification of assumptions (economic, commercial, marketing, and financial) hardly exhaust the list.

But UK experience may not afford a blueprint for US practice. The Institute of Chartered Accountants report on *The Accuracy of Profit Forecasts* in Bid Situations shows approximately two-thirds of the UK projections covered a period of three months or less (The Institute of Chartered Accountants in England and Wales, 1969). Since forecasts generally deteriorate with time, the longer term projections allowed by the SEC guidelines must presuppose even more careful attention to assumptions (Securities and Exchange Commission, 1973, 1975).

Table 8 extracts representative statements of assumptions from budget documents recently published in the United States. Items a through g were obtained from feasibility studies (new hospital facilities), a proposed offering of investment in a limited partnership and projections supporting applications for bank financing. In each case the forecasts were accompanied by a CPA's report describing the assistance rendered in preparing the projection, but disclaiming any opinion on the 'accuracy' of the estimates. Items h and i were included as assumptions supporting an annual forecast distributed to shareholders of a publicly traded company; the forecast document did not refer to the company's auditors.

The examples of assumptions included in table 8 reflect the general scope and quality of assumptions included in the documents examined. The authors did not endeavor to select particularly 'good' or 'bad' statements. The typical format of the financial data was as point estimates. The assumptions disclose little regarding company forecasting methods and do not provide the wherewithal to evaluate the reasonableness of the assumptions and the projections or to reach any conclusion regarding the achievability of the forecast.

With the objective of isolating from among a great many reasonable assumptions those which are 'material' to a given forecast, management might undertake a sensitivity analysis to focus on those factors which *all things equal* may induce variations greater than a specified range. Some authorities advocate a range of 10 to 15 percent of net-income as the line of demarcation (Bernstein, 1967). Accepting 15 percent as the rule, management would alert investors to

Table 8. The quality of published assumptions: recent U.S. examples.

Published reports

a.   Sales are based on the average monthly sales for the seventeen month period ended September 30, 1970, and have been adjusted to reflect anticipated increases in demand as expected by the company.

b.   Cost of sales . . . reflect unit cost changes in relation to increased sales volume and other factors anticipated by the company.

c.   Operating expenses . . . assume no changes for inflation or otherwise during the life of the project. General operating expenses for 1973 and 1974 are based on assumptions of partial occupancy.

d.   Gross revenues . . . are based on past trends and current charges adjusted for managerial policies contemplated for the proposed expanded facilities and anticipated price level changes in the future.

e.   Historically the . . . rates have been increased to absorb the rising costs of health-care services and accordingly have maintained a satisfactory margin of income over expanses. It is the opinion of . . . management that this trend will continue.

f.   The mix of furniture to be rented has been assumed and a weighted average computed. This resulting theoretical set costs $509.40 and rents for $41.20 per month.

g.   Although salaries and other costs will increase in the future, advertising costs should decrease at the assumed level of activity per store. For this reason, total expenses are assumed to remain constant.

h.   Our outlook for continued rapid growth . . . is based on expansion of the boat and motorcycle trailer market, increasing market penetration, expanded geographical distribution, the introduction of new products, and of course, the past record of the company.

i.   We expect . . . to have another good year in 1973, but operating projections are less reliable than in some other . . . operations . . . This projection is based on the expectation that a new labor agreement will be successfully negotiated . . . and that appropriate rate increases will be granted.

Source: See Table 7.

those assumptions where variations might cause net-income to depart by 15 percent or more from the published estimate.

But a 10 or 15 percent standard is not sacrosanct. The standard could be set probalistically to identify a range of variation with, for example, a 75 percent chance of containing the actual net-income. Circumstances (the nature of the market, technological and financial characteristics of the industry) alter cases and it is management's responsibility to judge what is 'material' in the company's projection. Note also, no reference is made to accuracy in the sense of establishing a cut-off to govern the publication of forecasts. Accuracy standards cannot be generalized; they relate to firm and industry characteristics (Clark and Elgers, 1972, 1973, 1974).

Sensitivity analysis to identify material assumptions might take the following form on publication:

a. Product X comprises 20 percent of the company sales dollar. In the coming year its patent expires and immediate foreign competition is expected to cut sales by 5 to 15 percent. All other factors constant, a 15 percent fall in sales could result in a decline of approximately 25 percent below projected net-income.

b. The firm's labor contract expires in June of next year. If the tentative demands of the union are met, cost of sales will increase by 5 percent. Since management does not expect to be able to raise prices, *all other factors constant*, net-income would decline approximately 15 percent below the amount projected.

c. Company forecasting procedures establish a range of plus/minus 15 percent from the projected earnings before taxes. Accepted statistical techniques indicate a 75 percent certainty that actual earnings will fall within the range, all things equal.

These assumptions warn the investor not to expect proportional changes in assumptions and net-income and specify a variance in net-income resulting from a change in an assumption, *subject to the qualification of other things constant.* The latter is fundamental for it would rarely be possible to prophecy all possible combinations of factors which could conspire to change materially the sales and net-income estimates. Specifically, individual assumptions, evaluated in isolation may seem material; however, when likely combinations of variations are considered, the net impact may prove insignificant. Conversely, separate assumptions appearing immaterial in impact may occur in combinations which seriously affect the estimates. In this respect, if management employed a sensitivity analysis to identify material current period assumptions, *the basis of the selection should be set forth with a specific disclaimer that other events or combinations of events may impel net-income beyond the estimated range of variation.*

8. What can assumptions accomplish for the investor?

We may now respond to the questions raised above on the role of assumptions in published financial forecasts. Clearly, assumptions put the investor on notice about the multiple sources of uncertainty surrounding the estimates. In addition, the investor gains some insight into specific factors which may cause the actual incomes to depart significantly from the forecast. This is a valuable and necessary display for any appraisal of the forecast.

However, given the complex interactions among assumptions, the investor may or may not ascertain the *direction* of change in the forecast if he substituted other values for those contained in the assumptions. Except in very rudimentary circumstances, they would not permit him to trace the effect of a change in an assumption through criss-crossing packages of sales and costs to a specific variation in net-income. The number and diverse combinations of variables which intervene between sales and net-income raise a formidable obstacle to such calculation and would entail a substantive extension in the disclosure of information now viewed confidential. At a minimum, it would imply publication of the full forecasting model and operating structure of the firm. Unless the users of financial forecasts appreciate the limitations on the role of assumptions, the issue will certainly arise as to whether management exercised good faith in providing background data to interpret the reasonableness of the companies' projections.

Appendix A

| | General Electric | | | | | | Armstrong Cork | | | | | |
| | Sales | Moving Average Forecasts | | | Curve Fitting Forecasts | | Sales | Moving Average Forecasts | | | Curve Fitting Forecasts | |
Period	(000,000)	(1)	(2)	(3)	(4)	(5)	(000)	(1)	(2)	(3)	(4)	(5)
1	7.18				6.72	7.01	512.2				480.2	490.9
2	7.74		8.46	7.92	7.40	7.52	535.1		557.3	539.4	505.9	511.1
3	8.38		8.79	8.44	8.09	8.07	539.6		571.8	561.1	531.5	532.1
4	8.45	9.14	9.27	9.07	8.77	8.66	576.4	580.2	581.3	567.3	557.1	554.0
5	8.73	9.56	9.55	9.29	9.46	9.28	552.3	601.6	604.4	601.1	582.8	576.7
6	9.43	9.89	9.83	9.46	10.15	9.96	485.8	607.3	604.2	582.7	608.4	600.4
7	10.24	10.24	10.32	10.12	10.83	10.69	564.0	589.4	570.5	521.1	634.0	625.1
8	11.58	10.84	10.97	10.91	11.52	11.46	684.5	585.2	592.8	585.3	659.6	650.8
9	13.41	11.79	11.96	12.20	12.20	12.30	795.1	629.3	664.3	700.1	685.3	677.6
10	13.40	13.11	13.37	13.97	12.89	13.19	889.3	732.4	755.3	811.2	710.9	705.4
MAD		.723	.664	.420	.525	.408		77.5	116.9	52.2	49.6	47.4
STD		.871	.764	.567	.612	.251		67.7	74.2	64.3	63.1	61.5

R. H. HAASE AND J. J. CLARK

General Electric

1. Three-Year Moving Average with Trend Adjustment: Each three period average is used to forecast sales two periods ahead. The Trend (i.e. units rise per period) is the slope of the least squares trend line and equals 0.686. The trend adjustment equals

$$\left[\left(\frac{n-1}{2}\right)+1\right](.686) = \left[\left(\frac{3-1}{2}\right)+1\right](.686) = 1.372$$

Example:

$$F_4 = 9.14 = \tfrac{1}{3}[7.18 + 7.74 + 8.38] + 1.372$$

2. Exponentially Weighted Moving Average with Trend Adjustment (weight = 0.5): The forecast for each period is computed by

F = Previous Average + W (current sales − previous average) + Trend Adjustment
W = smoothing constant = 0.5
Trend Adjustment = $(1/W)(.686) = 1.372$
Starting value for Previous Average for period 0 was set equal to 7.00

Example:

$$F_2 = 8.46 = 7.00 + (.5)[7.18 - 7.00] + 1.372 = 7.09 + 1.372$$
$$F_3 = 8.79 = 7.09 + (.5)[7.74 - 7.09] + 1.372 = 7.42 + 1.372$$

3. Exponentially Weighted Moving Average with Trend Adjustment (weight = 0.9): The forecast for each period is computed by the same method as (2) above with $W = 0.9$ and the trend adjustment equal to $(1/W)(.686 = .762$.

4. Linear Curve Fitting: The best least squares line is fitted to the data for: $Y_F = a + bt$ where

Y_F = forecasted sales values
a = value at point of origin (i.e. $t = 0$)
b = average change in sales per period of time
t = a particular time period (i.e. 1, 2, 3, ... etc.)

For the given data:

$$Y_F = 6.03 + 0.686t$$
$$Y_{10} = 6.03 + 0.686(10) = 12.89$$

5. Exponential (logarithmic) Curve Fitting: The best least squares line is fitted to the data for: $Y_F = ab^t$ where

Y_F = forecasted sales values

a = value at point of origin (i.e. $t = 0$)
b = constant rate of change
t = a particular time period

For the given data:

$$Y_F = (6.534)(1.0728)^t$$
$$Y_{10} = (6.534)(1.0728)^{10} = 13.19$$

Mean Absolute Deviation (MAD): The DEVIATION is the difference between actual sales and forecasted sales for a particular time period. The ABSOLUTE deviation is the numerical magnitude, without regard to sign. The MEAN absolute deviation is the average of these magnitudes.

Standard Deviation (STD): The DEVIATION is the difference between actual sales and forecasted sales for a particular time period. All of the deviations are squared and summed. The sum is divided by the number of deviations. The STANDARD deviation is the square root of this average of the squared deviations.

Armstrong Cork
1. Three-Year Moving Average with Trend Adjustment: Trend Adjustment = 51.2
2. Exponentially Weighted Moving Average with Trend Adjustment (weight = 0.5): Trend Adjustment = 51.2
3. Exponentially Weighted Moving Average with Trend Adjustment (weight = 0.9): Trend Adjustment = 28.4
4. Linear Curve Fitting: $Y_F = 454.6 + 25.63t$
5. Exponential (logarithmic) Curve Fitting: $Y_F = (471.54)(1.0411)^t$

Appendix B

COVARIANCE MATRICES AND CORRELATION ASSUMPTIONS

Assumption 1: Sales distributions (S) independent; variable costs (V) perfectly correlated to sales; fixed costs (F) independent.

	S_A	S_B	V_A	V_B	F_A	F_B
S_A	$(20)^2$	0	$(-1)(20)(11)$	0	.0	0
S_B	0	$(5)^2$	0	$(-1)(5)(2)$	0	0
V_A	$(-1)(20)(11)$	0	$(11)^2$	0	0	0
V_B	0	$(-1)(5)(2)$	0	$(2)^2$	0	0
F_A	0	0	0	0	$(12)^2$	0
F_B	0	0	0	0	0	$(5)^2$

Assumption 2: Sales distribution (S) perfectly, positively correlated; variable costs (V) perfectly correlated to sales; fixed costs (F) independent.

	S_A	S_B	V_A	V_B	F_A	F_B
S_A	$(20)^2$	$(1)(20)(5)$	$(-1)(20)(11)$	$(-1)(20)(2)$	0	0
S_B	$(1)(20)(5)$	$(5)^2$	$(-1)(5)(11)$	$(-1)(5)(2)$	0	0
V_A	$(-1)(20)(11)$	$(-1)(5)(11)$	$(11)^2$	$(1)(11)(2)$	0	0
V_B	$(-1)(20)(2)$	$(-1)(5)(2)$	$(1)(11)(2)$	$(2)^2$	0	0
F_A	0	0	0	0	$(12)^2$	0
F_B	0	0	0	0	0	$(5)^2$

Assumption 3: Sales distributions (S) perfectly, negatively correlated; variable costs (V) perfectly correlated to sales; fixed costs (F) independent.

	S_A	S_B	V_A	V_B	F_A	F_B
S_A	$(20)^2$	$(-1)(20)(5)$	$(-1)(20)(11)$	$(1)(20)(2)$	0	0
S_B	$(-1)(20)(5)$	$(5)^2$	$(1)(5)(11)$	$(-1)(5)(2)$	0	0
V_A	$(-1)(20)(11)$	$(1)(5)(11)$	$(11)^2$	$(-1)(11)(2)$	0	0
V_B	$(1)(20)(2)$	$(-1)(5)(2)$	$(-1)(11)(2)$	$(2)^2$	0	0
F_A	0	0	0	0	$(12)^2$	0
F_B	0	0	0	0	0	$(5)^2$

SUMMARY

	Assumptions 1	2	3
Variance of total sales (S^2)	\$ 425	\$ 625	\$ 225
Standard deviation of total sales (S)	20.6	25	15
Variance of operating profit (S^2)	259	313	205
Standard deviation of operating profit (S)	16.09	17.69	14.32

Note: The normality assumptions permit the use of the following rules for sums and variances of random variables in the above calculations:

$$E \sum X_i = \sum E(X_i)$$

and

$$\text{Var} \sum X_i = \sum_i \sum_j \text{Cov}(X_i, X_j).$$

See Ya-lun Chou, *Statistical Analysis* (Holt, Rinehart and Winston) pp. 179–181.

References

American Accounting Association, Committee on Concepts and Standards Underlying Corporate Financial Statements, 1957, 'Accounting and Reporting Standards for Corporate Financial Statements, 1957 Revision', *The Accounting Review* (October).

Asebrook, Richard J. and D. R. Carmichael, 1973, 'Reporting on Forecasts: A Survey of Attitudes', *The Journal of Accountancy* (August), pp. 34–48.

Bernstein, Leopold A., 1967, 'The Concept of Materiality', *The Accounting Review* (January).

Clark, John J. and Pieter Elgers, 1972, 'Inclusion of Budgets in Financial Reports: Investor Needs v. Management Disclosure', Accounting and Business Research, The Institute of Chartered Accountants in England and Wales (Winter).

1973, 'Forecasted Income Statements: An Investor Perspective', *The Accounting Review*, (October).

1974, 'The Role of Assumption in Financial Forecasts', *Journal of Accountancy*, American Institute of Certified Public Accountants (July).

Clark, John J. and Richard Speagle, 1974, *Publishing Financial Forecasts: Benefits, Alternatives, Risks*, (Philadelphia: Laventhol, Krekstein, Horwath, and Horwath).

Issuing Houses Association, 1972, 'City Code on Take-overs and Mergers', (April 1969); Practices Note 4 and 6, (February 16 1972).

Lippitt, Vernon G., 1969, *Statistical Sales Forecasting* (New York: Financial Executive Research Foundation).

Nelson, Charles R., 1972, *Applied Time Series for Managerial Forecasting* (San Francisco: Holden-Day, Inc.).

Securities and Exchange Commission, 1973, 1975, *Statement by the Commission on the Disclosure of Projections of Future Economic Performance*, February 2 1973 and April 28 1975.

The Institute of Chartered Accountants in England and Wales, 1969, *Accountants' Reports on Profit Forecasts* (July).

Westwick, C. A., 1972, 'The Accuracy of Profit Forecasts in Bid Situations', The Institute of Chartered Accountants in England and Wales.

INDEX